Greeks,
Romans
and
Barbarians

LO
―――
CUN

Barry Cunliffe

Greeks, Romans and Barbarians

Spheres of Interaction

B. T. Batsford Ltd · London

First published 1988.

Typeset by Opus, Oxford
and printed in Great Britain at
The Bath Press, Avon

Published by B. T. Batsford Ltd
4 Fitzhardinge Street, London W1H 0AH

British Library Cataloguing in Publication Data

Cunliffe, Barry
   Greeks, Romans and barbarians: spheres
   of interaction.
   1. Rome—History—Germanic Invasions,
   3rd–6th centuries   2. Greece—History
   —To 146 B.C.
   I. Title
   937   DG311

   ISBN 0-7134-5273-0

To the memory of

Glyn Daniel

who taught me that
archaeology is fun

Contents

List of illustrations

Preface

This book had its genesis a long time ago when I sat enraptured at the feet of Glyn Daniel in Cambridge, learning about the Celto-Ligurian art of southern France and absorbing his infectious enthusiasm for the country. More recently my excavations at Hengistbury Head and Mount Batten have caused me to look in detail at the western French material — providing a delightful excuse to visit different parts of the country for several weeks every year, in the guise of working holidays, meeting colleagues and exchanging ideas. I remember with particular pleasure and gratitude the kindness of Christian Goudineau and Andre Tchernia in Aix-en-Provence, the Taffenals at Maillhac and many friends in Brittany including Pierre-Roland Giot, Loïc Langouët and Patrick Galliou. Gradually the stage widened. On one memorable trip to Italy Andre Carandini guided Martin Frederiksen, Molly Cotton and myself around Cosa and his remarkable excavation at Settefinestre, while frequent visits to Belgium and Holland have introduced me to the work and ideas of many colleagues there.

These travels over the years have impressed on me, with increasing force, the geography of western Europe, with its routes and barriers which have controlled and channelled the movements of goods and people in the past. It is one thing to be theoretically aware of the Carcassonne Gap or the Rhone corridor but quite another to experience them in reality.

A second impetus to the production of this book has been a growing sadness with the way in which archaeology has become compartmentalized and particularly with the unfortunate divide between 'classical' and 'prehistoric' archaeology. The cultural developments of mainland Europe and the Mediterranean Basin cannot be understood in isolation before AD 400 any more than they can after that date, but such is the pace of study that it is quite impossible for anyone to master the vast range of material now available. One way forward, however, is to explore a few of the themes which bind the two regions, within limited geographical constraints. It is in this context that the present book is offered.

This book has grown in parallel with a course of lectures given at the Oxford Institute of Archaeology and has benefited enormously from discussions with colleagues and students. Without the incomparable facilities of the Ashmolean Library it would never have been finished and without the skilled support of Lynda Smithson, who prepared the typescript, and Christina Unwin, who drew the illustrations, my task would have been immeasurably more difficult.

It would be easy to give the impression that the book was written in a worthy fit of missionary zeal — perhaps there is some element of this — but I can't help remembering Glyn Daniel's advice, received in my impressionable years, 'After all, why does one write and lecture except to amuse oneself?'.

Oxford
June 1987

1 Themes and approaches

For far too long the study of the classical world of the Mediterranean and of the barbarian communities of temperate and northern Europe have remained very separate disciplines. The dichotomy began in the eighteenth century and, as the academic structure of archaeology crystallized in the late nineteenth and first half of the twentieth centuries, the divide became formalized, manifesting itself in the specific titles of lecturership and professorship. But this is not to say that all scholars were prepared to be compartmentalized. The great art historian Paul Jacobstahl, studying the art of the barbarian Celts, ranged wide across the classical world in searching for the threads of inspiration which helped to generate the new art, and in defining by what mechanisms the barbarian and the Mediterranean communities interacted. Others like Sir Mortimer Wheeler, though classicists by training, actively researched the indigenous cultures of the areas they were studying. Yet still the divide persisted and, even today, is all too evident.[1]

The differences between prehistoric and classical archaeology were far more than simply differences in chosen period or place: the two branches evolved fundamentally opposed methodologies and research strategies, so much so that communication became difficult and data-sets were impossible to compare. This is entirely understandable. The archaeologist working in classical countries is usually embarrassed by a profusion of riches — tons of pottery and other artefacts, ample structural evidence and, frequently, a range of relevant documentary material. It is hardly surprising therefore that classical archaeology has tended to emphasize art historical, architectural and historical approaches. The prehistorian, on the other hand, has to search far harder for his data: it is fugitive, unspectacular and labour-intensive to extract. Without historical constraints to act as a guide, the prehistorian has had to develop his own methods of analysis, relying heavily on anthropological models to provide an interpretative framework.

The two camps viewed each other with some disdain. To the classical archaeologist the prehistorian was a person infatuated by technique, wallowing in a sea of trivia, intent upon learning more and more about less and less. To the prehistorian, classical archaeology was static, and without a developing methodology — a mildly exotic form of stamp collecting. Stark characterizations of this kind do, of course, underestimate the middle ground, yet they have a validity.[2]

Since the 1960s the situation has begun to change and at many points there is now a heartening *rapprochement*. This has been brought about largely by two developments. In the first place, archaeologists have become more and more interested by the systems at work in society — themes such as economic strategies, the nature of exchange and trade, the relationships between a civilized core and its periphery — and, more importantly, by the changing trajectories of the socio-economic systems. With the development of these concerns has come an increasing awareness of the potential of studying Mediterranean and barbarian Europe together as part of one system, given the high quality of the historical data and the scholarship that is making it available, as well as the meticulously studied archaeological record of temperate and northern Europe.

The second development has been the emergence of a school of ancient historians concerned with the ancient economy, who approach their study not anecdotally, as was the tradition in the past, but in terms of model-building, using a wide range of analogies and supporting their arguments with quantified data susceptible to statistical testing.[3]

The convergence of interests between the archaeologists reared in the prehistoric cradle, and the economic ancient historians, is a most exciting development. Both groups share aims, methodology and, quite often, data-sets. The divide that has been with us for so long is at last beginning to break down. The result is that archaeologists working on classical sites in the Mediterranean are at last beginning to employ the techniques of extraction and analysis developed by prehistorians, while archaeologists studying the barbarian fringes are paying far greater attention to contemporary developments in the classical world. A new and creative dialogue is underway.

Europe and the Mediterranean together provide an ideal study area. The Mediterranean, by virtue of its favourable climate, wide range of resources and ease of communications has for much of the last 5000 years been an area of innovation and power. The earliest European civilizations began to emerge c. 3000 BC in the Aegean, centred on Crete, and after a period of development the focus of power spread to the Greek mainland. This Minoan-Mycenaean cycle lasted until the twelfth century BC, by which time complex networks of exchange extended from the coasts of Asia Minor in the east to Sicily and southern Italy in the west and penetrated deep into barbarian Europe. Although the extent and degree of Mycenaean influence in Europe is still hotly debated, few would deny that the requirements of the Mycenaean socio-economic system bound many of the communities of central Europe to the east Mediterranean in systems of exchange which can be recognized only dimly in the archaeological record. The collapse of the Mycenaean system was accompanied by rapid culture changes among the communities of central Europe. To what extent this was direct cause-and-effect is highly debatable, not least because other complex folk movements were in progress at the time. Nonetheless, the collapse of the Mycenaean core — a core consuming raw materials — cannot have failed to have had some effect on the central European periphery where many of the consumables were produced.

Core-periphery relationships of this kind pervade the rest of history. The emergence of the Greek city-states around the fringes of the Aegean in the eighth century once more created a central core to which raw materials and manpower flowed from the barbarian periphery. As the Greek colonial settlements spread out, north-eastwards into the Black Sea and westwards, first to southern Italy and Sicily and later to southern France and Spain, so areas once peripheral soon became engulfed in the expanding core. This is the point at which the main theme of this book begins.

With the rise of Rome came a major change of scale both geographically and volumetrically. By the second century AD the core — the Roman empire — had grown so quickly that it had engulfed its periphery without fully integrating it. In the vast region under Roman domination it is possible to define three distinct zones. In the centre was the inner core, Rome and Italy, consuming raw materials, manpower and cash in enormous quantities, far above its own productive capacity, in order to maintain a high urban population and the full apparatus of the state. In simple terms, the inner core was a tax-importing zone. Around it lay an inner periphery of rich provinces — Spain, Gaul, Asia, Africa — producing far in excess of the local needs. That is, they were tax-exporting, part of their product going to maintain the inner core and part to the third zone, the outer periphery of the frontier

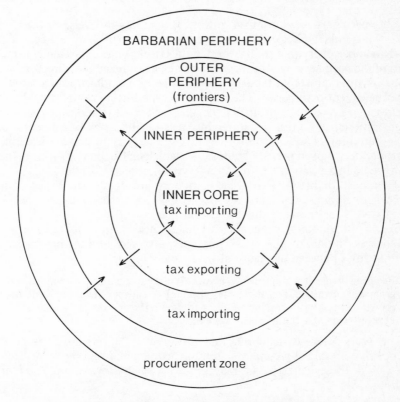

1 Model to show the relationship of the principal economic zones into which the Roman world can be divided

regions, where the fighting forces had to be supplied and paid.[4] Outside all this lay the barbarian periphery, a zone from which, by processes of exchange and trade, a further range of manpower and raw materials, some unobtainable elsewhere (like spices, ivory and exotic animals for beast shows), were drawn into the empire. This model is over- simplified but it helps to focus on the complexities inherent in the Roman system (fig 1).

The breakdown of the Roman system brought to an end the Greco-Roman cycle. Out of its remnants emerged, for a time, a more disparate network of small cores with their own peripheries. This development culminated, in the fifteenth century, in the emergence of western Europe as a single dominating economic force. From this new, but politically divided core, by a series of remarkable overseas adventures, a new periphery was created in America, Africa and the east.

The three European-centred cycles, Minoan-Mycenaean, Greco-Roman and West European, provide ample scope for studying core-periphery relationships. But sufficient will have been said in the brief outline given above to show that variations in scale can be enormous. One of the themes of this book is to explore aspects of these relationships in one sector of the Greco-Roman cycle.

Core-periphery relationships can work at a variety of levels. At the lower end of the scale, a Greek colony planted on a barbarian shore is a core to its barbarian periphery, but to the world of the Greek Aegean the colony itself is part of the periphery. On the mega-scale, we have already seen, in the case of the Roman empire, that the core itself can be broken down into a series of interdependent peripheries. The problem is even further complicated by the fact that no single relationship is static, and each set of relationships develops along different trajectories at different rates. The best way to appreciate the range of complexities inherent in a real situation is to explore a defined territory over a given period of time, as we will do in Chapters 2–9. Only then will we be in a position to offer a few generalizations (Chapter 10).

Relationships between core and periphery are dominated by economic exchanges administered under a variety of political systems. Let us consider briefly the two aspects of this contention.

Any consideration of economic exchanges must begin with Karl Polanyi's famous definition of the three processes involved in the movement of commodities between one cultural group and another:

> Reciprocity denotes movements between correlative points of symmetrical groupings: redistribution designates appropriational movements towards the centre and out again: exchange refers to vice-versa movements taking place between 'hands' under a market system.[5]

Some years later, in exploring the *two-sidedness* of organized trade (as opposed to one-sided *pre-trade* — hunt, expedition and raid) he formalized a view of the three main types of trade: *gift trade*, *administered* or *treaty trade* and *market trade*:

> *Gift trade* links the partners in relationships of *reciprocity*. . . . The organization of trading is usually ceremonial, involving mutual presentations, embassies, or

political dealings between chiefs or kings. The *goods* are treasure, objects of elite circulation. . . .

Administered or *treaty trade* has a firm foundation in treaty relationships of a more or less formal nature. On both sides the import interest is determinative, and for that reason the trade is organized through governmental or government-controlled channels. . . . The mutually imported goods are standardized, according to quantity and package, weight or other easily accessible criteria. . . .

Market trade is the third typical form of trading. Exchange is here in the form of integration that links partners to each other. . . . The range of tradable goods — the commodities — is practically unlimited. . . . The market mechanism is adaptable to the handling not only of the goods, but of every element of trade separately — storage, transportation, risk, credit, payments, and the like.[6]

These concepts and definitions are very useful in exploring and describing the various relationships encountered in Europe during the Greco-Roman period.

The different types of trade were carried out at different locations. Gift trade could operate practically anywhere. Administered trade would normally be practised at a *port-of-trade* (or emporium) — a place set aside for commercial transactions giving protection to the foreign trader and usually situated at a route node such as a good harbour. Market trade could be enacted at external markets, like ports-of-trade, or internal markets to which foreign traders were admitted. It was through the internal markets that the products of long distance trade could most easily be integrated into the 'local' socio-economic system.

Polanyi's concept of port-of-trade has been the subject of lively discussion.[7] Polanyi saw the port-of-trade in broad terms as a neutral place to which either buyers or sellers travelled to exchange goods with resident buyers or sellers. Other writers have tried to limit the definition, leading to some confusion. More recently Kenneth Hirth has developed the geographer's concept of the *gateway community* to serve archaeological needs:

Gateway communities develop either as a response to increased trade or to the settling of sparsely populated frontier areas. They generally are located along natural corridors of communication and at the critical passages between areas of high mineral, agricultural, or craft productivity; dense population; high demand or supply of scarce resources; and at the interface of different technologies or levels of socio-political complexity. They often occur along economic shear lines where cost factors change and where there are economic discontinuities in the free movement of merchandise. The function of these settlements is to satisfy demand for commodities through trade and the location of these communities reduces transportation costs involved in their movement.[8]

Hirth's definition is of considerable relevance to the region and period to be considered below. The quality of its fit is a matter to which we will return in Chapter 10.

Hirth goes on to make two further points of general significance to our discussion. First, he contrasts the *central place* — a hierarchically dominant settlement which lies towards the centre of a symmetrical service, or distribution, zone and the gateway community, which is located on one edge of their hinterland. Individual communities throughout the hinterland are linked directly to the gateway community by a linear or dendritic market network which need not be circumscribed by political boundaries. Moreover, while the central place is characterized by an emphasis on retail economic activity, gateway communities are commercial middlemen indulging more in wholesale activity. The kind of model most applicable to the situation which concerns us can be characterized as the multiple gateway case (fig 2). Secondly, Hirth considers the potential effects of competition from hinterland central places. The gateway community may lose part of its hinterland and decline to an economic level similar to its competitors; it may take on an even greater central place activity itself; new areas may be brought under the gateway's control; or it may cause the development of more complex forms of socio-political authority. This last possibility could precipitate militarism, leading to the conquest of the hinterland. These possibilities are all of potential relevance to western Europe in the Greco-Roman period, where the pace of change was rapid.

We have said that core-periphery relations concerned economic exchange administered under a variety of political systems, although the discussion so far has been concerned essentially with the mechanisms of exchange. The Greco-Roman world was characterized by two contrasting political systems, the city-state and the empire, and the passage of time from the sixth century BC to the second century AD saw the transformation of one into the other. The

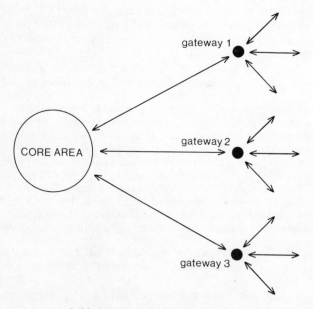

2 Model of a multiple gateway system

change was accompanied by continuous reordering of the exchange systems binding the interior to the exterior. To begin with, from the sixth to the end of the second centuries, the pace of change was comparatively slow. The core remained small, the interface with the barbarian world had not spread much beyond the boundary of the Mediterranean ecozone and the barbarian periphery was immense. Stability had allowed a complex of exchange systems to evolve, based largely on the process of gift trade. Towards the end of the second century BC Roman militarism became a dominant force, and within the space of barely 150 years the frontiers had advanced through Europe so fast that those new exchange patterns which developed in front of it were rapidly overtaken and absorbed. It was not until the middle of the first century AD that a new stability emerged, but now the empire was so large, and protected by a resident military élite stationed along the barbarian interface, that entirely new systems of administered trade came into force, while the internal structure of the empire was itself divisible into several levels of economic interdependence.

Europe in the Greco-Roman period provides an ideal study area within which to consider core-periphery relationships and the mechanisms of trade which enabled the two parts of the system to articulate. The reasons for this are not difficult to see. In the first place the geography is varied. For much of the period, the traditional core zone occupied a single ecological niche, the Mediterranean ecozone, while the periphery comprised another — temperate Europe. By the middle of the first century AD the core zone (in its broadest sense) had expanded to engulf temperate Europe, creating a new interface roughly coincident with the southern boundary of the coniferous zone of northern Europe. There is a satisfying neatness about this which, given a detailed knowledge of the subsistence strategies of the various regions, based on intensive archaeological research, allows the intricacies of the regional economies to be assessed and compared with changes brought about by developing patterns of trade.

The second reason is the quality of the historical data available for much of the area. Generations of scholars working on a tolerably large corpus of texts have provided a framework of aspirations, motives and events against which to see the unfolding economic pattern. While the historical sources often fall short of providing the quantified data necessary for statistical assessment, and while archaeological evidence seldom has a sufficiently precise chronology, it can fairly be said that the combined data provided by classical and archaeological research makes Europe one of the richest study areas available.

In this present volume we make use of a small tithe of what is to hand, restricting our study largely to western Europe. The reasons for this are several. In the first place, the sheer volume of data available makes some selection necessary, and it is with western Europe that the writer is most familiar. But the western zone has a distinct cultural character which distinguishes it from the east. For the most part the communities were sedentary and there is little evidence of major dislocations of population. In eastern Europe, on the other hand, the presence of nomadic and semi-nomadic communities, coming ultimately from the Russian steppes, introduces a distorting factor which, fascinating though it is in its own right, is difficult to contend with when exploring the comparatively simple models of core-periphery and of trade which are our principal concern here. The problems of eastern Europe deserve a full treatment in their own right.

The physical structure of the landscape of western Europe constrained the way in which the different communities developed. Some, occupying central positions on major routeways, or commanding access to rare resources, remained in contact with more distant regions and were receptive to outside influences, while others, cut off by features of the natural landscape or lying well away from the main routes, developed in isolation.

The cognitive geography of Europe, of someone brought up in the Mediterranean, must have been very vague, until, that is, the Roman conquests of the first century BC began to open up the interior. In simple terms it must have appeared as if the Mediterranean was backed by a wall of mountains. Beyond lay a vast expanse of undulating country, scored by great rivers which flowed into an ocean (Atlantic, English Channel and North Sea), and across that ocean lay a group of islands. It would have been widely understood that the ocean could be reached by sailing northwards after passing through the Pillars of Hercules (Straits of Gibraltar).

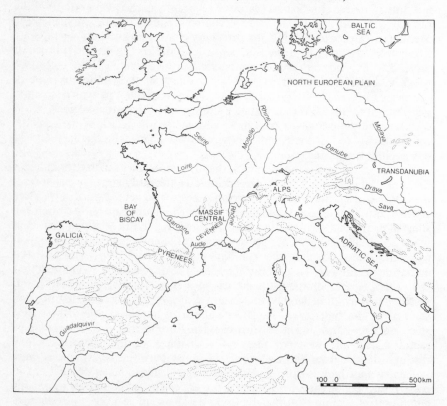

3 The physical structure of western Europe

There were two stretches of the Mediterranean coast which provided comparatively easy access through the mountain barrier: the southern coast of Gaul and the head of the Adriatic. From the Gaulish coast two routes led deep into the hinterland. A northern route followed the Rhône valley, passing between the western fringe of the Alps and the Massif Central and Cevennes, to link up the river system of the Seine, Loire, Moselle and Rhine; the other took a western route along the Aude and through the Carcassonne Gap to the Garonne, and thence to the Bay of Biscay (fig 3).

The head of the Adriatic also offered two routes to the interior. One followed the River Po to the Italian lakes, and provided access to the major Alpine passes, which led eventually to the upper reaches first of the Rhine and then of the Danube. The second route led north-east, through the Julian Alps to the headwaters of the Sava and Drava, providing access to Transdanubia, and along the eastern foothills of the Alps (roughly the present Austrian/Hungarian border) to the crucial route node in the vicinity of modern Bratislava on the Danube. From here, the Danube led east or west, while the river Morava led north to the north European plain and the Baltic beyond.

These routes have all played a decisive part in the cultural development of Europe, not only in the prehistoric and Greco–Roman periods but also into medieval and early modern times. In times of peace they provided axes of communication by which traded goods and the traders themselves could pass, while in times of war they served as lines of entry for invading armies.

The resources of western Europe were considerable and, in many cases, particularly desirable. Most important were metals, in particular tin and copper, and to a lesser extent gold and silver. Two regions were particularly well-endowed: the hinterland of the river Guadalquivir in southern Spain, and what we can call the Atlantic province — including Galicia in northern Iberia, Armorica, south-western Britain, south Wales and parts of southern Ireland. The Carthaginian domination of southern Iberia and the Straits of Gibraltar was soon to render the Guadalquivir deposits inaccessible to the Greeks, who were forced, inevitably, to develop the routes through Gaul in order to tap the riches of the Atlantic province. Other metal-rich deposits were to be found in the eastern Alps and the mountains of Bohemia.

In addition to essential raw materials like copper and tin, and in the later period the more widespread iron, a whole range of luxury commodities were traded across Europe — amber from the Baltic, furs from the north European plain, wild animals for the arena, hunting dogs, rare herbs and relishes, pigments, etc. Less exotic goods included leather and woollen fabrics, together with a range of foodstuffs, some of which, like Gaulish hams, were regarded as delicacies by the Roman consumers. No doubt there was much more besides, unrecoverable from the classical and archaeological sources. One commodity which should not be underestimated is manpower, which was imported into the Greco–Roman core in several forms, as slaves, mercenaries and auxiliary troops. Quantification is very difficult but there can be little doubt, from the classical literature, that the slave trade had reached very considerable proportions by the first century BC. This massive consumer demand for slaves cannot have failed to have had a dramatic effect on the social structure of the barbarian communities from which they were culled.

The constant outflow of raw materials and manpower from barbarian Europe to the Greco–Roman world was matched by reciprocal imports in the form of consumer durables, often fossilizing high labour input, for use and redistribution by the barbarian élites. In this way, social systems were created and maintained, and if the flow faltered, élites could collapse. By these processes the interdependence of the Greco–Roman and barbarian systems was assured.

Throughout the thousand years or so covered in this book political changes of considerable magnitude took place, constantly shaping and reshaping the links between the Mediterranean and barbarian worlds. In the seventh century the links were tenuous. Traders from the east Mediterranean were probing the coastal regions of Gaul and Iberia but it was not until *c.* 600 BC with the foundation of the Phocaean colony of Massalia (Marseilles) that the Greeks established a permanent foothold in the region. Thereafter, more colonies followed, often as daughter settlements from the mother city, until the entire coastline from the valley of the Ebro to the Maritime Alps was fringed with Greek-occupied trading ports. The prime attraction to the settlers was easy access to the mineral and other wealth of the interior, and oversight of the coastal shipping lanes leading south and west along the Iberian coast.

Routes to the interior were developed and regular exchange took place with the chiefdoms of west central Europe, the trade reaching a peak of intensity about 500 BC. Thereafter, internal developments led to an increasingly unstable situation, which erupted, in the middle of the fifth century, with the breaking out of Celtic warrior bands. Bands of raiders soon swelled into marauding, migratory hordes, who swept southwards through southern France and into Italy, and eastwards through the Balkans to Greece and even to Asia Minor.

Such a movement disrupted established patterns of exchange, and it is not until the beginning of the second century BC, which saw the final stages of the Roman domination of Italy, that regular systems of exchange can begin to be recognized again, linking the Mediterranean to the north. But by now the political configuration of the Mediterranean had changed. Rome had become an imperial power, and a few decades later, in the single year 146 BC, had destroyed its two most powerful trading rivals, Carthage and Corinth. From this point on, the economic exploitation of the European hinterland went largely unchecked.

The Roman state had now developed socio-political and socio-economic systems which required the constant inflow of raw materials and manpower to maintain their stability. This need, and the endemic militarism of the state, led inexorably to a process of economic exploitation of peripheral areas, followed by conquest. In this way the army and the traders leapfrogged over each other across barbarian Europe, absorbing the largely Celtic tribes into the Roman system.

The Rhine-Danube line was, effectively, the northern boundary of the empire, even though temporary advances had been made beyond it, and here a long-lasting interface with the barbarians was established. The trading relationships with the barbarian north echoed in many ways the systems established by the Greeks along the Mediterranean coast 800 years before. Social systems emerged in free Germany comparable to those in west central Europe, and the rise of Germanic warrior bands and their subsequent move south had something in common with the earlier Celtic migrations. It was the turmoil they caused in the fourth and fifth centuries AD that brought the Greco–Roman world to an end.

The varied geography of Europe, and the response of the Greco–Roman world to it, provide an ideal context against which to study core-periphery relationships and the trading systems accompanying them. In the following chapters, aspects of the story will be considered, roughly in chronological order, selecting those themes which best reflect classical and native interaction in the socio-political and socio-economic sphere. In the final chapter we will return to the question of general models to see what can be learnt from this particular case study.

2 The Greek adventure: 600–400 BC

The little Turkish town of Eski Foca, some 50 km (31 miles) north of Smyrna, overlooks a wide, well-protected harbour, almost closed by a rocky island and a humpbacked peninsula. An imaginative onlooker could be excused for thinking them to be seals breaking the surface of the water. *Phoce*, the Greek word for seal, is the probable origin of the classical name for the city — Phocaea. Nowadays, there is nothing left to be seen of the once-famous town, and it is difficult to imagine the impact which the settlers of this dour coast had on the barbarians of western Europe; yet the Phocaeans were among the most adventurous of the Greeks, who, in a brief century and a half, 734–580 BC, were to establish colonies throughout the length and breadth of the Mediterranean.[1]

The reasons for the period of colonization were many, and will have varied in relative significance from one mother city to another.[2] The reason most usually given by classical writers was over-population, and there is no doubt that in many areas population was growing fast. In Attica, for example, where the cemeteries have been well-explored, it is estimated that the population increased by a factor of six during the years between 800 and 700 BC. An annual four per cent increase is considerable, even by modern Third World standards.[3] In a place like Attica — fertile and thinly peopled — the rise could be absorbed to generate new prosperity through industrialization. In consequence, Athens played little part in the colonizing movement, but elsewhere, where available land was limited, the only solution was to select a body of surplus population and send it off to find a new ecological niche in which to develop. So it was with the Therans. Their island (modern Santorini), though fertile was of finite extent, and after a seven year drought the situation had reached crisis point. The oracle at Delphi had earlier been consulted and had advised that a colony be sent to found a city in Libya. Not knowing where Libya was, the islanders were reluctant to act, but the drought forced their hand and the unwilling colonists had to be chosen by lot from among the young men. Herodotus gives details of what happened:

> The expedition sailed to Libya but did not know what to do next, so returned to Thera: but the Therans stoned them as they were putting in and would not allow them to land, telling them to sail back again. So under compulsion they sailed back and established a settlement on an island off Libya, called Platea.[4]

Later, we are told, the settlers moved to the better site of Cyrene. The story is of particular interest as an example of society's response when population level approaches or exceeds the holding capacity of the land.

It would be wrong to overstress population pressure as a direct causal factor in colonization. It was undoubtedly important, but there were other factors too, less directly demographic. The alleviation of social tensions by migration has been used as a solution many times throughout history (though quite often the tensions themselves are caused by demographic stress). The lure of equality and freedom from conventional restraints, together with the potential opportunities for acquiring wealth, would have been a considerable incentive to society's malcontents, encouraging them to move off to new lands. When the poet Archilochos, describing the colony on Thasos — 'three times lousy city', characterizes the population by saying 'the dregs of all the Greeks have run together in Thasos' he may not have been painting too inaccurate a picture of at least some early colonies.

One overriding incentive to colonize, was trade. The Greeks made a distinction between a settlement away from home (*apoitia*) and a trading post (*emporion*), but quite often the differences were blurred and one would merge into the other. A casual settlement of traders could become the nucleus of an organized settlement while a planted colony would not fail to exploit the resource potential it could command.

Greek and Phoenician colonization in the western Mediterranean (fig 4)

The Greek penetration of the western Mediterranean in the eighth century must have been largely motivated by the desire to acquire raw materials, in particular metals, by establishing regular contact with the metal-producing peoples of the west, among them the Etruscans of north Italy and the Tartessans in south-western Iberia.[5] One of the earliest of the colonial settlements was at Pithekoussai, on the island of Ischia at the northern end of the Bay of Naples.[6] According to tradition, it was created by an expedition of Euboeans from Eretria and Chalcis, and the earliest pottery from the excavations suggests that trade was already underway by *c.* 770 BC. Situated on an easily defensible promontory on an offshore island, the traders were admirably placed to serve as middle men between the highly receptive and metal-rich Etruscans and the Greek home markets (fig 5). Analysis of the considerable quantities of iron slag and associated industrial debris show that iron ore was being imported from Elba in bulk, and here worked into blooms for trans-shipment to Greece.[7]

Not long after the establishment of Pithekoussai, the Chalcidians founded a new settlement on the adjacent mainland, at Cumae, where an acropolis and landing beach could be found, protected from landward approach by a marsh.[8] The earliest pottery suggests links with Euboea going back to even before 770 BC, but the first Greek tombs are no earlier than 730.

The pioneering trade centres at Pithekoussai and Cumae had been thrust into a semi-barbarian unknown on the fringes of the Etruscan sphere of influence. What now followed was a consolidation of the approach to this interface with the foundation of a series of colonies on eastern Sicily and southern Italy. Thucydides provides the outline: 'Of the Greeks the first to come were Chalcidians from Euboea sailing with Thoukles as founder; they

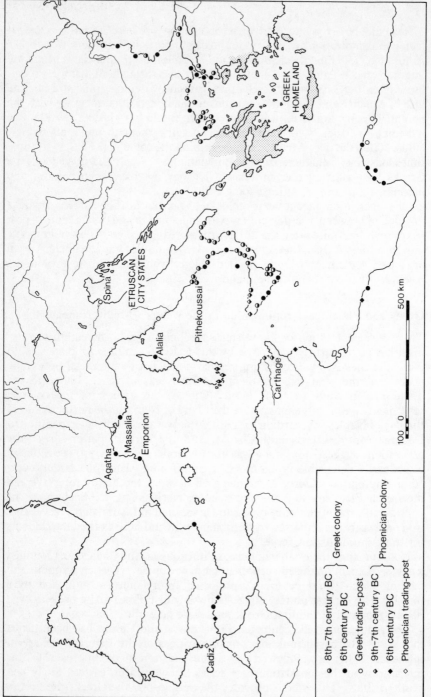

Legend:

◑ 8th–7th century BC } Greek colony
● 6th century BC

○ Greek trading-post

◈ 9th–7th century BC } Phoenician colony
◆ 6th century BC

◇ Phoenician trading-post

Map labels: GREEK HOMELAND, ETRUSCAN CITY STATES, Spina, Alalia, Pithekoussai, Carthage, Agatha, Massalia, Emporion, Cadiz

Scale: 500 km / 100 0

4 *The Mediterranean world in the ninth–sixth centuries* BC

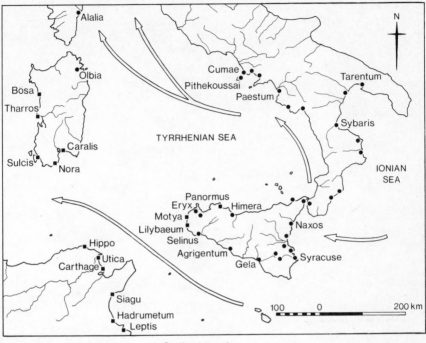

• city of Greek foundation   ■ Carthaginian city

5 The routes between the east and west Mediterranean and the cities controlling them

established Naxos, and set up the altar of Apollo the Leader which still exists outside the city'.[9] Naxos, just south of Taormina, on the east coast of Sicily, was ideally located to be a port-of-call for Greek ships rounding the toe of Italy. According to Thucydides, it was established in 734 BC. A year later, the Corinthians set up a colony to the south, at Syracuse, commanding the best deep water harbours in the area. Other groups of colonists arrived not long after, and within eighty years, by 650 BC, eastern Sicily and southern Italy had been transformed into an extension of the Greek world by successive waves of immigrants — Euboeans, Achaeans, Spartans, Rhodians and Cretans — as well as by second and third generation colonists expanding into new territories as their original settlements could no longer hold the swelling populations. The cities of *Magna Graecia*, as the area became known, grew rich through their command of the western trade routes, as well as from the exploitation of their rich agricultural hinterlands.

It is against this general background that the activities of the Phocaeans must be seen. Phocaea was never a large city. It had little good agricultural land but it was blessed with a magnificent harbour and inevitably its citizens took to sea-faring, and in particular to exploration. It was they, more than any other people, who were responsible for opening up the mineral-rich west

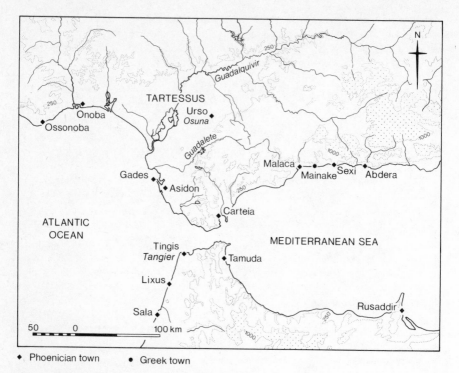

6 *The cities of the Mediterranean/Atlantic interface
controlling the Straits of Gibraltar*

for the Greeks. Herodotus thought it worth remarking that the Phocaean adventurers sailed not in merchant ships but in *pentekonters* — fifty-oared war galleys — a sensible precaution because they were vying with the Phoenicians from Carthage for control of the western Mediterranean.

The Phoenicians, themselves a sea-going colonial people, came from the shores of the Levant, and from the ninth century began to establish colonies on the north African coast.[10] One of the earliest, Utica, was soon eclipsed by Carthage (in Phoenician Kart-Hadasht, the New City) close to the modern city of Tunis. From here, Phoenician traders and warships sailed west along the north coast of Africa to the metal-rich region of Iberia. For the next three centuries or so these two great maritime powers contested the western Mediterranean (fig 5). The Greeks, holding most of Sicily and southern Italy, commanded the Straits of Messina, the Tyrrhenian sea and the northern coast-hopping route to Iberia. From what is now modern Tunisia, and with towns established in western Sicily (e.g. at Motya) and on southern Sardinia, the Carthaginians were able to control the southern route along the coast of the Margreb to the Pillars of Heracles and beyond.

It was into these contested waters that the Phocaean warships sailed in search of metals. 'The Phocaeans were the first of the Greeks to make long voyages, and it was they who opened up the region of the Adriatic, Etruria, and Spain and Tartessus', writes Herodotus.[11] Tartessus features frequently in ancient accounts: it was the rich metal-producing region of the river Guadalquivir, which flows into the Atlantic between Cadiz and Huelva.[12] To reach it ships would have had to sail out through the Straits of Gibraltar into the unknown Atlantic (fig 6). Herodotus continues:

> When they went to Tartessus they became very friendly with the king of the Tartessians, whose name was Arganthonios . . . . So friendly with this man were the Phocaeans that he first asked them to leave Ionia and live wherever they wished in his territory, but afterwards when he could not persuade them, and heard that the Persian power was increasing in that area, he gave them the money to build a wall around the city: he gave them a great deal, for the circuit of the wall is considerable, and it is all made of large well-fitted stone blocks.[13]

The episode dates to the period 640–550 BC and implies a long-established relationship. The attraction of the ready supplies of tin, copper and silver, as well as the friendliness of the natives would have been a considerable incentive to the Phocaeans to return frequently once the route had been established. There is some place-name evidence to suggest that the Greeks may even have established settlements on the Mediterranean and Atlantic coasts of Africa, but if so they were short-lived, engulfed by the rise of Carthaginian power.

Most Greek traders would have used the northern route — to Syracuse, then on to Cumae, and then north and west following the coasts of Italy, southern France and Spain. The journey was long and there would certainly have been landfalls on the way where camps were established, some of them developing into trading settlements of varying degrees of permanence. Such may have been the sites of Saint-Blaise and La Couronne, close to the mouth of the River Rhône, where Corinthian and east Greek pottery, dating from the late seventh century, has been found.[14]

As time went on and the routes became firmly entrenched, so colonial settlements were founded (fig 7). Massalia (Marseilles) was the first to be established, in about 600 BC by a colony of Phocaeans.[15] Some daughter colonies followed: Emporion (Ampurias) on the coast of northern Spain not long after, with Tauroention (Le Brusc), Antipolis (Antibes) and Nicaea (Nice) a little later. Olbia, near Hyères, came into being *c*. 330–300 BC. All four of the colonies in France were intended to be strongholds against pressure from the Celto-Ligurian tribes. The Phocaeans also had a colony on Corsica at Alalia (Aleria), founded about 560 BC.[16]

The power of the mother city was short-lived. In 544 BC the Persians besieged the town and in the period of turmoil which followed half the population sailed away to join the colony at Alalia, founded two decades before. The sudden increase in population on Corsica provoked the Carthaginians and Etruscans to a joint attack in *c*. 537 BC, no doubt in an attempt to circumscribe Greek influence in the western Mediterranean. The Phocaeans won the battle of Alalia but their fleet was severely mauled and they withdrew to the safety of southern Italy to found a new and highly

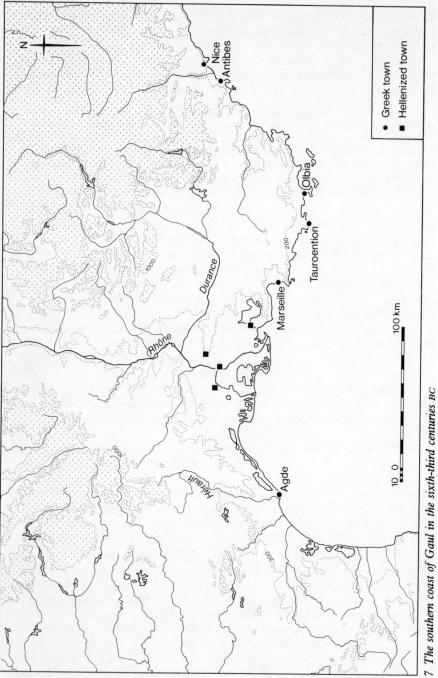

7 *The southern coast of Gaul in the sixth–third centuries BC*

successful city at Elea (Velia), leaving the Carthaginians to consolidate their position in the western Mediterranean.

The eighth and seventh centuries BC saw the Carthaginian hold on the north coast of Africa and the southern shores of Iberia strengthening. Phoenician settlements clustered around the Straits of Gibraltar effectively closing the passage to the Atlantic and the western seaboard of Iberia while the port of Gades (Cadiz) controlled the approach to the Guadalquivir valley. Settlements spread over Sardinia and the Balearics and along the Mediterranean coast of Spain: Carthago Novo (Cartagena) was established by 226 BC and Phoenician influence spread as far north as Saguntum, making the River Ebro the effective frontier between the Greek and Phoenician spheres. The battle of Alalia in *c.* 537 BC had effectively established Carthaginian maritime supremacy in the area; thereafter, the Greek traders were restricted to the northern shores of the western Mediterranean. It was to barbarian Gaul and beyond that they now had to look for supplies of exportable raw materials.

The port of Massalia (figs 8 and 9)

The Phocaeans were wise to choose the site of Marseilles as their principal port-of-trade on the Gaulish coast. The prime attraction of the area was the River Rhône, providing a means of easy access to the barbarian north and to the headwaters of the Loire and thus the Atlantic seaboard. We have already seen that traders probably established themselves at Saint-Blaise and La Couronne, close to the Rhône mouth, in the late seventh century, but both sites had shortcomings. By choosing a site 50km (31 miles) to the east, the marshes of the Rhône delta and the exposed rocky coast of the Chaîne de l'Estanque were avoided and the Phocaean sailors could have a far more congenial anchorage — a deep narrow bay, or *calanque* (more extensive than the present Vieux Port which occupies part of the former inlet), dominated on the north by a narrow, rocky promontory, ideal for settlement and defence.

Little is known of the earliest settlement.[17] Traditionally its founder on arrival married a local princess and the new colony lived in harmony with the indigenous population. By 525 BC the city was rich enough to establish a treasury at the Greek sanctuary of Delphi. Archaeological evidence is sparse, but recent excavations at the Bourse have established the line of the main approach road between the northern end of the *calanque* and the marsh beyond, which protected the eastern side of the promontory. Traces of a possible sixth-century defensive wall were found, which had been replaced by the more massive Hellenistic wall of the second century BC. Just outside the defensive line were several funerary enclosures of the fourth century. The significance of the discovery is that it establishes the eastern limit of the early city, implying that settlement extended across the three peaks of the peninsula, St Laurent, Les Moulins and Les Carmes. Archaeological material collected from within the settlement area from time to time yielded an impressive array of imported pottery, including material from Etruria, Corinth, Athens, Sparta as well as from the eastern Greek area — Rhodes and

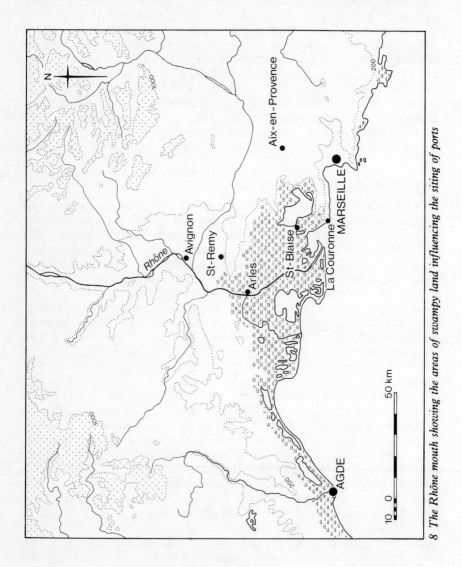

8 *The Rhône mouth showing the areas of swampy land influencing the siting of ports*

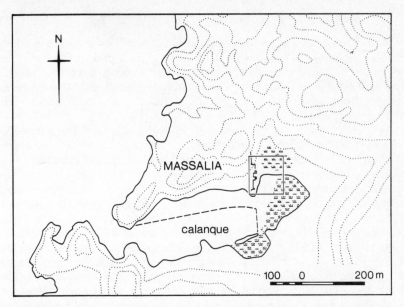

9 *The city of Massalia (Marseilles) in the pre-Roman period (redrawn after Euzennat 1980, figs. 1 and 2). The inset (below) shows the eastern approaches and the Hellenistic city wall exposed during the excavation of the Bourse*

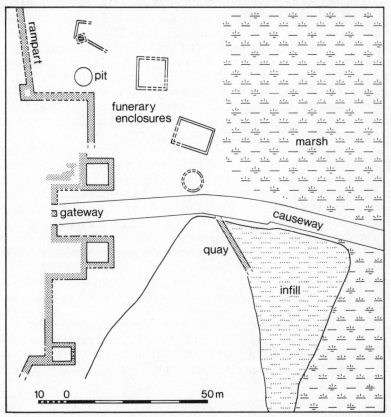

Chios, including a range of wares of Phocaean origin or inspiration. Sherd counts of the more closely datable Attic wares show a peak at the end of the sixth century BC, with a rapid drop in the fifth suggesting (but not necessarily proving) a decline in trade with the east Mediterranean after about 500 BC. Evidence from neighbouring sites tends to reflect a similar pattern.[18] The problem is one to which we shall return.

The range of imports is impressive; so too is the industrial development of the new colony.[19] Brown-painted 'Ionian wares' and comb-decorated grey 'Phocaean wares' were widely copied to be used locally, and exported to the barbarian hinterland and along the coastal routes. Wine growing was also introduced, the wine being transported in large amphorae. Preliminary fabric analysis of the so-called Massaliot amphorae has identified four different locations of manufacture: two on the coast of Provence, along the Massif des Maures (between Hyères and Fréjus) and the Massif de l'Estrel (beween Fréjus and Antibes); in the region of the Drôme-Rhône confluence, and also possibly in the region of Nice. If the wine was produced in the regions where the amphorae were made, which seems probable, then the region controlled by Massalia must have been far larger than has previously been thought.[20]

Massalia and its daughter cities occupied a comparatively fertile coastal zone, where vines and olives could be grown in plenty, together with lesser quantities of corn. The climate and the soils were ideal for the production of herbs, relishes, medicinal plants and resin (as a visit to the market at Nice will remind us today), while the coastal position ensured plentiful supplies of fish, salt, coral and purple dye from the *murex* shell. From not far inland, and particularly in the Montagne Noire, a range of metals could be extracted.

Perhaps the simplest way to see Massalia is as a focus for exchange, set in resource-rich territory, able to articulate the complex processes of trade between three spheres: Iberia, the barbarian north, and the states of the central and eastern Mediterranean.[21] It was the balance point of a complex dynamic system in a state of unstable equilibrium. Deflect any one component and the whole system was liable to dislocation.

The relationship between Massalia and the Etruscan cities of northern Italy, involving as it did long-established trading practices and complex political alliances, was a crucial element in the broader system. There is ample pottery evidence from the Greek cities of southern Gaul, and from the peasant settlements of the hinterland, to show that trade with Etruria was well developed in the sixth century BC — Etruscan black bucchero ware is everywhere to be found. The reason is not difficult to understand, for the Etruscan coastal cities, sited midway between the ports of Magna Graecia and Massalia, were the obvious stopping-off point, added to which Etruria produced a ready market for craft products brought from the east Mediterranean, and metals and other raw materials from the barbarian north and west.[22]

In the mid-sixth century BC this pattern was disrupted by the foundation of the Phocaean colony at Alalia on Corsica, the effect of which was to attract Greek shipping, cutting out the need to stop off on the northern Italian coast. To what extent this affected trade with the Etruscan coastal towns it is impossible yet to judge, but the battle of Alalia in c. 537 BC between the Massaliots on the one side and the Etruscans and Carthaginians in alliance on the other, and the strained relations which followed, may well have led to a wholesale breakdown in relations, and the possible exclusion of Etruscan ships from Greek ports in the western Mediterranean.[23]

The expansion of Etruscan influence

The Etruscan response was to develop new trading systems northwards through the Appenines to the Po valley. Etruscanization of the material culture of the area is well-recognized in the period 535–25 BC, with the foundation of cities such as Marzabotto and Felsina (Bononia) commanding the routes through the Appenines. The Po valley, with its rich corn-lands, was an attractive area to settlers and traders alike, but for the Etruscans it provided two important interfaces now denied to them in the west Mediterranean: direct access to the resources of the barbarian north, through the communities of the Alpine foothills and the Italian lakes, via the eastern Alpine passes; and access, through the coastal towns of Spina and Adria, to the Adriatic sea and the markets of Greece.[24]

Excavations in the cemetery of Spina show that Etruscans and Greeks lived side by side, though who initiated the settlement is not yet clear. The earliest imported vases from the graves, almost all of them Athenian, date to c. 520 BC and herald the beginning of a period of prosperity that was to last until about 300 BC. The archaeological evidence from Adria suggests a slightly earlier date of foundation.[25]

The two Adriatic ports, whether Greek or Etruscan by foundation, are a reflection of Etruria turning its back on the west Mediterranean and realigning its trading axes. The Greeks could obtain copious supplies of grain from the Po valley settlements, as well as high-quality horses from the neighbouring Veneti, while metals from Etruria would find a ready market. The Etruscan cities for their part had easy access to supplies of Greek luxury products and could also look northwards to the productive barbarian lands beyond the Alps.

The progressive isolation of the Etruscans from the markets of the west Mediterranean continued for the next half century, exacerbated by the increasing dominance of the cities of Magna Graecia, and culminating in the closing of the Straits of Messina to Etruscan shipping by the tyrant Anaxilas in the 470s. In two major sea battles, fought in 474 BC off Himera and Cumae, Etruscan fleets were defeated by the Greeks. Thereafter, the coastal cities of Etruria were in decline and Etruscan trade with Massalia and other cities of southern Gaul dwindled as the north-eastern sector of the west Mediterranean became an exclusively Greek preserve. This major readjustment in the exchange system, caused by the political squabbles of 540–30 BC and culminating in the sea battles of 474, had, as we shall see, a significant knock-on effect in developments north of the Alps.

Massalia and the barbarians of the north

Massalia's position on the coast of southern Gaul was well chosen: it was admirably sited for controlling the longshore trade between metal-rich Spain and the ports of Italy and beyond, but it was also located sufficiently close to the Rhône mouth to command the major route leading northwards to the heartland of Celtic Europe. Along both routes, and in both directions, commodities would have passed, but inevitably there were changes with time, and as the political configuration of the Mediterranean evolved, so the patterns, directions and intensities of trade altered. The dynamics of the systems are dimly reflected in the archaeological data; inadequate though it is, there is no other way in which the problem can be approached.

North of the Alps, in a great swathe of territory stretching from the Paris Basin to the valley of the Morava, and from the Alps to the north European plain, the numerous communities shared a broadly common culture, known archaeologically as the Western Hallstatt culture (fig 10). It was a patchwork of local groups, differing in a variety of respects, but sufficiently similar to be regarded as ethnically homogeneous.[26] In the early Hallstatt period (roughly 800–600 BC) there is comparatively little evidence for great distinction in wealth. A few individuals were important enough to be buried with a funerary cart, or the horse gear appropriate to it; rather more were warriors, their rank denoted by their swords, but the great majority of the population were interred with little more than their personal ornaments and a range of pots containing food offerings. Cemeteries were generally small, reflecting the dispersed nature of settlement, and suggesting that the average unit was occupied by the extended family or, at the most, a small cluster of families. Apart from the horse-gear and weapons, and rarely carts, the only luxury objects found in graves ('luxury' in the sense of representing fossilized work) were elaborately decorated pots, though exotics such as gold, glass, amber and coral occurred sparingly.

Although evidence for economy and social structure is still extremely patchy, the overall impression given is of a high degree of cultural stability. The society was producing what it needed to maintain an equilibrium, but little more; that is, it was a sufficer economy. Since prestige was not at this stage equated with the ability to dispense goods on a lavish scale, there was little need to produce unnecessary surplus. This, in very broad outline, was the situation by c. 600 BC when Massalia was founded.

What followed in the next 150 years (c. 600–450 BC) was the transformation of Western Hallstatt culture (archaeologically the change from Hallstatt C to Hallstatt D). Greek, Etruscan and Massaliot luxury goods are found in quantity in Western Hallstatt territory; a hierarchy of very rich graves appears; and a number of fortified hilltop sites display features redolent of powerful aristocracies. It is difficult to resist the conclusion that the presence of the Greek trading port created a demand for commodities from the north and that this led to the emergence of powerful chiefdoms in the core of the barbarian area, able to command the flow of luxury objects

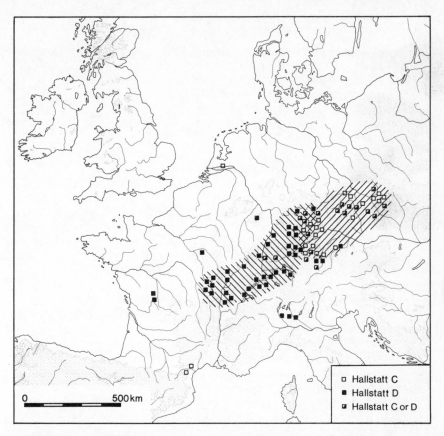

10 *Wagon graves of the Hallstatt period showing the westerly shift in emphasis between Hallstatt C and Hallstatt D*

from the south. This generalization is worthy of more detailed consideration.[27]

The range of Mediterranean imports found in the settlements and burials of the Western Hallstatt zone has been extensively studied (figs 11 and 12). It includes Attic pottery, Mediterranean amphorae and a variety of bronze vessels of Greek and Etruscan origin associated with the wine drinking ritual — a *krater*, a *hydria*, cauldrons and tripods, *stamnoi*, jugs and bowls. In addition to items belonging to the wine-set, smaller objects of ivory, amber and gold of Mediterranean manufacture have been recorded. The dating of the individual imports cannot always be precise, and is liable to periodic reassessment; there is also the unanswerable question of how long an object of value remained in use before burial.[28] But aside from these constraints, the earliest items found are the *oinochoai* ('Rhodian flagons') from Vilsingen and Kappel, now thought to have been manufactured in the last third of the seventh century BC. The *hydria* from Grächwil was probably made in

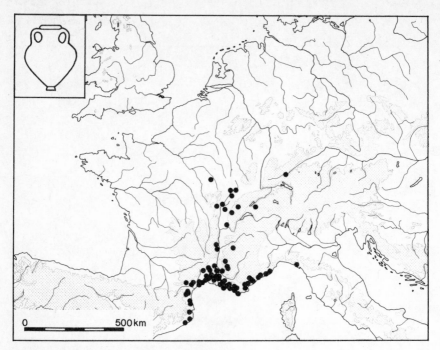

11 Above: distribution of Massaliot amphorae.
Below: distribution of Attic black figured ware.
(After Kimmig 1983, Abb. 27 and 28)

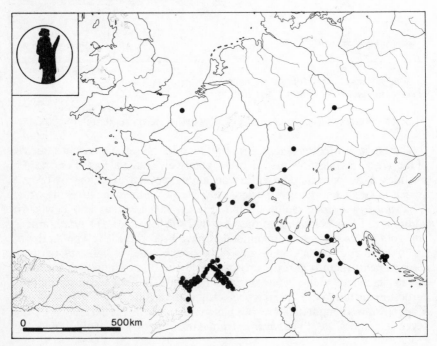

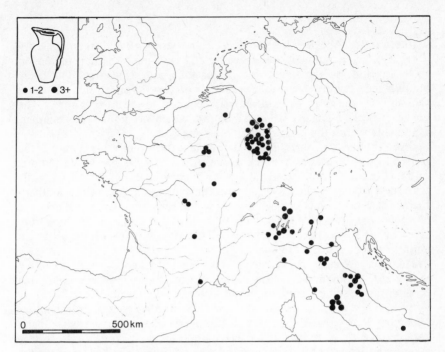

12 Above: distribution of Etruscan beaked flagons.
Below: distribution of Attic red figured ware.
(After Kimmig 1983, Abb. 29 and 32)

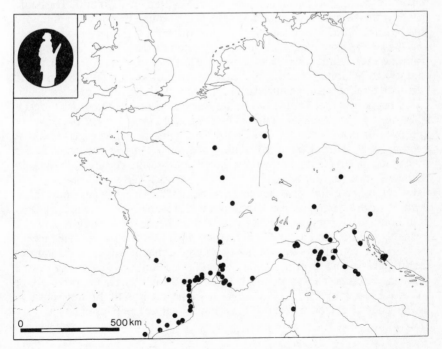

southern Italy in the decade 580–70 BC. Thus there is a likelihood that luxury wine drinking equipment was being traded into the barbarian regions at about the time of the foundation of Massalia and soon after. The black figured Attic pottery, which occurs on a dozen or so sites, dates to about 530–500 BC, the rarer red figured ware belongs to the fifth century. The Etruscan beaked flagons (*schnabelkannen*), which occur in some number, were made within the century or so after 525 BC.

Given the various constraints on dating, and the fragmentary nature of the archaeological evidence, it is impossible to say how the volume of imports varied with time, but the clear impression is given that trade built up rapidly after the battle of Alalia in 537 BC and the consequent loss of the southern Iberian markets to the Carthaginians. It would seem that the Massaliots were now looking northwards for the commodities that had previously come from the west. The further implications of the distributions of the different imports will be returned to later.

There is no clear cut evidence to show what goods were exported southwards from west central Europe but the prime needs of the Mediterranean states were for raw materials and manpower. Metals are likely to have bulked large among the former category, not least when we remember that after Alalia access to the metal sources of southern Iberia became severely restricted. It has been argued that tin from south-western Britain and Brittany was now brought to the southern Gaulish ports via the Seine or the Loire and the Saône-Rhône river system. The only positive evidence that can be presented in support of this is the development of a port-of-trade on the promontory of Mount Batten in Plymouth Harbour, between the seventh and third centuries BC.[29] Mount Batten was admirably situated to command the source of stream tin around the Dartmoor fringes and the silver-rich copper ores of the Callington district. Exotic bronze finds from the site include *fibulae* closely similar to those made in Aquitania and a solitary trilobate arrowhead of 'Greco-Scythian' type. The evidence is permissive rather than persuasive, but there is nothing inherently implausible in supposing that British/Breton tin was one of the commodities to reach Massalia by the overland route. That Massaliot sailors were occasionally approaching south-western Britain by sea, perhaps on voyages of prospection, is clear from the sixth century Massaliot *Periplus* preserved in the much later poem of Avienus and by the accounts of the voyage of Pytheas in the late fourth century BC.

Of the other metals that would have been attractive, copper could have been extracted from nearer at hand, in the Montagne Noire or the Pyrenees. Iron could have come from west central Europe, from Burgundy and the Franche Comté, and gold from further north, but positive evidence of extraction for trade to the south is lacking. Other northern commodities might have included resin, pitch, honey, wax, amber, salt, hides or the woollen products and salted pork listed by Strabo as choice products of eastern France in the first century BC. The chance of finding positive archaeological evidence for the bulk movement of such products is very slight.

In addition to raw materials, the Mediterranean states needed a constant and abundant supply of manpower in the form of slaves and mercenaries. Nothing is known of a slave trade with west central Europe at this time, but in view of the rate of consumption of slaves in the Mediterranean world, and the lively slave trade which existed with barbarian Gaul in the first century BC, it seems highly likely that the acquisition of slaves for export was a significant activity in the West Hallstatt chiefdoms. Nor should we forget the importance of mercenary armies in Mediterranean warfare. There is nothing inherently unreasonable in supposing that the provision of a well-armed fighting force was one of the services that the Hallstatt chiefs could offer.[30]

The effects of the developing patterns of long-distance trade on the Western Hallstatt community were dramatic. In the Hallstatt D period (roughly 600–450 BC) there emerge a number of powerful chiefdoms, represented in the archaeological record by strongly defended hilltop enclosures — thought to be the residences of the nobility — around which cluster richly appointed 'aristocratic' burials (figs 13 and 14). The hillforts (*Fürstensitze*) — places like Mont Lassois in Burgundy, Heuneburg in southern Germany and Châtillon-sur-Glâne in Switzerland, have all produced evidence of the presence of Mediterranean luxury goods, together with the signs of a range of local manufacturing activities. At Heuneburg, the remarkable defensive wall of phase IV, built of mud-bricks on a drystone

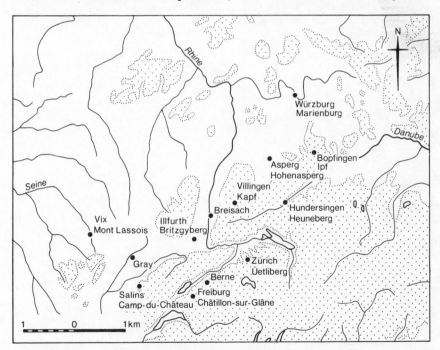

13 The principal chieftains' hillforts of the late sixth century BC in western central Europe (Based on Kimmig 1983, Abb. 45)

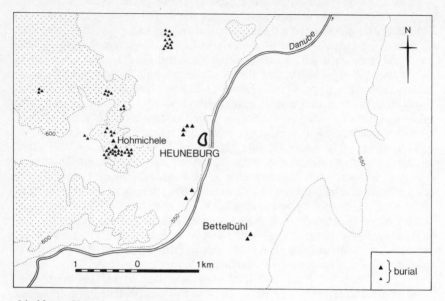

14 *Above: Heuneburg and its environment.*
Below: Mont Lassois and its environment.
(Based on Kimmig 1983, Abb. 47 and 51)

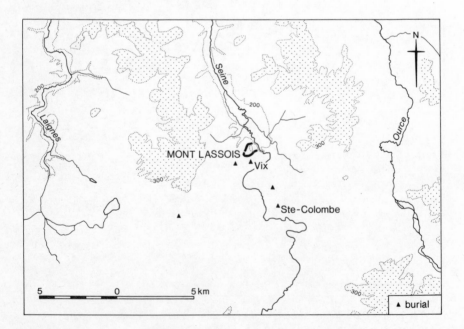

foundation, with rectangular bastions at intervals, is so directly inspired by contemporary Greek architecture that its construction may well have been overseen by a Greek engineer.[31]

The aristocratic burials (*Fürstengräber*) associated with residences of nobility frequently contained imported Mediterranean luxury goods. The great burial at Vix, near Mont Lassois, produced a complete wine-drinking set, including a huge Greek bronze *krater*, 1.64m (5½ ft) in height, together with two basins, a bowl and a beaked flagon of Etruscan origin and three Attic cups (*kylikes*). A rather different grave, at Grafenbühl, in the vicinity of the hillfort of Hohenasperg (near Stuttgart), though robbed in antiquity, yielded a tantalizing array of fragments left behind by the robbers, including the feet of a Greek bronze tripod, two bronze vessels, two carved sphinxes — one of bone and amber, the other of ivory, probably from Magna Graecia — and an ivory plaque and ivory lion's foot, both probably of Greek origin. There were in addition locally-made items such as a wagon and several gold ornaments. Among the other exotic imports from Hallstatt burials we may note the silk textile from Hohmichele, the Greek tripod and cauldron from La Garenne and the Greek *hydria* from Grächwil. The concentration of these imported luxuries in the vicinity of the comparatively few fortified *Fürstensitze* and their associated burials strongly suggest the emergence of an aristocracy able to command the inflow of Mediterranean luxury goods and to retain them in their own ambit.[32]

The type of socio-economic system which has been modelled to explain the archaeological evidence is known as a prestige goods economy.[33] Society is seen as strictly hierarchical, and political advantage is gained by controlling access to resources that can only be obtained through external trade. The distribution of these resources down through the social group provides a mechanism for maintaining the hierarchy. In such a society the various groups are linked together by competitive exchange in cycles of continuous rivalry. In reality this would mean that the dominant chief has to redistribute sufficient quantities of prestige goods to his subordinates, and thus down the chain, to maintain, not only his own position, but also that of the chain of subordinates. If he fails, the system collapses from the bottom up. A further implication is that for the system to retain a level of stability, the subordinate lineages must not be allowed to take part in external trade.

A detailed study of groups of burials within defined territories has suggested that it might be possible to distinguish the different social levels of the occupants. In the Heuneburg region, for example, distinction has been made between the burials of paramount chiefs, vassal chiefs and sub-chiefs. The *paramount chief* burial is typified by inhumation in a wooden chamber accompanied by a wagon and horse trappings. This is a reflection of high status which developed in the preceding Hallstatt C period but, in addition, we now find a range of imported luxury goods including bronze vessels for wine-drinking, gold, silk and other fabrics, glass, amber, and coral. The *vassal chief* burials are similar, but without the range of imports; instead there are weapons and jewellery, probably produced in the paramount settlement. The *sub-chief* burials are similar again, but less elaborately furnished. They often contained daggers and belt fittings, together with lignite arm bands, all locally made. Further down the hierarchy, wagon burials and imported goods are entirely lacking.

Thus, it is argued that those of chieftain status are afforded wagon burial; the lower orders are not. The paramount chieftain maintains his position by retaining all imported goods, only occasionally allowing such commodities as coral to be distributed down to the lower echelons. His relationship with his vassals is articulated by gifts of quality items made in his own workshops.

An economy of this kind requires that the paramount chief is able to accumulate, through gift exchange, the commodities for export — the raw materials and the slaves considered above. He then engages in direct transactions with the Mediterranean entrepreneurs. How this was articulated presents problems. The virtual absence of luxury goods in the intervening territories would imply the absence of middlemen. This would, in turn, suggest the use of expeditions either from the West Hallstatt chiefdoms to the south or, more likely, from the Mediterranean cities northwards. Further archaeological discoveries may yet throw light on the complex mechanisms demanded.

The *Fürstensitze*, and the economic system which they represent, spread in a broad arc from Burgundy to the middle Rhine and the comparatively even spacing of the major fortified sites gives the impression of a territorial stability throughout the period.[34] At one level this is true, but a more detailed study of the chronology of the aristocratic graves shows, as one might expect, fluctuations in the fortunes of the individual domains. In the early period (Hallstatt D1, roughly 600–550 BC) there were two paramount settlements, Magdalensberg and Heuneburg. By Hallstatt D2/3 (c. 550–450 BC) the Heuneburg domain had contracted, while that of Hohenasperg had risen to dominance. It is probably in this period that Mont Lassois reached the height of its power. In the final stage (Hallstatt D3/La Tène A, c. 450–420 BC) the Hohenasperg declines at the expense of a political unit which emerges at the confluence of the Rhine/Moselle in the Hunsrück-Eifel area. In the eastern part of the zone, Mont Lassois appears to lose its pre-eminent position, perhaps being replaced by Châtillon-sur-Salins.

The causes for these shifts of power were no doubt many and various, and mostly beyond the range of recovery, but events in the Mediterranean must have had an effect on the Hallstatt chiefdoms since the social system was entirely dependent upon the regular supply of luxury goods, and any fluctuation in Mediterranean interest would have rocked the unstable barbarian economy. The apparent decline in Greek activity via Massalia after 500 BC, and the increase of Etruscan interest in the north, using the Po valley, following the development of the Adriatic ports of Spina and Adria, may well have been the prime cause for the shift of power eastwards to the Saarland (the Rhine-Moselle confluence). Significantly, it is in the burials of this region that the prime Etruscan export to the north — the beaked flagon — concentrates.[35] In addition to the external causes of change, there was also the inherent instability of the prestige goods economy, so structured that, given the appropriate stimulus, it would collapse like a house of cards.

Social transformation in barbarian Europe in the fifth century BC

The collapse of the Western Hallstatt chiefdoms appears to have been sudden, and in places there is direct evidence that it was violent. In the fifth century BC the defended *Fürstensitze* were destroyed, and from Burgundy to Bohemia the practice of aristocratic burial under a tumulus came to an end. It was at this time that the *Fürstengräber* appeared, quite suddenly, in the Hunsrück-Eifel region, an area which had previously been sparsely settled. One suggestion is that the new prosperity resulted from the exploitation of local, high-quality iron ore under direct stimulus from Etruria.[36] A further link with Etruria is the adoption of the two-wheeled chariot to accompany the dead chief in his grave. An even more dramatic development was the emergence of a distinctive and vigorous art style, generally referred to as Celtic or La Tène art, used in the ornamentation of aristocratic goods. To the west, in the Marne region of northern France, parallel changes can be identified, with the appearance of flat grave inhumations and a series of well-furnished chieftains' graves like those at Somme Bionne and La Gorge-Meillet.[37]

Although considerable problems of chronology still exist, it would appear that the collapse of the Western Hallstatt chiefdoms in the core zone was roughly contemporary with the emergence of a new and vigorous warrior society in the northern periphery, with two foci, in the Marne and Hunsrück-Eifel. What had, in the sixth century BC, been an undeveloped peripheral region, became, in the fifth century, the core of a cultural complex known as the Marne-Moselle group of the western early La Tène culture province (fig 15).

The lack of a precise chronology, and our inability to establish exact synchronisms across west central Europe at this time, make a stage-by-stage account of the intricate shifts in power impossible to construct with any degree of assurance. However, many archaeologists would now agree that the last stages in the development of the old West Hallstatt chiefdoms (Hallstatt D3, *c.* 500–450 BC) were running roughly parallel with the emergence of the Marnian and Hunsrück-Eifel cultures (La Tène A), and that in these peripheral regions the continuation of the La Tène A culture, with its aristocratic art style, outlived the collapse of the chiefdoms.[38] Thus, at its simplest, it might be suggested that the power to command long distance trade shifted north during the fifth century BC from the core to the periphery, rather like the outward growth of a toadstool ring, the old core decaying whilst vigorous growth continued along its perimeter. As a simple descriptive generalization this has a value, and we have already seen, in the intensification of Etruscan trade with the Hunsrück-Eifel area, a potential cause for part of the shift. But the overall situation was far more complex.

The economy of the West Hallstatt chiefdoms was based upon extracting surplus produce from a subservient peasant population and concentrating it in centres of power for subsequent 'export'. In return, the lower echelons of society were provided with manufactured goods produced under the

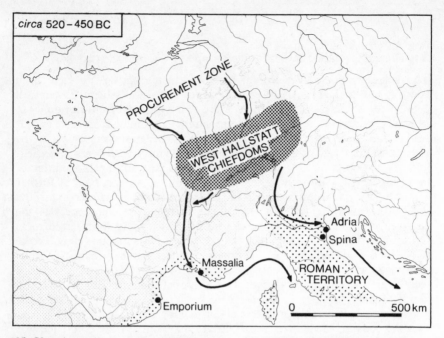

15 Changing socio-economic systems in western central Europe 520–400 BC. In the upper map the arrows represent the movement of raw materials, in the lower map they indicate the principal routes of the Celtic migrants

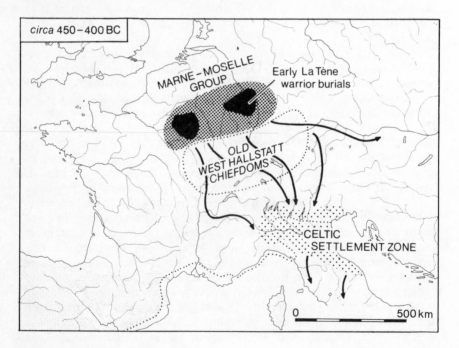

authority of paramount chieftains. Thus, it was in the interests of all to maintain order, so that the delicately balanced economy could continue to function. Apart from the fortification of the *Fürstensitze*, which was probably as much for display as for defence, signs of aggression are noticeably absent.

The communities of the periphery developed along somewhat different lines, and are best characterized as warrior societies. Males buried were frequently heavily armed, and by the fifth century BC, when rich aristocratic burials appeared, no regional centres of power comparable to the *Fürstensitze* had developed. Such a situation is best interpreted as a Celtic warrior society in which prestige was based on qualities of leadership and the ability to gather plunder.

The simple model which can be generated from these observations sees the emergence, in the sixth and fifth centuries BC, from a common Hallstatt C cultural continuum, of a complex socio-economic system, composed of two sub-systems in symbiosis: a *core* — the chiefdoms of the West Central Hallstatt zone, producing surplus locally, and a *periphery* — the warrior chieftains, whose surplus, of plunder and captives, was acquired by raiding in the zone *beyond*. The conversion of the combined surpluses into luxury goods from the south was articulated by the chiefdoms.

This system was in unstable equilibrium. Two factors can be detected which may have contributed to its downfall: the first, the outflanking of the core by those manipulating trade with Etruria, has been discussed above; the second was a rapid rise in population in the periphery. In both the Marne region and the Hunsrück-Eifel, the archaeological evidence would seem to suggest a consistent and substantial increase in population from about 600 to 450–400 BC. Assuming the evidence to be properly interpreted (and whatever the cause), an increase in population would mean a rise in the number of young men wishing to compete for status. This could well have created a dangerous instability.

There is a third factor which should be briefly explored. The prestige goods economy of the core zone was based on conspicuous consumption. To demonstrate status, the lineage group of the paramount had flagrantly to dispose of wealth. This was a mechanism by which rare status-giving goods could be kept in short supply. One method by which this was done was by burying quantities of luxury goods every time a member of the lineage died. In such a system it is quite possible for a momentum of expectation to be generated which exceeds the productive capacity of the group. Such a situation would, of course, be destabilizing.

In summary, after the middle of the fifth century BC a rise in population in the peripheral zone, a possible loss of production relative to expectation in the core zone, and a realignment of the trading axes brought about by political changes in the Mediterranean, together with a range of other factors so far undetected, seem to have instigated the collapse of the socio-political system of west central Europe. The immediate aftermath saw the beginnings of the Celtic migrations.

The Celtic migrations

Just before 400 BC, war bands of Celtic warriors began to move southwards and eastwards from their homeland in northern Gaul and the mid-Rhine. The southern thrust reached Rome on 18 July, 387 BC, and then moved on southwards deep into Italy. The bands forcing their way eastwards besieged the Greek sanctuary of Delphi in 279 BC, the next year crossing the Bosphorous into Asia Minor. It is not our purpose to examine these events in historical detail, fascinating though they are, but we must consider why the movement took place and what effects it had on western European society.[39] There are two ways to approach the problem: through the classical texts, and by offering explanations for the patterns observed in the archaeological evidence.

The Elder Pliny provides a succinct explanation:

> The Gauls, imprisoned as they were by the Alps . . . first found a motive for overflowing into Italy from the circumstance of a Gallic citizen from Switzerland named Helico, who had lived in Rome because of his skill as a craftsman, had brought with him when he came back some dried figs and grapes and some samples of oil and wine: consequently we may excuse them for having sought to obtain these things even by means of war[40].

Here then, two reasons are given: the restricted territory and the desire for southern luxuries.

Pompeius Trogus[41] gives emphasis to the second reason. The Gauls, he says, outgrew their land and sent 300,000 men to seek new lands, adding that internal discord and bitter dissension spurred on the movement into Italy where they expelled the Etruscans and founded a number of towns including Milan, Brescia and Verona. Livy, on the other hand, embroiders the first theme, reporting that the Gauls were lured south by a native of Clusium to bring vengeance on the city. But later he provides a more factual account: the most powerful of the Gaulish tribes was the Bituriges, who were ruled by King Ambigatus. They grew rich in corn and the population increased to such an extent that governing them was difficult. The king 'wished to relieve his kingdom of the burdensome throng'. Accordingly he chose two warriors — his sister's sons, Bellovesus and Segovesus — to lead a mass emigration. By augury, Segovesus was pointed in the direction of the Hercynian hills, while Bellovesus was sent to Italy.[42]

Taken together, then, the classical sources are agreed that the prime cause for the beginning of the migrations was over-population leading to strife, which was alleviated by sending out massive folk movements. The southern and easterly directions which the migrations took were no doubt conditioned to some extent by the knowledge that in these directions lay the sought-after luxuries.

Turning to the area from which the migrations might have originated — the peripheral zone around the northern fringe of the West Hallstatt chiefdoms — there is evidence to suggest an apparently rapid increase in population in both the Champagne and the Hunsrück-Eifel regions during the fifth century BC (La Tène 1a). It is the subsequent development of this culture (La Tène 1b) of fourth century date that is found in a wide territory stretching from the periphery, across the old West Central Hallstatt area and the Alps, and into the Po valley. It was this material culture that the migrating Celts carried with them. One further point is worth stressing: two of the tribal names of groups known historically to have settled in the Po valley — the Lingones and Senones — also occur in the Marne region, from where, it is tempting to believe, the warrior bands may well have set out.

Although the archaeological evidence is not as sharply focussed as one would like, it does seem that the peripheral zone, from Champagne to the Hunsrück-Eifel, where in the fifth century a warrior aristocracy emerged, was the centre of dispersal of the Celtic migrants. This is not to say that all the chieftains left their homeland. In the Marne, the chieftain's burial at Somme-Bionne is quite late, sharing many characteristics with La Tène Lb styles, while in the Hunsrück-Eifel, the rich burials of Reinheim and Waldalgesheim are a generation or two after 400 BC. Thus the old warrior aristocracy continued to manifest itself in the homeland, in rich tombs of traditional types, well after the migrations had begun.

The distribution of flat inhumation graves of La Tène 1b and later reflects the extent of the settlement of the migratory groups, but in no way indicates the maximum penetration of the marauding bands. The story of the migrations is beyond the scope of this book, but suffice it to say that the main advances took place in the fourth and early third centuries BC. So serious was the threat of dislocation in the Balkans that Alexander the Great himself was forced to intervene. After the middle of the third century BC the Gauls came under increasing pressure, in the south from the Romans, in the east from the Hellenistic kingdoms and in the north from the Dacians and the Germans. In the face of these pressures, folk movement continued. One of the last was in 58 BC when the Helvetii made their abortive attempt to move west from their Swiss homeland. We will return to the details of these events in Chapter 6.

3 The southern shores of Gaul

The native towns of southern Gaul

The southern coastline of Gaul provided an interface between the developing Mediterranean states and the barbarian peoples of inland Europe. In the previous chapter we examined something of the interactions between the two systems in the two centuries following the foundation of Massalia in *c.* 600 BC. The concept of the coast as a semi-permeable membrane is not altogether inappropriate: commodities passed through it both ways — but selectively — using the Greek ports of Massalia and her daughter colonies, Tauroeis (Tauroention), Olbia, Antipolis (Antibes) and Nicaea (Nice) to the east, and Agatha (Agde) to the west. These cities belonged to the Mediterranean, but away from the coast was a rich hinterland, rendered productive by its mild climate, which supported a dense and stable population throughout much of the first millennium BC.[1]

The coastal zone, stretching from the Italian border to the Pyrenees, is of varying width (fig 16). To the east, between Nice and Marseilles, the Alpes Maritimes come close to the sea in the Massif des Maures and the Esterel. Valleys like those of the Var and the Argens allow limited access to the interior, but the land is largely closed and inaccessible. This was the territory occupied by the warlike Ligurians and Salyens (Saluvii) living in the hundreds of small fortified sites scattered about the inland hills and valleys, and the Segobrigii, Camactullici and Oxubii of the more coastal regions.[2]

Westwards from Marseilles the land opens up to become the triangular Rhône delta, its base on the sea, its two sloping sides fringed by the Vaucluse and the Cevennes. The apex of the triangle is at Avignon, just above the confluence of the Rhône and the Durance. North of this point the Rhône valley narrows. The lower valley of the Rhône (Bouches du Rhône) was a widely settled and substantially Hellenized area. The two towns of St Blaise and Glanon, whatever their status, were both enclosed with well-built walls of Greek style in the fourth century BC.[3] The river formed something of a tribal divide. To the east were the Saluvii and the Cavares (north of the Durance) while to the west lay the Volcae Arecomici. The archaeological evidence tends to support the idea of a cultural boundary along the river course. Along the western fringe of the Golfe de Lion is the wide fertile land of Languedoc, stretching to the Cevennes and the Montagne Noire. The River Hérault offers access deep into the Cevennes, while the Aude provides the beginning of the vital east-west axis which led, south of the Montagne Noire, via the Carcassonne gap, to the Garonne, the Gironde, and the

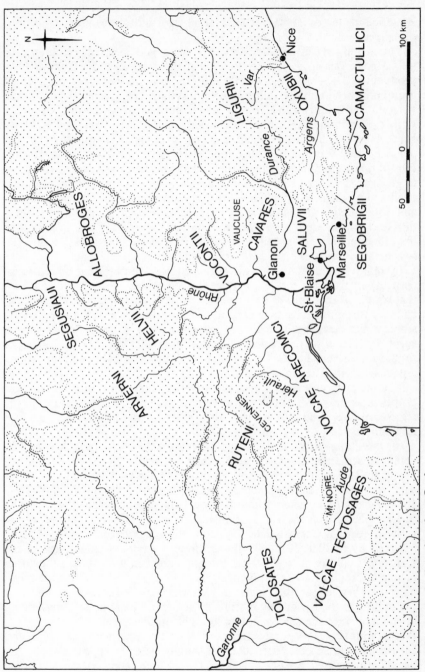

16 The principal tribes of southern Gaul

Atlantic. In this congenial region a number of hilltop fortified settlements developed.

The mixed, but essentially calcareous, soils of the coastal region and the mild Mediterranean climate combined to make the lands of the Golfe de Lion productive. The entire region lay within the zone in which the olive would grow and ripen naturally, and where vines suitable for wine production could be cultivated with ease. Olive production and the extraction of olive oil are well attested in the area, at Entremont for example, where olive presses have been found. The local production of wine is demonstrated by the comparatively widespread distribution of the so-called Massaliot amphorae. Recent fabric analysis has shown the problem of the origins of the wine to be more complex than previously realized, with at least four different production centres in operation — three on the coastal zone between Hyères and Nice, the fourth inland close to the Rhône-Drôme confluence.[4] If these different centres were producing wine under the auspices of Massalia then the economic territory of the colony must have been more considerable than is generally supposed.[5]

In addition to oil and wine the region must have produced quantities of corn. Apart from the fertile soils, the climatic advantages of the area meant that winter wheat could be harvested very early in the year, in the latter half of June. Just outside the inhabited area of Enserune, a large number of grain storage pits have been excavated, suggestive of a capacity for storing surplus.[6] The discovery raises the possibility that the coastal fringes of southern Gaul may have been involved in the production of grain for export, especially to the Roman army.

The majority of archaeologists commenting upon the cultural sequences proposed as the result of recent excavations in hilltop settlement sites in the region are impressed by the continuity of development throughout the first millennium BC.

In the Languedoc, the three classic sequences are provided by the defended settlements of Cayla de Mailhac, Enserune and Nages. The Cayla has an advantage in that the sequence can be traced back to the Late Bronze Age, and is manifest in two complementary sites: the defended hill of Cayla and the extensive cemeteries found on low-lying ground nearby (fig 17).[7] The earliest phase, Mailhac I, has similarities to the Urnfield culture of the western Alps, and must date to before the seventh century BC. This is followed by Mailhac II which, though local in style, is reminiscent of the Hallstatt C culture of west central Europe, and even incorporates the burial of horse trappings — very much in Hallstatt C style. The range of metal objects appearing at this stage also shows inspiration from Spain — a reminder that the Languedoc culture of the first millennium BC shared much in common with the Iberian coasts south of the Pyrenees.

It is with the third phase, Mailhac III, that contact with the Greek and Etruscan world becomes particularly apparent, with the appearance of Attic black figured wares, Etruscan black bucchero, Greek and Etruscan amphorae and 'Phocaean' wares. These imports, together with native copies, such as ochre-painted and grey bucchero wares indicate a date in the sixth century

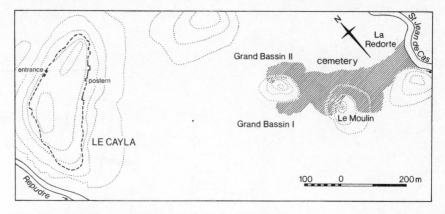

17 The settlement and cemetery of Mailhac in Languedoc.
(After Sandars 1957, fig. 87)

BC, by which time these long-established native sites were coming into regular contact with the trading communities of the south. Fifth-century Cayla, together with several other sites in the region, bears evidence of destruction by fire, which may reflect disturbances consequent upon the Celtic migrations. The problem is hotly debated, and by the nature of things must always be highly speculative. At any event, from the fourth century occupation continued and the settlement was not abandoned until well after the Roman conquest.

About 30km (18 miles) to the east, towards the sea, is the hilltop settlement of Enserune (fig 18). Enserune is a long narrow ridge rising above a fertile undulating plain just south of Beziers. Extensive excavations have brought to light the main cultural sequence.[8] The first phase (Enserune I) begins in the mid-sixth century and lasts until *c.* 425 BC. The structures, simple mud-built huts, grain pits, etc, are essentially indigenous but imported Greek and Etruscan pottery show that contacts with the Mediterranean, probably through ports like Agde, were well established. The second phase (Enserune II, *c.* 425–220 BC) sees an extensive redevelopment — the settlement was replanned and rebuilt in an orderly manner in stone, with rectilinear houses occupying much of the hilltop amid a network of roads. The entire hilltop was now enclosed with a massive stone-built rampart, within which, on the western part of the hill, lay the cemetery.

The cemetery was in continuous use throughout period II, but can be divided into two phases. In phase IIA the graves were furnished with a range of pottery, including Attic red figured ware and black glazed wares from Campania (southern Italy), together with items of La Tène type such as brooches, belt clasps and swords in their scabbards. In phase IIB, the main differences are that the cremations were now buried in imported Italian black *canthari* (as opposed to local ochre-painted wares) and are regularly accompanied by La Tène I and II metalwork, especially brooches, swords and shields.

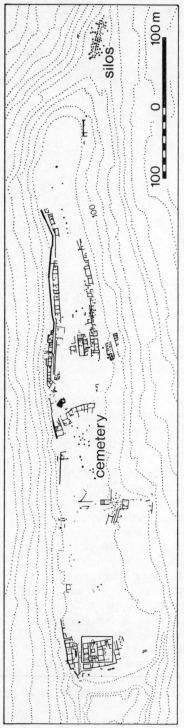

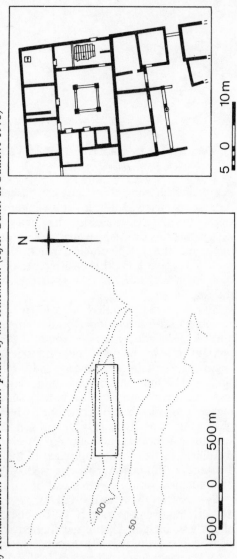

18 The hillfort of Enserune (Herault). The detailed plan is of a peristyle house in insula X indicating the degree of Romanization evident in the later phases of the settlement. (After Gallet de Sauterre 1978)

Throughout period II and into the succeeding period, close cultural similarities existed between Enserune and the settlements of the Catalan coast. This is underlined by the local script, known principally from graffiti scratched on pots. The language is uncertain but is thought to derive from a script found in the region of Ampurias, on the coast of Catalonia. Thus in period II, three major cultural influences are evident: the basic folk culture is an indigenous development which links the coastal zone from the Ebro to the Hérault. Superimposed on this is evidence of direct trade contact with the Mediterranean ports. More difficult to assess is the Celtic (i.e. La Tène) component. There is no need to see the appearance of La Tène weapons and jewellery as evidence of an intrusive ethnic group, but at the very least the presence of this warrior equipment in graves suggests a degree of cultural assimilation with Celtic groups occupying the hills to the north. Intermarriage, gift exchange, or even the employment of mercenaries could account for what is observed.

Towards the end of the third century there is evidence of destruction, possibly at the time of Hannibal's advance through southern Gaul in 218 BC, but immediate rebuilding (Enserune III) shows that the dislocation was of no cultural significance. The town now developed elaborate masonry buildings, and contacts with Italy increased. After the foundation of the Roman colony nearby, at Narbonne, in 118 BC, the pace of Romanization intensified, and several of the houses were remodelled with peristyle courts in Greco-Roman style (fig 18). Occupation continued into the first century AD, after which the site was abandoned in favour of the developing Roman towns in the nearby plain.

Enserune occupied a central position in the Languedoc. Not far from the Greek port of Agde and close to the River Aude, it commanded a route nexus linking the coastal plain with the metal-rich Montagne Noire and the westerly route leading to the Atlantic. After the establishment of Roman authority in the region, a main road linking Italy with Spain — the Via Domitia — was constructed only a short distance from the foot of the hill; and the principal planned settlement in the region — the colonia at Narbo Martius (Narbonne) — developed only 20km (12 miles) away. From their central position, the inhabitants of Enserune were able to absorb into their culture the many influences to which the area was subjected.

The third site, of considerable importance to the assessment of local cultural development, is the plateau of Roque de Viou in the commune of Nages, overlooking the Vaunages plain, not far from Nimes (fig 19). The earliest occupation, roughly equivalent to Mailhac I, dates to the eighth and seventh centuries BC. The second period, dating to the fourth century BC, saw the construction of a stone rampart with simple houses built against it, and is associated with quantities of Attic, Italiot and Massaliot pottery.[9]

In the early years of the third century BC the old settlement on Roque de Viou was abandoned in favour of the nearby Castels hill at Nages, which was defended by a stone-built rampart. Some time between 250 and 230 BC the first town of Nages was destroyed, possibly by the Celtic tribe, the Volcae Arecomici, but was immediately rebuilt on a grander scale (Nages II). The

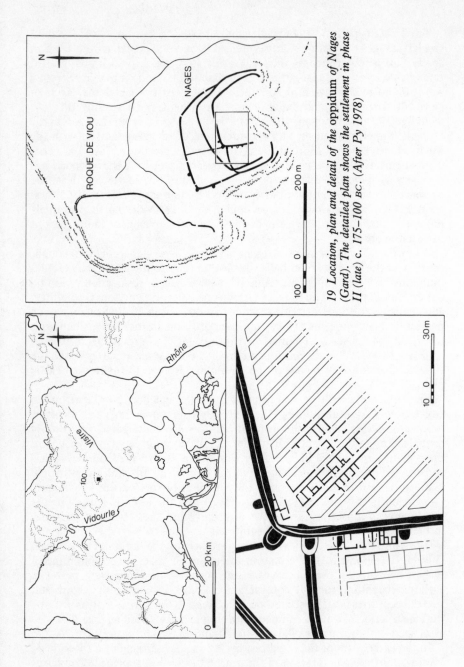

19 *Location, plan and detail of the oppidum of Nages (Gard). The detailed plan shows the settlement in phase II (late)* c. 175–100 BC. *(After Py 1978)*

rampart was provided with massive bastions, while inside, the settlement was laid out in a remarkably regular fashion, with a series of parallel streets defining long narrow *insulae*. In the early second century BC the streets were narrowed to allow the *insulae* to be enlarged. Throughout the period of Nages II (roughly 230 to 120 BC), trade with Italy increased dramatically, with the importation of black Campanian fine wares and amphorae. The third period, after the foundation of the Roman province, saw the settlement considerably enlarged. Occupation continued until the site was finally abandoned at the beginning of the first century AD.

Although Nages is more isolated from direct Mediterranean contact than Enserune, it shows a similar increase in the intensity of trade with southern Italy in the third and second centuries BC. The impressive replanning of the town in the late third century BC is also paralleled at Enserune a decade or two later, though the more constricted topography at Enserune made a regular street grid more difficult to impose. Taken together, the two sites suggest that the third century BC was a time of change, when the long-established hill-towns of the Languedoc were beginning to adopt a more distinct Mediterranean culture. A further implication is that the intensity of trade with Italy was building up. Detailed quantification is not yet possible but the overall impression given is that the volumes of Italian fine wares appearing in the third century were greatly in excess of the Attic and Etruscan imports of the fifth and fourth centuries BC.

Enserune and Nages provide the most impressive examples of the change in trading patterns coming about during the sixth to second centuries BC, but the same potential for assessment is offered by a number of other sites in Languedoc. The precursor of the Roman colony at Narbonne, known as Naro in the contemporary texts, has been identified on the hill of Montlaurés, 4km (2½ miles) north-west of the modern town.[10] It was the principal *oppidum* of the Elysicii and was sited to command the Aude route to the west along which British tin was transported.[11] By the time of the Roman conquest the town had grown to about 30ha, spreading from the acropolis down to the lagoons (fig 33). In the sixth century BC the now-familiar range of Attic, Ionic, Etruscan and Phoenician pottery is found in abundance; by the fifth-fourth centuries, western Greek ceramics and vessels from the region of Ampurias dominate, but by the end of the fourth century BC the first 'pre Campanian' wares appear. Thereafter, Campanian wares greatly increase in quantity, but Spanish imports are maintained at a high level (and, as at Enserune, Spanish script is widely used) until the final stage of occupation in the second century BC, when Italian products begin to dominate.

Naro, along with several other sites in the region (e.g. Pech Maho and Peyriac-de-Mer),[12] shows signs of an episode of destruction in the late third or early second century BC, which is generally assigned to the war-like activities of the Celtic tribe, the Volcae Tectosages, who are thought to have been moving through the region at about this time. The event had no lasting effect on the development of the *oppidum*.

The coast of the Golfe de Lion must have been peppered with small ports and harbours commanding the river routes into the interior (fig 20). The Greek

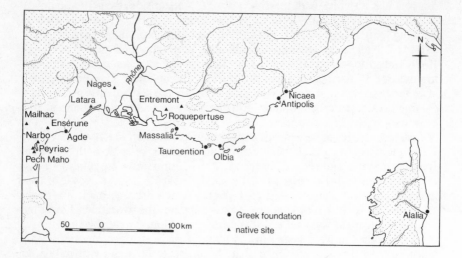

20 *Greek colonies and selected* oppida *in southern Gaul*

city of Agatha (Agde) lay close to the mouth of the River Hérault, only a few kilometres from the native *oppidum* of Bessan.[13] It was the only Greek city on the Languedoc coast and was carefully chosen to command both the Hérault and the Aude — both rivers leading to the metal-rich interior. The other ports were all native developments. Latara (modern Lattes just south of Montpellier) grew up at an important crossroads where maritime, river and road transport routes naturally converged.[14] Recent excavations have shown that occupation intensified in the seventh century BC, and continued on into the Roman period. Long-distance trade is well attested to by quantities of imported pottery, including Etruscan, Phocaean, Ionian, Attic and Ibero-Punic varieties, and extensive port installations show that Latara was a place of trans-shipment from sea-going to riverine vessels (fig 21).

Sufficient will have been said of the sites of the Languedoc to stress two points: the continuity of occupation over many centuries at most sites, in spite of episodes of destruction which may be linked to historical events; and the widespread trading activity, beginning in the sixth century BC and continuing to the period of Roman annexation, which linked the Languedoc to Iberian, Punic, Greek and Italian trading networks. Culturally, the Languedoc was part of a broad continuum stretching from the Ebro to the Hérault and beyond, manifest in their use of an Iberian script, and in the quantity of finds, mainly pottery, emanating from the region of Ampurias. These westerly, Spanish links will have brought the Phoenician pottery to the towns of southern Gaul. Superimposed upon this are the changing trading patterns with Greece and Italy — a decline in the volume of trade with the east Mediterranean during the fifth-fourth century BC, with a corresponding growth of commerce with southern and central Italy, reaching a crescendo in the third and second centuries BC. This 'Italianization' of southern Gaul must

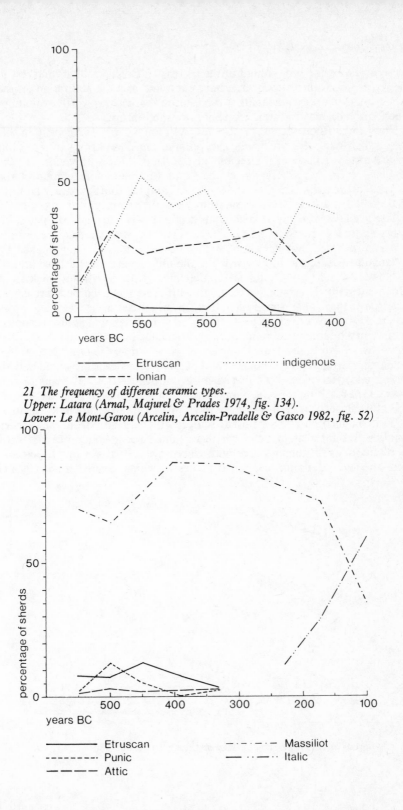

21 *The frequency of different ceramic types.*
Upper: Latara (Arnal, Majurel & Prades 1974, fig. 134).
Lower: Le Mont-Garou (Arcelin, Arcelin-Pradelle & Gasco 1982, fig. 52)

be seen against the background of the increasing Roman military interest in the region consequent upon the Punic wars, and also the realization on the part of Roman entrepreneurs that the Gaulish market was worth exploiting. These are both considerations to which we shall return.

The Lower Rhône basin is rather less well known archaeologically in this period than Languedoc (with the exception of the sites of the Vaunage), but on the eastern fringes of the region, just north of Aix-en-Provence, lies the *oppidum* of Entremont, capital of the Celto–Ligurian confederation of the Salyens (or Saluvii). The site was occupied from the fourth century BC until its destruction at the hands of the Romans in the campaigns of 125–3 BC.[15]

The *oppidum*, roughly triangular in shape, is divided into two parts, an upper and a lower town (fig 22). The upper town, which may represent the first fortified area, was enclosed by a well-built stone wall strengthened by rectangular bastions at intervals, while the much more considerable area of the lower town was more massively defended, with a wall 3m thick from which substantial rectangular bastions with rectangular corners project at intervals of 19m. That part of the settlement which has been excavated shows a regularity of layout, with a grid of cobbled streets defining *insulae* occupied by masonry-built houses. Some were quite small, single-room structures, but others were more substantial houses of five or more rooms. Decorative elements, including a crude mosaic and part of a clay facade ornamented with fluting and triglyphs, show that classical influences from Massalia (40km away) were reaching the site, along with a range of imported goods.

Built against the wall of the upper town was a long structure in the form of a portico, incorporating re-used sculptural fragments from an earlier building, the most dramatic of which was once a long column carved with representations of human heads with closed eyes. Part of a lintel, possibly from the same building, contained niches in which severed human heads

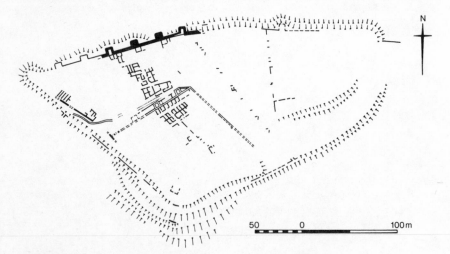

22 The oppidum *of Entremont, near Aix-en-Provence (Benoit 1981)*

could be put. An actual human skull, complete with the long iron nail driven into it for attachment, was found nearby, giving a grim reality to Diodorus' statement about head-hunting among the Celts.[16] Near to the portico, in road make-up layers, were found fragments of a range of remarkable statues in the round, including heroes adorned with breastplates or scale armour and torcs, sitting cross-legged, some with their hands resting on severed human heads. Other reliefs depict horsemen and severed heads.

The range of religious sculpture found at Entremont is paralleled by a similar collection from the nearby shrine at Roquepertuse.[17] Here, it is suggested that the seated figures sat in front of a portico composed of pillars, containing niches for human heads, surmounted by a lintel engraved and painted with a frieze of horses, birds, plants and geometrical motifs. Perched on the lintel was a fearsome, fantastic bird carved in the round. More unusual was a two-headed Janus-like figure, precisely carved and wearing a 'crown' of fleshy leaves. Little is known of the context of this remarkable collection, but Roquepertuse differs from Entremont in that it appears to have been a shrine with no adjacent settlement.

A number of other sites have been found in the lower Rhône region (in Gard and Bouches-du-Rhône) producing sculptured elements of these Celto-Ligurian religious complexes. The most dramatic of these is the Tarasque de Noves, a fabulous beast covered with scales, sitting on its haunches and holding two severed heads, one in each front paw. A human arm and part of a human foot appear once to have projected from its mouth. Even today, in the unemotional context of the Lapidarium of the Musée Calvet, Avignon, the beast has a distinctly awe-inspiring quality. In the context of its original shrine, accompanied by pillars of human heads, its effect on the unwary would have been devastating.

The Celto-Ligurian religious sculptures come from comparatively few sites, tightly distributed around the fringes of the Rhône delta. They represent a very distinctive religious iconography, incorporating much from Celtic religious practices, as presented to us by classical writers, but depicted in a milieu of stone sculpture which has clearly gained inspiration from the nearby Greek cities. Nonetheless, this can fairly be regarded as a native art of some quality, reflecting a high degree of ethnic cohesion among the inland tribes.

Inland trading centres of the Rhône axis (fig 23)

The native communities of the coastal region of southern Gaul grew rich on their ability to produce a range of goods for export (e.g. fish, salt, corn and spices) and to exploit the metal-producing regions of the nearby Cevennes, Montagne Noire and the Pyrenees. But, in all probability, they also acted as middle men in acquiring other goods, particularly tin, from more far-flung regions along the traditional routes of the Rhône and the Aude-Garonne. It is not surprising, therefore, to find a number of sites along these major routes which, by virtue of their positions on route nodes, were able to develop as centres of population and exchange. Two sites along the Rhône axis deserve special notice: Le Pègue and Vienne.

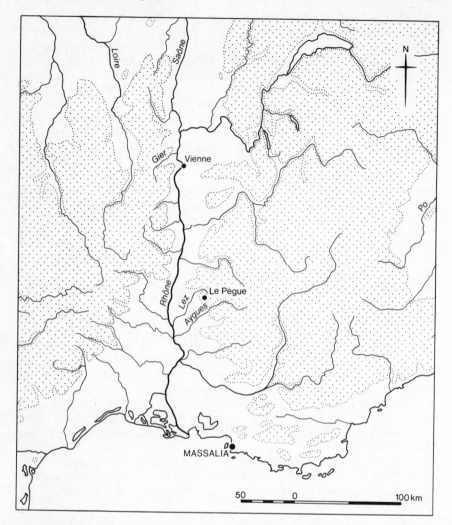

23   The Rhône valley route to the interior of west central Europe

Le Pègue is an *oppidum* on the west edge of the Alpine foothills, between
the valleys of the Lez and Aygues (both tributaries of the Rhône).[18] Its
position is a commanding one, controlling the route from the Rhône valley,
via the pass of La Madeleine, to the upper reaches of the Po valley. Intensive
occupation began in the sixth century BC, with the usual range of
Mediterranean imports, and continued (though with two phases of destruction, reflecting local problems), the contemporary levels yielding Attic red
figured vessels of the fourth century and later Campanian wares of the third
and second centuries BC, together with Massaliot coins (*obols*). Clearly, Le
Pègue remained in close contact with the Mediterranean coast throughout the

second half of the first millennium BC and was able to maintain its long-distance links by virtue of its favoured position in relation to the west Alpine passes.

Vienne actually lies on the Rhône, only 25km south of the confluence of the Saône and Rhône, at a point where the Rhône valley is considerably narrowed by neighbouring hills, but the real significance of its position lies in the fact that it commands the westward route through the Montagne du Lyonnaise, via the valley of the Gier, to the upper reaches of the Loire. This was one of the routes along which, later writers tell us, tin from the west was transported to Marseilles. Comparatively little is known of the early settlement of Vienne, but beneath the later Roman town, on the site of the Temple de Cybele, deeply stratified levels going back to the fourth century BC were discovered, producing Attic red figured ware, a range of Massaliot pottery and, later, Italian Campanian wares and Republican amphorae. From what has been said, Vienne's commanding position is self-evident.[19]

Many questions are raised by sites like Le Pègue and Vienne which the archaeological evidence is still too ill-focussed to answer. The most obvious area of interest is the attempt to gauge the changing intensity of trade from the fifth century BC to the first. Adequately quantified data is not available, but the general impression gained is of an increase in the volume of imported pottery in the third and second centuries BC. If this is so then it reflects what appears to be happening on the settlements of the coastal region and implies that distant trading centres like Vienne and Le Pègue were an essential part of the southern Gaulish economic system.

The western trading axis (fig 24)

The western route to the Atlantic, via the Aude and Garonne, is also likely to have been in operation as a major transport route for a range of goods. Here too there would have been *oppida* controlling trade. Evidence is slight, but the hilltop of Carcaso (Carcassonne) and the site of Tolosa (Toulouse) on the Garonne were both occupied from the sixth century BC or before, and both have produced Attic red figured pottery. However, excavation has not yet been sufficient to allow the status and intensity of occupation of these sites, and others, to be assessed.[20]

That the trade between Aquitania and Languedoc was of an organized kind is nonetheless suggested by the occurrence of a long-established coinage in the area — the so-called *Monnaies-à-la-Croix*. These coins were derived from silver drachmas issued by the Rhodian colony of Rhode (now Rosas) not far from Ampurias. The prototype had the head of a nymph on one side and a rose on the other. Both degenerated in the copying, the rose becoming a cross-like motif, hence the name *monnaies-à-la-croix*. It is widely believed that *monnaies-à-la-croix* began to be issued in the early years of the third century BC and continued into the Roman period. Their wide distribution, from the Rhône to the Gironde, including the valleys of the Aude, Ariege, Tarn, Lot and Dordogne, and the regional variation in style, are taken to reflect a series of distinct but similar coinages belonging to different tribes —

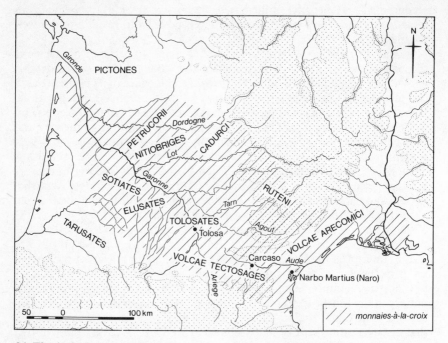

24 The Aude-Garonne route to the Atlantic showing principal tribes

the Volcae Tectosages, Tolosates, Volcae Arecomici, Nitiobriges, Petrucorii, Cadurci and Ruteni. The development of such a widespread coinage, continuing to evolve over several centuries, is indicative of organized exchange between the tribes occupying the western corridor.[21]

We have already stressed the occurrence of metals, especially silver and copper, in the mountains on either side of the corridor, the Montagne Noire and the Pyrenees. Coins of recognized value would have aided the exchange and transport of these essentially local products, but it is tolerably certain that tin from Britain was also passing this way to the Mediterranean ports. Extracted as stream-tin from the river deposits around the granite masses of Cornwall and Devon, ingots were exported via ports like Mount Batten,[22] presumably in a series of short- haul jumps to the mouth of the Gironde. The Atlantic tin sources were well known.[23] A Phocaean sailor had explored the west coasts some time in the sixth century BC (his exploits were incorporated much later in Avienus's *Ora Maritima*), and in about 325 BC Pytheas from Massalia had sailed the same route, circumnavigating Britain into the bargain. There is no need to assume that these journeys were particularly unusual; they merely reflect a long-term interest in western tin.

Some details of the tin trade are given by later writers. Diodorus Siculus, writing in the first century BC, is evidently drawing on an earlier source (possibly Pytheas) when he describes the friendly inhabitants of Belerium, a promontory of Britain, who extract tin and turn it into ingots which are then taken to an offshore island called Ictis. There, the metal is purchased by merchants and trans-shipped to Gaul '. . . and finally, making their way on foot through Gaul for some thirty days they bring their wares on horseback to the mouth of the river Rhône'. The route is not given, but the timing of 30 days would suggest either the Loire-Rhône route or, more likely, the Gironde-Aude. Later on, Diodorus tells us that tin was carried to Marseilles and Narbonne.[24] The sailing directions quoted in the *Ora Maritima* provide the additional information that the journey from the Mediterranean to the Gironde took seven days — this presumably referring to the situation in the sixth century BC.

The documentary evidence is admittedly scrappy and inadequate, but taken together it implies the use of the Aude-Gironde route as early as the sixth century BC. By the end of that century, the closure of the Straits of Gibraltar to Greek shipping by the Carthaginians would have given increased importance to the cross-Gaul routes, at least until the Romans took Gades (Cadiz) in 206 BC, bringing Carthaginian domination to an end. By that time the riverine routes were probably so well established that they continued to be used, if less consistently, until the late second century BC when, as we shall see, the Roman annexation of southern Gaul provided a new impetus.

The Romans and southern Gaul (fig 25)

Rome's interest in southern Gaul began to intensify towards the end of the third century BC, when Rome was drawn into conflict with the Carthaginians in Spain.[25] In 226 BC, in an attempt to stabilize relations, Rome and Carthage concluded the Ebro Treaty, which defined the river as the legitimate boundary between the spheres of interest of the two superpowers. For Rome this provided a much needed respite, allowing them time to clear the Gauls from Italy. Six years later, however, Hannibal attacked the town of Saguntum, which had previously come under the protection of Rome, and in the autumn of 219 BC the town capitulated after an eight-month siege. In March 218 Rome declared war on Hannibal, and thus began the Second Punic War.

The Ebro Treaty was swept aside as Hannibal and his army marched through southern Gaul, reaching the Rhône and crossing it before the Roman expeditionary force, led by Publius Scipio, could arrive at the mouth of the river. Finding Hannibal already heading for the Alps and northern Italy was a devastating blow to Scipio, and he was left with little choice. Sending his force to Spain under the leadership of his brother Cnaeus he returned by sea to northern Italy to assume command of a new force sent north to block Hannibal's advance. Thus it was that in the late summer of 218 BC two legions landed at Emporiae to open hostilities.[26]

The war ended in 206 BC with the surrender of Cadiz to the Roman army. Rome was now committed to Iberia, and the struggle against the Iberian tribes continued until the strength of the resistance was finally sapped and the last symbol of Celtiberian independence, the stronghold of Numantia, fell to Scipio in 133 BC.

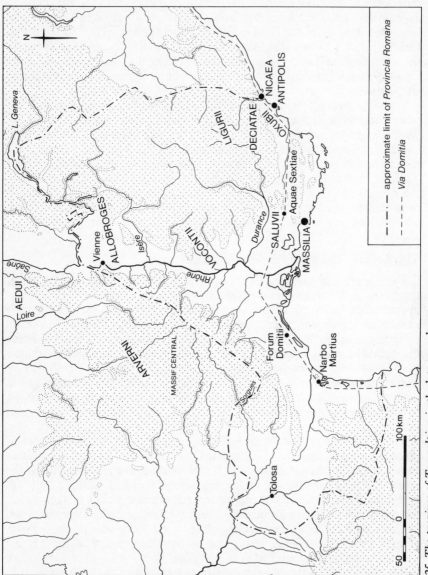

25 *The province of Transalpina in the late second century BC*

For eighty-five years, from the outbreak of the Second Punic War, Rome had been constantly involved in military activities in Iberia. During this time, the Roman commanders and their supply trains would have come to know well the land route between Italy and Spain and the various small ports around the coast. Inevitably, southern Gaul became a supplier for the army: corn, food and wine, hides and metals were all sought-after commodities, much in demand by the Roman quartermasters willing to pay prices inflated by the war. It was against such a background that the enormous increase in imported Italian products, evident in the archaeological record of various southern Gaulish towns after the middle of the third century BC, should be seen. But while the dramatic growth in Italian imports was a direct result of Roman military involvement in Spain, we should not underestimate the effects of the civilian entrepreneurs following in the wake of the army, eager to explore the new markets. The archaeological evidence does not allow a distinction to be made between these two prime causes of economic change.

Roman interest in southern Gaul, both military and commercial, was firmly established by the beginning of the second century, but this reliance on a friendly coastal zone took with it certain responsibilities of policing. After the Hannibalic War, the eastern part of the land route became very unsafe, and throughout the 190s there was almost continuous trouble from the Ligurians and Gauls.[27] In 189 BC a governor, *en route* to Spain with a force of 7000, was attacked by the Ligurians and died a few days later in Massalia. In 173 BC another governor died in uncertain circumstances while on his way to his Spanish command, and news of his death was taken to Rome by Massaliot envoys. He too may have suffered Ligurian attack, but if so the fact is unrecorded. Nor was it only the overland route that was unsafe. Ligurian pirates were making sea travel a dangerous business. In 181 BC the Massaliots complained to Rome, with the result that Gaius Mattienus was sent with ten ships to rid the seas of pirates.[28]

Matters finally came to a head in 154 BC, when Massaliot envoys appealed to Rome to help them against the Ligurians, who were now threatening the two coastal Greek cities of Nicaea and Antipolis.[29] A commission of enquiry soon established that the hostile tribes were the Oxubii and Deciatae, who occupied the territory south and west of the Var. The consul, Quintus Opimius, was quickly dispatched, and in two decisive battles brought the Oxubii and Deciatae to their knees. Their territory was now made over to Massalia, to whom several lesser tribes were required to submit hostages. That the Roman army remained in the region throughout the winter is an indication of how serious Rome considered the danger to the overland route to Spain to be. The settlement they imposed shows that Rome was coming increasingly to look on Massalia as the guardian of her interests in the area.

In 125 BC Roman policy towards southern Gaul underwent a significant change. The immediate cause of Roman intervention was another call for help from Massalia, this time to protect her against the aggressive activities of the Saluvii, who occupied the territory immediately to the north of the city up to the valley of the Durance.[30] The Saluvii, it seems, were being urged on by the powerful confederation of tribes led by the Arvernii of the Massif

Central. Rome responded by sending two legions under the command of the consul, M. Fulvius Flaccus. He arrived late in 125 BC, and early in the new campaigning season won battles against the Saluvii, the Ligurians and the Vocontii. However, no permanent settlement was in sight, and in the next year (123 BC) another consular army, under C. Sextius Calvinus, was sent to fight the same three tribes. It was probably in this campaign that Entremont, capital of the Saluvii, was finally destroyed.

A few kilometres to the south of Entremont, Sextius founded a *castellum* which he named Aquae Sextiae (Aix-en-Provence). He then set about organizing a permanent settlement. The coast was cleared of Gauls to a depth of 8 to 12 stades (1–2 miles), and the territory was put under the control of Massalia. In this he was simply restoring the arrangements made thirty years before by Opimius. The Saluvii he forcefully moved from their hilltop capitals, selling large numbers of them into slavery. But some of the Saluvian chieftains, including King Tutomotulus, managed to flee north to the safety of the Allobroges.

By this stage the Romans must have realized that the problem they were facing was of considerable dimension: beyond the immediate fringes of troublesome tribes lay the more remote Allobroges, and beyond them the inestimable force of the Arverni. To stabilize the situation in the south-west meant campaigning deeper and deeper into the unknown heart of Gaul. But there may have been another reason for their evident concern for the region: the Rhône valley was a commercial route of some importance. By penetrating it the Romans may have been hoping to establish a degree of control over the passage of goods.

It is at this stage that we hear for the first time of the Aedui as allies of Rome. The Aedui lived in the Morvan, well north of the Arverni; in fact they occupied a central position between the Saône, Seine and Loire, crucial to the control of many of the trade routes crossing France. By establishing friendly relations with them, the Romans were surely well aware of the commercial opportunities which were likely to arise. The only problem was that between the now-peaceful land of southern Gaul and the territory of the Aedui lay the aggressive Allobroges.

In 122 BC the consul, Cn. Domitius Ahenobarbus, was sent out to continue the war, accompanied by a herd of elephants with which to terrorize his opponents. The next year he began his attack on the Allobroges, very probably using Aquae Sextiae as a base. He was met by a Gaulish ambassador representing Bituitus, king of the Arverni, but refused to be drawn into diplomatic debate and pushed on across the River Durance towards Allobrogic territory. Somewhere close to the confluence of the Sorgue and the Rhône he encountered the enemy army and won an overwhelming victory.

It was now that the enormity of the task which the Romans had taken on began to be realized and Domitius sent to Rome for additional urgent help. A new Roman force of 30,000 troops was dispatched under the command of Q. Fabius Maximus, arriving in Gaul in the summer of 121 BC. Fabius went immediately into action against a colossal force of Allobroges and Arverni, and in a pitched battle, fought close to the confluence of the Isère and Rhône, he won a decisive victory. Contemporary accounts gave the size of the Celtic force as between 180,000 and 200,000, of whom three-quarters were killed. Allowing some degree of exaggeration, it was still a spectacular success for the Romans.[31]

The campaigns of 125–1 BC had been fought entirely to the east of the Rhône, and were clearly intended to break the power of the Celtic tribes occupying the Rhône valley. In the settlement that followed, the Allobroges became subject to Rome, thus giving her free access to the valley as far north as the Rhône-Saône confluence and eastwards to Lake Geneva. Significantly, at about this time, the Allobroges modified their coinage to match the Roman *denarius*. The Arverni in the Massif Central were left to their own devices, but the allies of Rome, the Aedui, were now within easy reach of Roman territory, no longer isolated by the hostile Allobroges. As long as this situation remained stable, Roman entrepreneurs had free access to the barbarian markets of the north and west.

In the period of consolidation which followed, the western part of Transalpina was gradually brought under Roman control. Domitius is generally credited with much of the basic organization, and in particular the creation of the great western highway into Spain which bears his name — the *Via Domitia* — though the road in some form must have already existed for decades.[32] He may also have been responsible for founding the market town of *Forum Domitii* (just north of Sete). But the single act which sealed the future was the foundation of the citizen colony of *Narbo Martius* in 118 BC.[33] The site chosen was significant: it was where the *Via Domitia* crossed a navigable branch of the River Aude, close to a sheltered inlet from the Mediterranean and only 4km from the long-established native *oppidum* of Montlaurès (fig 26). There can be not the slightest doubt that the founding fathers chose the one crucial route node in western Transalpina that commanded the movement of goods from Italy to Spain by the land route, and from the Mediterranean to the Atlantic by the ancient 'tin route' via the Aude and Gironde. The subsequent history of the colony was to justify the wisdom of their choice.

It was not long before the Romans turned their attention westwards, taking a firmer control of the way to the Atlantic. At about the time that Narbo Martius was founded, a treaty was struck with the natives at Tolosa (Toulouse) allowing a Roman garrison to be sited there. It was a wise move: in doing this the Romans had effectively secured the safety of the Carcassonne gap. Tolosa was now essentially a frontier town, the garrison keeping a watchful eye, not only on the locals, but on the *mélange* of traders of all nationalities, who were eager to exploit the newly enhanced commercial possibilities of the area.

The raw instability of the situation was soon demonstrated during the Cimbric War which followed. In brief, a mixed horde of Celts and Germans were rampaging through Europe. After defeating a Roman army on the Danube in 113 BC they crossed the Rhine in 109, and for a decade terrorized Gaul. It was in 109 that a Roman army was severely mauled somewhere in the north of Transalpina, and in the mêlée that followed, the local Celtic tribes, the Tigurini and the Volcae Tectosages joined in. Somewhere not far from Bordeaux, in 107 BC, the Roman army led by Cassius Longinus was defeated and forced to submit to the ignominy of marching under the yoke. Encouraged by their success, the Volcae slaughtered the Roman garrison at Tolosa. These events demonstrated the weakness of the Roman presence in the west, and also the vital strategic importance of Tolosa. Accordingly, in 106 BC the city was sacked by the Roman army of Caepio, who destroyed the native temple and appropriated a vast amount of gold from the sacred places.[34]

Rome suffered further reverses. In 105 BC two consular armies were defeated at Orange by the Cimbri and Teutones, who now threatened Italy itself. In the panic which ensued, the most famous commander of the day, Gaius Marius, was sent to regain control. After a period of reorganization he defeated the Teutones near Aquae Sextiae in 102 BC, and the Cimbri at Vercellae in northern Italy in the following year.

The events of 109–101 BC had been a frightening reminder to the Romans of their vulnerability to the northern barbarians. It was a fear on which Caesar was to play forty years later, but more than anything it had impressed on the Roman mind the vital need to maintain a firm control over Transalpina, in the interests of national security.

Standing back from the complexities of the Roman involvement in southern Gaul, it is possible to see a general pattern emerge. From about 250–125 BC Transalpina was used by the military, and exploited by the entrepreneurs with increasing intensity. The events of 125–118 BC were essentially a response to the need both to maintain freedom of passage and to develop the main trading routes to the north and west. Rome's involvement at this time, culminating in the foundation of the citizen colony of Narbo Martius, can only really be understood against the background of the social revolution which was being enacted in Italy during the same period, aspects of which will be considered in the next chapter.

Economic consolidation was well underway by 118 BC, but there is little sign of tight provincial control being exerted at this time, or in the following decade, and it was only after the shock of the Cimbric Wars (109–1 BC) that Transalpina began to be organized on a regular provincial basis. But in spite of these vicissitudes, trade intensified, and in the early years of the first century BC showed signs of exponential growth. These are matters to which we shall return in Chapter 4.

4 Roman estates and entrepreneurs

Social change in Italy

For the last two centuries before Christ, Rome was almost constantly at war. These were not minor skirmishes in distant frontier zones, but major wars involving a colossal input of manpower, estimated at ten per cent of the adult population. How this situation came about does not strictly concern us here; suffice it to say that in Roman society warfare was endemic — it was an essential part of the social system. The élite of Rome was a military élite and status was maintained by prowess on the field of battle. By the institutionalized display which followed — the triumph — the success of the individual was communicated to the masses while the militarism of the state was seen to be glorified. Only in matters of scale and style did Rome's system of social militarism differ from that of the Celts.

Until the third century BC the extent of Rome's military involvement in the Italian Peninsula was contained, and the system within which it worked was in equilibrium with the gradually evolving structure of the state. At this time, most Romans worked the land and most were under-employed. The system adopted, in common with that of most primitive peoples, was a sufficer-system: that is, the investment of work was sufficient to produce a small surplus, but not to extract from the land the maximum it could produce. One estimate for the typical Roman peasant economy envisages 60% of the product going towards the peasants' subsistence, 20% providing the seed for the next year and a further 18% being devoted to tax and rent paid in cash or in kind. The remaining 2% surplus provided a few necessities, often additional food, but also manufactured goods purchased in the towns. Even though the surplus was so small, with the demands of several million peasants to satisfy, a network of small towns could be maintained to provide the necessary goods and services.[1]

The state taxed labour in two ways: it taxed the product of labour in cash and in kind, and it taxed surplus labour in the form of military service. Citizen farmers were required to provide the armies commanded by the élite. The mere size of these armies, and the not inconsiderable period of time each year when the land would be depleted of its active manhood, is convincing proof of the view that peasant labour was chronically under-employed.

At the élite level, the system of continuous warfare provided the Roman nobility with the means to compete for glory. Commands were assigned by lot on a yearly basis. In this way opportunities were fairly shared, while the build-up of excessive power in the hands of a single successful individual was prevented.

The peasants called to take part in the annual summer campaigns suffered considerable hardship. Many were killed. In the first half of the second century BC it can be shown that 100,000 died — about a tenth of the total adult male population.[2] Before the second century the numbers lost were less, but even so, the percentage killed each year would have been a major factor in maintaining the balance of the rural population in relation to the holding capacity of the land. The equilibrium was a delicate one. A decline in warfare could have led to dangerous over-population and a peasantry with too much free time on its hands. This did not happen; in fact it was exactly the reverse — from the end of the third century BC, when Rome was drawn into the Hannibalic war, warfare escalated and for the last two centuries BC was continuous and often intense. Such a shift had irreversible effects on the rural economy, and indeed on the very structure of the state.

The many threads are tightly interwoven and to tease them out is to risk over-simplification, yet the main trends are clear enough. Prolonged absence from the land by an increasingly large proportion of the adult male peasantry began to cause social and economic disorganization. Families were unprovided for and farms became increasingly encumbered by debt. Inevitably, farms were sold and land began to accumulate in the hands of the rich. Parallel with this, the pool of hired labour diminished. Traditionally, the free peasantry had been employed as temporary labour on the farms of the rich, particularly at harvest time. It was an efficient system: peasants had surplus time which could be utilized for short periods on the larger estates, thus relieving the larger landowners from the wastefulness of employing a full-time labour force. The decrease in the availability of peasant labour as the result of prolonged war meant that a new source had to be found. Dispossessed peasants and their families were not much use: as peasants they had the sufficer mentality, and as citizens they had legal rights. Far better to replace the traditional free labour force with slaves. Slaves were, after all, a product of warfare, and were becoming more readily available. Thus the balance changed. As peasants left the land, so their holdings were bought up by the rich and merged into larger and larger estates which could be run efficiently with a force of agricultural slaves.

The decline of the rural peasantry was in reality a massive replacement of population. Where did they go? Some of course were killed or maimed in battle but many remained for much longer periods in military service. Prolonged wars brought to an end traditional patterns of citizen recruitment. For the poor and landless the attraction of the army was considerable and so there emerged the professional soldier employed on a long-service contract. The scale of the change was massive: it has been estimated that in the early second century BC in excess of half of all citizens served in the army for less than seven years, but two centuries later one sixth of all Italian-born citizens served a twenty-year term.[3]

The large-scale 'emigration' of peasants, mainly the landless and the poor, in the service of the army provided only temporary relief. Many returned; some were settled in the Italian countryside, but this created unrest not least because land had to be appropriated for them, which meant that others had to be dispossessed.[4] Moreover, a man who had spent his adult life as a soldier would have found readjustment to a peasant's life difficult — both skills and motivation were lost. Against this background it is possible to understand the mass migration to Rome which swelled the population of resident plebeians. In summary, the rural poor, given aspirations by years of military service, became the urban poor, and so migration from the land was intensified.

The third quarter of the second century BC was a turning point for Rome. One hundred years of continuous warfare had brought its rewards. In the single year, 146 BC, Rome had sacked two of the greatest cities in the Mediterranean — Corinth and Carthage — and thus become master of Greece and Africa. But the pivotal year was 133 BC. Numantia fell after a long and bitter siege, and Rome's ascendancy in the Iberian peninsula was assured: with Carthage gone she was now master of the western Mediterranean. As if by an act of the gods, the same year saw the legal transfer of the powerful kingdom of Pergamum to the Roman state in the will of the last of the Pergamene dynasty, King Attalus III. The largest power bloc in Asia Minor was now a direct and legitimate Roman concern. If the cares of empire were now piling fast on Rome, so too were the problems of civil unrest at home.

In 133 BC the cumulative effects of the concentration of land in the hands of the rich became evident. Its problems were now apparent to any thinking man looking about the country. The slave-run estates of the élite had grown vast, at the expense of the smallholdings of the free peasantry. From this followed two consequences: the rural poor and dispossessed flooded to the cities, and this created a volatile urban mob while at the same time drastically reducing the number of property-holders from whom the army could be recruited.

In 133, Tiberius Gracchus, a nobleman by birth, recently returned to Rome from military duty in Spain, was elected tribune of the people.[5] He fully understood the problem facing the Roman state and immediately set about solving it, in doing so riding roughshod over convention and trampling on the law. Gracchus's Land Laws were to the point. Public land — that is land acquired by the state through requisition, gift, debt repayment, etc. — was governed by an ancient law which forbade any individual from holding more than 500 *iugera* (125ha). The law was defunct and enormous holdings of state land were now concentrated in the hands of the wealthy aristocracy. Gracchus reaffirmed the ancient law and set up a commission to reallocate surplus state land to the poor. In addition to this he proposed to appropriate the new revenues derived from Asia Minor to provide cash grants for the new farmers, to enable them to stock their farms.

Both proposals were against the vested interests of the rich, and, more to the point, had they been successful they would have greatly enhanced Gracchus's reputation as a benefactor and popular hero. The dangers inherent in this, and the abhorrence felt by the conservative faction for the unconstitutional way in which Gracchus went about his reforms, brought the episode to its well known, violent end: Gracchus and four hundred of his followers were assassinated by a lynch mob of vigilante senators.

The Land Commission continued with their programme of redistribution after Gracchus's death, but momentum slowed as opposition grew, and it was eventually abolished in 119 BC. Meanwhile, a new palliative was being tried — the creation of citizen colonies in far-flung parts of Italy.[6] However, Italian land was expensive for the state to acquire, and inevitably eyes began to look abroad, to the newly-won provinces where land could be taken at little or no expense. Gaius Gracchus (brother of Tiberius) championed the idea, and in 123 BC proposed the setting-up of a citizen colony, to be called Junonia, on the site of devastated Carthage. The idea of a transmaritime colony met with violent opposition, fueled by superstition about the 'cursed' site of Carthage,[7] but with Neptunia (Taranto) and Minervia (Squillace), Gracchus was more successful.

The creation of colonies, or the promise to create them, now began to be a political ploy: it was approved of by the masses and was used by the unscrupulous as a means of acquiring a popular following. Gradually, opposition to overseas settlement was overcome. Mobility was in the air; in two generations, between 80 and 8 BC, it is estimated that about half the free adult males in Italy were resettled in Italian towns or on new farms in Italy or the provinces, and between 45 and 8 BC about one hundred colonies were established overseas.[8] Thus, in a single generation a quarter of a million adult males from Italy — one fifth of the population — were shipped off abroad.

The location of some of these colonies implies much about their function. There was clearly a military aspect: Narbo Martius founded in 118 BC was intended to protect the road between Italy and Spain from the potentially dangerous Volcae Tectosages; Dertona (Tortona), founded in 109 BC, guarded the difficult route between the Ligurian Alps and the Po valley, while Eporedia (Iurea), founded in 100 BC at the entrance to the Val D'Aosta in Piedmont, controlled the approaches to the Saint Bernard passes and was there to keep an eye on the native Salassi. No one would doubt the strategic sense which lay behind the siting of these foundations, but route nodes were attractive for trade as well, and the senators who put their names to these programmes will not have been unaware of the commercial possibilities that the new colonies created.

To understand what was happening in the Italian countryside in the last two centuries BC it is necessary to reiterate one basic premise: land and the facility to work it efficiently formed the basis of wealth generation throughout Roman history. Status and expectation depended on the size and fertility of one's landholding for probably as many as 90 per cent of the population before the social changes beginning in the third century BC. This is reflected in social attitudes enshrined in law. In the *plebiscitum Claudianum* of 218 BC, no senator or senator's son was permitted to own an ocean-going ship (one with a capacity for more than 300 amphorae), though small ships were allowed of sufficient size to carry crops from the farms. Livy's gloss on the law puts it in perspective: 'every form of profit making was regarded as unseemly for senators'. Or, as Licinius Crassus said, 'to increase the size of one's inherited fortune . . . is not consistent with *nobilitas*'. But these were pious statements, reflecting the old order; by the first century BC senators were widely involved in loan finance and, through middle-men, in trade. As Cicero remarks in *De Officiis*, 'trading must be regarded as undesirable unless engaged in on a grand scale'.[9] Even so, the opportunities for investment of capital in the Roman economy were few, and returns could be uncertain. The traditional high status of land-owning ensured that land remained the basis of wealth acquisition.

The growth of large estates probably began in early Republican times and escalated after the Hannibalic wars.[10] The dislocation of peasants, through army service and the drift of the rural poor to towns, were, as we have seen, significant factors in putting land on the market for the rich to acquire. Moreover, vast areas of Italy had been desolated by Hannibal's invasion. Peasants were reluctant to return, and in the financial crisis of the time the government had little option other than to make over great areas to its creditors at a nominal rent. This, probably more than any other factor, began the race of the land-hungry rich. In the later second and first centuries BC civil war and massive confiscations brought many of the recently created estates onto the market intact — for those who survived to acquire. As the profits of empire accrued to the senatorial class, so their ability, indeed their need, to invest in land grew. In other words continuous military involvement overseas not only freed the land of Italy from its peasant owners but it also provided the capital which the rich needed to purchase it.

The growth of estates brought with it a revolution in working the land. The peasant system had been a sufficer economy — that is, only such effort was invested that was needed to provide a small margin of surplus. The large estates were run differently: the rich had invested capital in the land and it had to be made to yield a good percentage return — in the order of five or six per cent.[11] Thus the traditional sufficer economy was abandoned and replaced by one which exploited land and labour to the full — a maximizer economy. Since the revolution in agriculture took place in a period of minimum technical innovation, to improve yields it was necessary to harness labour more efficiently. Advice was forthcoming in a number of treatises on estate management, of which the works of Cato, Varro and Columella are all that now survive. The emphasis was on profitability, and all were agreed that the most efficient way to run an estate was with slave-labour.

Slaves, though quite expensive to buy and in need of constant supervision, allowed considerable economies of scale to be made.[12] They could be organized into gangs of the appropriate size, taught specific skills and made to work long hours. Without the impediments of wives and children to feed, male slave gangs, properly organized, could yield considerably more than they consumed — far more than the hired labourers. Thus in terms of investment a slave offered a better return than a free peasant. But there had to be a balance: unlike the hired labourer who could be laid off when the task was done, the slave had to be maintained the year round, even through slack periods. It was even more important, therefore, for the estate to be so run that there was always work of one kind or another to be done. Columella was mindful of this when he advised that a duplicate set of tools should be kept so that if one was lost or broken work would not be held up, since 'the loss in labour exceeds the cost of replacement'.[13]

It would, however, have been inefficient to keep enough slaves to cope with all the estate work at times of peak activity, since the surplus labour at slack periods would have been too great to gainfully employ. Varro, writing in the first century BC, describes the kind of mixed labour force then in favour. He advises the use of hired labour 'contracted for the heavier work of the farm, such as harvesting or haymaking . . . it is more profitable to work unhealthy land with free wage labourers than with slaves; and even in healthy places, the heavy tasks such as the storage of the harvest can best be done by the free labourers'.[14] All the time that hired labour was available, such a system would have been sensible, but as the rural poor migrated, so an increased reliance had to be placed on slaves.

By the mid first century BC it is estimated that there were in excess of one million agricultural slaves employed in Italy. Given the limited life expectancy of the time, this means that a regular and substantial supply of slaves had to be maintained. We will return to these matters later (pp.77–8).

One feature of the drive for agricultural efficiency was the change from mixed farming to monoculture as the large estates concentrated more and more on the bulk production of a limited range of crops.[15] For much of Italy the system most commonly employed was probably a mixture of arboriculture and grain cultivation, the cereals being intercultivated with vines and olives. Both Varro and Columella speak of Italy as one vast orchard. Classical writers agreed that the most profitable of all crops was the vine. Indeed, Pliny said that wine production could be even more profitable than trade with the Far East. Periodic crop disease and over-production, or an exceptionally good harvest, could seriously affect profits, but even so, vine-growing spread rapidly throughout Italy and the provinces.[16]

The problems of over-production were always present. Cicero refers to an incident in the late second century BC which implies a ban on vine- and oil-growing among transalpine Gauls settled in the Po valley,[17] while Domitian passed an edict in AD 92 prohibiting the extension of vineyards in Italy, ordering that half the vineyards in the provinces should be destroyed. This Draconian measure coincided with a grain famine, and may in part have been aimed at restoring a balance in a farming system that had drifted too far towards monoculture, attracted by high cash returns.[18]

The olive was also an attractive possibility. The trees took longer to mature and to become productive, and the return was lower than with vines, but olive trees needed comparatively little attention, saving considerably on labour costs, while the wide spacing it was customary to adopt allowed ample room for cereal- or legume-growing.

It would be wrong to give the impression that pure monoculture was the norm. The ideal estate was one that could be self-sufficient, and the wise manager would ensure that adequate stocks were laid in to guard against shortage or crop failure. To have to buy in corn or wine to feed the resident slaves would have been economically disastrous. But the tendency to specialize in a single crop, especially wine, was irresistible to those interested in making a fast return on investment. Columella provides details and costings for setting up a new vineyard.[19] When due allowance is made for a number of uncertainties it is clear that, given a favourable soil and an average yield, then the annual return was likely to be between seven and ten per cent. Compared with the five to six per cent return estimated for ordinary mixed arable farming, wine-production had evident attractions to the landowner interested in a quick profit.

The *Ager Cosanus* (fig 26)

It is surprising how little archaeology can yet add to our understanding of the late Republican agricultural estates. One region, however, the *Ager Cosanus*, has recently been studied in sufficient detail to offer a range of useful new data.[20] Cosa lies on the coast of southern Tuscany, close to the island of Orbetello. Originally the territory belonged to the Etruscan city-state of Vulci, but it came under the control of Rome after being defeated in 280 BC. Soon after, in 273 BC, a colony was settled 30km from Vulci, and on the coast 'a city somewhat above the sea; the cove ends in a lofty knoll on which the town stands' (Strabo). The town was walled and laid out with a regular street grid containing the usual range of public buildings, as well as houses for the colonists. How many were originally sent and what percentage lived in the town itself it is impossible to say, but estimates for the original force of *coloni* range from 2500–4000.

Each colonist would have been given about 6 *iugera* of land (1.5ha) and most would have lived on their smallholding somewhere within the centuriated area around the town. In 197 BC a second group of colonists were sent out, presumably requiring more land allotments to be made from the previously uncultivated waste.

The *Ager Cosanus* suffered the fate of much of the west of Italy. When Tiberius Gracchus travelled along the Via Aurelia in the 130s he saw abandoned fields with only slaves herding the livestock and working the land. By this time, larger estates owned by absentee landlords and worked by slaves had replaced the many smallholdings of earlier times.

The centres of these new estates were often quite luxurious villas. Several are known, and one, built in the early first century BC, has been extensively excavated on the hill of Settefinestre.[21] The main house is a perfect square of 150 Roman feet (44m) with an enclosed courtyard behind and the *villa rustica* (farmhouse) to one side (fig 27). Walled gardens lie to the south and west of the villa. The arrangement is such that the main villa opened onto a west-facing loggia, providing a magnificent view across the western garden, enclosed with a turreted wall, to the sea 3km away. The decorative fittings of the villa, its painted walls, mosaic floors and elaborate terracottas, as well as the care taken in landscaping, show it to have been a building of some pretension.

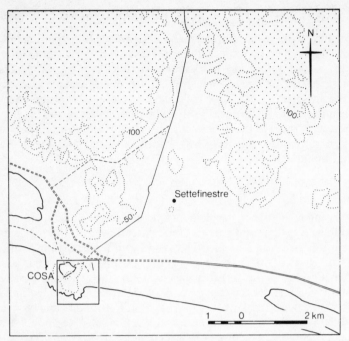

26 Above: Cosa and its hinterland. Below: the city of Cosa and its port.
(Lower plan based on McCann 1979, fig. 2)

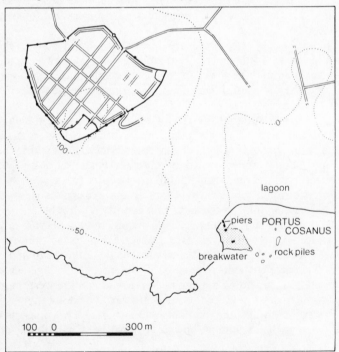

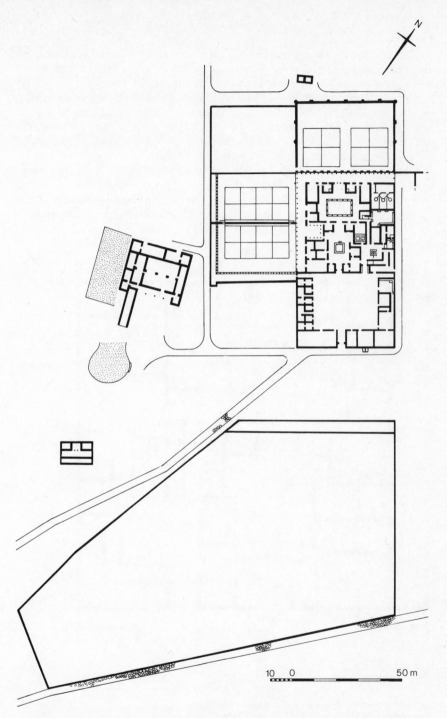

27 *The villa complex at Settefinestre (Carandini 1985, I, 139)*

The eastern third of the main building was at some stage separated off from the main villa and given over to industrial use (fig 28). The fittings are of unusual interest. One room contained an olive mill (*mola olearia*) with an olive press room nearby housing a single press and two settling tanks for the oil. In the same range were the wine presses — three arranged side-by- side in a single large room. From each, a runnel led to an adjacent room entirely occupied by a wine vat. A drain in its base would have allowed the liquor to be run off into amphorae in the storage area below.

The excavation of the area immediately adjacent to the industrial range could not be completed. Here, there may have been further industrial installations, perhaps *cellae vinariae* and *oleariae*. The incompleteness of the picture unfortunately prevents a quantitative assessment of the estate's

28 *The residential block at Settefinestre showing the*
agricultural installations for the manufacture of wine and olive oil
(Carandini 1985, I, 151)

output from being proposed with any assurance; nonetheless, what we do know presents a fascinating insight into the organization and style of a medium-sized estate. According to Cato, three wine presses would be appropriate to the cultivation of 100 *iugera* of vines. Allowing a further 50 *iugera* for olives, and bearing in mind the need for the estate to be self-supporting, the approximate size would probably have been *c.* 250 *iugera*. Cato's models would suggest the ideal slave complement to be about 20, but to make a reasonable profit of, say, seven per cent it has been estimated that it would have been necessary to buy in the labour of free peasants on a regular seasonal basis; to have run the estate on slaves alone would not have been financially viable. The implication, then, is that far from being a slave-dominated landscape, the 'Ager Cosanus' must have supported a considerable free peasantry working land of their own and maximising on their own labour to produce a surplus cash income.[22]

Excavations at the port of Cosa have thrown much light on the economy of the region.[23] The port was presumably created in 273 BC, when the colony was founded. In its present form, with harbour protection constructed on the basis of a series of concrete piers, it dates to the late second or early first century BC, when the prosperity of the region was at its height. Close to the port, some 250m away, behind a zone of sand dunes, excavation has revealed convincing evidence of a commercial fishery. Here a natural lagoon was modified to improve conditions for fish-breeding, by providing a fresh-water supply to help regulate the temperature and salinity of the water. Two substantial fish tanks were built, either to hold live fish ready for market, or to raise the fry before turning them loose in the lagoon.

The discovery of the fishery is of particular interest because the size of the installations suggest that fish or fish products formed a major element in the local economy. Live fish could have been transported to Rome in specially constructed boats with fish-wells, but this would have been expensive and is unlikely to have accounted for more than a small percentage of the product. It is far more reasonable to suppose that most of the catch was treated to produce the fermented fish-liquor known as *garum*. *Garum* was much in demand in the Roman world as an additive to cooking, and was sometimes drunk in its natural state. That it was a valuable commodity is emphasized by Pliny, who writes, 'scarcely any other liquor except unguents has come to be more highly valued, bringing fame even to the nations that make it'. No direct evidence has yet been found of its manufacture; nor is it certain how the *garum* was transported, unless, as has been suggested, it was in one of the types of amphorae (Dressel 1C) made locally. Nonetheless, there can be little doubt that the production and export of *garum* was one of the mainstays of the economy of the *Ager Cosanus*.

The principal product of the area, however, was wine. The evidence for this is overwhelming — the discovery in the town, and at the port, of a vast number of amphorae. About half of them are of Dressel 1 type (fig 29), dating from the late second century and throughout the first century BC, strongly suggesting that the peak of prosperity of the port was in the late Republican period. A number of the amphorae were stamped with a maker's

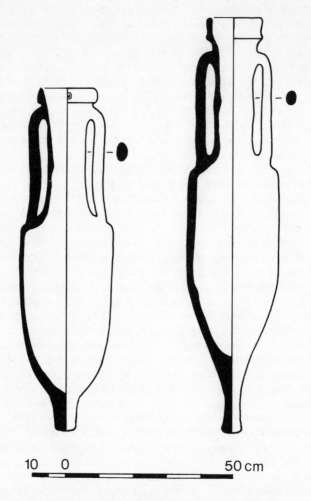

29 Amphorae of Dressel type 1: left 1A, right 1B

name, and of these, 43 per cent bear the name of Sestius. Preliminary analysis of the fabrics, and the sheer quantity of the Sestius product, leave little doubt that the vessels were made locally for the export of Cosan wine.[24]

There is some uncertainty about the significance of name stamps on amphorae. They could refer to the manufacturer of the amphora, the producer of the wine or the shipper, but these distinctions are likely to have been blurred. The owner of a large estate may well have had his own kiln complex, staffed, in slack periods, by surplus slave-labour. He may also have owned ships to transport his products.

Something is known about the Sestius family from historical sources.[25] Lucius Sestius Quirinus, *consul suffectus* in 23 BC, was engaged in the manufacture of roof tiles, many of which, bearing his name, have been found both in Rome and the *Ager Cosanus*, and two varieties of amphorae, both Dressel 1B types, stamped with the name of Lucius Sestius, have been found at Cosa. There can be little doubt then that the Sestius family were involved in the wine trade in the late first century BC. His father, Publius Sestius, was a praetor in 54 BC and proconsul of Cilicia in 49–8. Publius was a friend of Cicero, and through him we learn a little more: Publius was wealthy (and indeed Cicero asked him for financial help on one occasion); he had a villa at Cosa, and the family appear to have owned 'splendid ships' (*navigia luculenta*). The poet Catullus was also impressed by the 'costly dinners' which Publius was accustomed to provide.

The picture which emerges of the Sestii is of a wealthy aristocratic family owning an estate at Cosa, where they made amphorae, presumably for their own wine, and commanded a fleet of merchant ships which in all probability was employed to carry the vintage to market.

The earliest amphorae bearing the stamp of Sestius are of the Dressel 1A type which is currently dated to the late second and early first centuries BC. While the chronology does not preclude the possibility that Publius began the family business, it is more likely that it was started by his father, the elder Lucius, who was a tribune some time between 100 and 90 BC. Instead of proceeding to hold more illustrious offices, Lucius appears to have retired from public life, for such is the implication of Cicero's enigmatic statement that Sestius 'did not so much wish to hold other offices as to appear worthy to hold them'. This is a little unusual and it is tempting to believe that Lucius gave up his public career in favour of pursuing his more lucrative business activities from Cosa. It seems, then, that three generations of Sestii were involved in the wine business at Cosa during the period *c*. 120–20 BC.

Roman trade with southern Gaul

Archaeological evidence has shown, with an unusual clarity, one aspect of how the Sestii organized their business. The distribution of their stamped amphorae in Europe vividly demonstrates that they were aiming specifically for the Gaulish market (fig 30), and the detailed pattern of find-spots suggests that they were using the ports of Marseilles and Narbonne.[26] One of the ships carrying Sestius amphorae sank off the Grand Congloué rock, 24km east of Marseilles, in the early first century BC.[27] A little later we learn that Publius Sestius paid a visit to Marseilles, presumably in the interests of the family business. Cosa was well sited to trade with southern Gaul, and the enormous opportunities opening up in the new province would not have been overlooked by the entrepreneurs and estate owners of Italy.

The activities of the Sestii were by no means unusual. By this time, the traditional attitudes to commerce were fast breaking down. This is vividly shown by another case which has recently been examined, in which we can recognize a commercial grouping comprising a senator, C. Sempronius Rufus, a municipal notable from Puteoli, C. Vestorius, and a commoner, M. Tuccius Galeo.[28] The three men were involved in a shipping venture which,

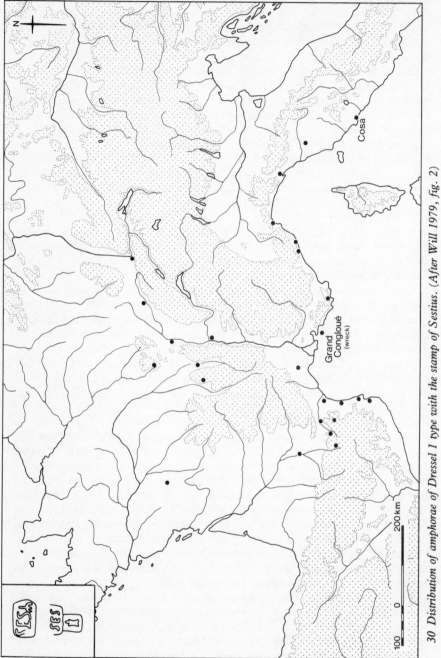

30 Distribution of amphorae of Dressel 1 type with the stamp of Sestius. (After Will 1979, fig. 2)

it seems, met with disaster in the middle of the first century BC. The interest of the case is considerably increased by the discovery of a wreck found off the island of Planier south-west of Marseilles.[29] The vessel was carrying a mixed cargo including amphorae, probably of oil, stamped 'M. Tuccius Galeo', and made in the region of Brindisi in Apulia. Also included were a number of dyes: realgar (*sandaracoi*), lithage (*molybditis*) and *caeruleum*, all of which can be found in the region of Puteoli. Even more of a remarkable coincidence is the statement by Vitruvius that C. Vestorius initiated the production of *caeruleum* at Puteoli. The third element of the cargo was fine ceramic table ware.

The implications of this evidence are tolerably clear. Oil amphorae were being shipped up from Apulia to the port of Puteoli, either to be trans-shipped to another vessel or, more likely, to take on board a consignment of dyes and fine wares before sailing north to Marseilles — and to disaster. The example is particularly interesting in that it shows commerce in action in the mid-first century BC. The products of Italy — both agrarian and industrial — were being systematically shipped off to the lucrative markets of Gaul. There can be little doubt that the late Republican estate owners and entrepreneurs saw the Gaulish market as the ideal place to dump their surpluses.

The evidence quoted above is essentially anecdotal; it throws light on trade patterns but does not allow any quantitative assessment of the commerce to be made. There are, however, some ways in which the question can be approached. The first, and perhaps the most direct, is by assessing the number and date of wrecks along the treacherous southern coast of Gaul. Although there are difficulties inherent in this approach, not least the impossibility of dating wrecks accurately, a most informative pattern is produced, showing a dramatic increase in the number of wrecks after 150 BC, peaking at the end of the first century BC (fig 31).[30] If one accepts that the number of wrecks is directly proportional to the volume of shipping then the only possible conclusion is that Roman trade with southern Gaul saw an exponential growth from the middle of the second century BC.

Although virtually all ships caried mixed cargoes, by far the commonest type were ships devoting in excess of 75 per cent of their cargo space to amphorae. When it is remembered that a ship like that wrecked at Madrague de Giens near Hyères *c*. 60–40 BC carried 400 tons of cargo, and this included 6–7000 amphorae, then the sheer volume of the wine trade to Gaul begins to become evident.[31]

The direct effect of this on the southern Gaulish communities can easily be judged from the considerable quantities of Italic amphorae and Campanian pottery found on native sites. The statistics published for the ceramic sequence at Nages are particularly revealing.[32] Converted to diagrammatic form (fig 32) it is possible to appreciate the dramatic increase in Italian wine at the expense of Massaliot wine after *c*. 175 BC, rising to a virtual monopoly after 100 BC. Against this, the figures for percentage of amphorae in relation to other pottery forms show a sharp increase in amphorae from about 100 BC. In other words, two distinct trends are evident: the collapse of the local wine

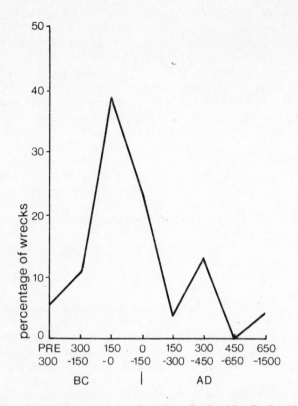

31 Dates of wrecks off the coast of central southern Gaul. (After Parker 1984, fig 6)

market in the face of Italian competition is well underway at least half a century before the conquest; and, following the conquest, the overall consumption of wine increases. It is tempting to assign both changes to the deliberate marketing policies of the Roman entrepreneurs.

The effects of this rapidly escalating trade on the Gaulish communities will be explored in detail in the next chapter, but here we must briefly consider the volume of the trade in the first century BC. The first point to make is that at some sites, particularly Toulouse and Chalon, the actual quantity of Dressel 1 amphorae discovered is enormous. At Chalon, where large quantities were dredged from the Saône in the nineteenth century, it has been estimated that some 24,000 have been recovered of a potential quarter to half a million that might have been deposited. From Toulouse the numbers were probably even greater.[33]

Impressed by these figures, and using the number and capacity of the wrecks as a starting point for a quantitative guess, André Tchernia has suggested that the annual import of Italian wine to Gaul in the first century BC probably reached 100,000 hectolitres, accounting for 40 million amphorae over the century.[34] At first sight the figure might seem excessive, but seen

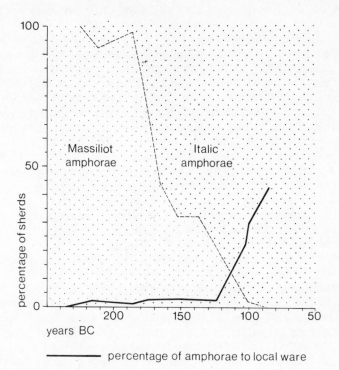

*32 Quantification of amphorae from the Vaunage
(from figures quoted in Goudineau 1983)*

against an independent suggestion that the annual output from the *Ager Cosanus* alone was about 50,000 hectolitres[35] then Tchernia's figure may, indeed, prove to be too conservative. To understand the order of magnitude of what is being suggested, the figures quoted for Italian exports to Gaul in the first century BC should be compared to the 750,000 hectolitre export of wine from Gascony to Britain and Flanders in the early fourteenth century AD, which is generally considered to have been the largest trade system operative in pre-industrial Europe.

Production and consumption in late Republican Italy

Sufficient will have been said above to have demonstrated something of the size of the Gaulish market that was being opened up to the Italian producers in the second and first centuries BC. In Gaul, the surplus products of the Italian estates, particularly wine and to a lesser extent oil, could be off-loaded in return for raw materials and, more important, slaves. The evidence for this exchange we will examine in detail later (pp.77–8, 81–7), but here it is necessary to stress the vital importance of the Gaulish market to the economic stability of late Republican Italy. The Hannibalic war had opened up southern Gaul to Rome and its traders; few could have failed to have understood the colossal potential of the rich, boundless hinterland, with its great rivers providing easy communication to the interior. It is impossible now to untangle the aims and aspirations of those who led Rome into the Gallic wars of 125–1 BC but it would be naive to suppose that commercial considerations were not to the fore. Indeed it would be possible to argue, though difficult to substantiate, that had it not been for the development of the Gaulish market in the second century BC, and its consolidation in the first, the stability of the Italian economy might have been in jeopardy.

The other great consumer market was, of course, Rome itself. The affluence and life-style of the rich had been greatly enhanced throughout the second and first centuries BC, and consumption had accordingly increased. But to this must be added the phenomenal increase in population which the city had experienced as the result of the continuous influx of rural poor. By the end of the first century BC the total population probably approached one million. All had to be fed, on however low a level.

Gaius Gracchus first came to terms with feeding the plebeians when, in 123 BC, he passed a law which guaranteed to all citizens living within the city a monthly allowance of corn at a fixed subsidized price. After 58 BC, it seems that the agreed monthly measure was given free. By 46 BC the number of citizens benefitting was in the order of 320,000.[36] Economically this made good sense since it provided an assured market for the wheat produced on the large Italian estates, and in this way filtered a proportion of state income, from taxes, plunder, etc., into the hands of the estate-owning aristocracy. It also increased the spending power of the masses who, freed from the necessity to buy wheat, could spend what surplus they had on other consumables such as oil, wine, fruit and meat, thus benefitting the estates once more.

The third type of market, far more difficult to assess, was that created by the colonial settlements in Italy, where, as we have seen, large numbers of the urban and rural poor were settled. Although they were presumably self-sufficient in food, and were therefore unlikely to have needed to import staple agrarian products, the aggregated surplus wealth of a population of 5–10,000 will have provided a market for a range of luxuries and other consumable durables, some considerable part of which, like for example fine pottery, would have been estate-produced.

Of the three main consumer markets, the colonies, Rome and the provinces, and their hinterlands, the first was small, the second finite, the third without apparent bounds. Given the accumulation of wealth in the hands of an estate-owning aristocracy, combined with increasing capital investment in the estates as the principal means of wealth generation, then the state had little option but to capitalize on the tradition of endemic warfare. Foreign wars and the acquisition of provinces became an integral and essential part of the socio-economic system.

Slaves

Finally we must return to the question of the fuel which generated the energy for the system — slaves. We have already explored the system's loop: continuous warfare leading to the rise of large estates, leading to the need for a constant supply of slaves, leading again to continuous warfare. Here we must briefly consider the size of the demand and the sources of supply.[37]

Something of the scale of the slave trade can be grasped by considering some *ad hoc* figures. Each year, according to Cassius Dio, there were about a quarter of a million slave sales in the open market and no doubt many more that went unrecorded and untaxed.[38] At the great slave market on Delos, Strabo casually tells us that there was nothing unusual in 10,000 slaves changing hands in a single day's trading. Figures such as these, together with Galen's assertion that at Pergamum (in Asia Minor) there were as many slaves as freemen in the second century AD, give a vivid impression of the extent to which Rome was a slave society. Current estimates suggest that at the end of the first century BC, in Italy, out of a total population of six million, one-third were slaves.[39] This pool of labour had to be maintained, since wastage, through manumission and, more significantly, low life expectancy, was considerable. A replacement rate of about 7 per cent per annum is by no means unlikely. Thus, simply to maintain the Italian labour force in the late first century BC would have required the generation of 140,000 slaves a year. Replacement by breeding would certainly have contributed, but, as an industry, it had not yet got underway on a large scale. At a rough estimate, therefore, well in excess of 100,000 new slaves had to be acquired every year, assuming a situation of non-growth in the rural estates.

Slaves came from three different sources: by capture during war; through piracy; and by means of regular trade with territories beyond the frontiers. Acquisition through warfare was an uncertain business, but the haul could be very considerable. Caesar's campaigns in Gaul beween 58 and 51 BC yielded an uncountably high number ('a hundred myriads') and in one campaign alone, against the Aduatuci in 57 BC, he enslaved 53,000.[40] At such times, demand could probably have been met by the results of warfare and there might even have been a glut in the market.

Piracy certainly kept the slave markets well supplied, but it was a mixed blessing. In the east Mediterranean, Delos thrived by selling captives taken by land and sea, particularly along the southern coasts of Asia Minor, but the disruption caused to normal commerce was so considerable that in 67 BC Pompey was given a special commission to suppress piracy. His success must have had a dramatic effect on the supply of slaves.[41]

Rome's slave-based economy required a regular and reliable flow of slaves; it could not, therefore, rely solely upon the fluctuations of military campaigns and pirate raiding to supply its needs. In this context the importation of slaves, acquired as a commodity by trade across frontiers, takes on a particular importance. Rome's frontiers with the barbarian world were long, and the barbarian communities beyond were ready to readjust their social systems to provide a crop of captives when required. Once the channels of exchange had been established, the Roman entrepreneurs could control the volume of through-put to compensate for the vicissitudes of the slave market in general.

Some indication of the nature of cross-frontier trade is given in the classical sources. Strabo, writing of the entrepôt of Aquileia at the head of the Adriatic, lists the imports coming from the barbarian lands beyond to the Roman world as 'slaves, cattle and hides', in return for which the Romans gave oil, wine and 'the products of the sea'. The same writer, describing Tanais on the Black Sea, lists as exports from the Cimmerian Bosphorus 'slaves, hides and other such things as nomads possess', and from Britain came 'grain, cattle, gold, silver and iron' together with 'hides, slaves and hunting dogs'. A century or so later, Tacitus tells the story of a cohort of Usipi who, after various adventures, were caught by the Frisii north of the Rhine frontier and were 'sold as slaves and passed from hand to hand till they reached our bank of the Rhine'.[42] These examples, admittedly anecdotal, show that slaves were regularly supplied along the length of the northern frontiers.

To arrive at any idea of the volume of the trans-frontier slave trade is extremely difficult, but for Gaul, in the first century BC, Tchernia has offered an estimate. Basing his calculations on figures given for the ethnic composition and numbers of slaves taking part in a slave rebellion led by Spartacus in 74–1 BC, he arrives at 300,000 as the total number of the Gallic slaves in Italy. Assuming a replacement rate of 7 per cent, and also that the proportion of Gallic slaves was maintained, then the annual export of slaves by trade in a non-war year must have been about 15,000.[43] Sufficient will have been said of the calculations to show that the figure can be regarded only as a best guess, rather than an estimate, but nevertheless it offers an order of magnitude.

Regular trade must of course be seen against the periodic gluts in the market caused by military campaigns. Ample surpluses of Gaulish slaves would have been available in 200–190, 154, 125–121, 107–2, 90, 83, 77–2 and 58–1 BC, but the suppression of the Ligurian pirates in 181 BC, and of piracy in the east Mediterranean in 67 BC, would have created widespread shortages not only in Italy but elsewhere in the Empire. There is no reason why the slave trade should not have been well organized before 125 BC. After the establishment of Transalpina, apart from brief campaigns necessary to quell unrest, there was no major offensive until Caesar arrived in 58 BC. We would therefore expect to find the Gaulish slave trade organized on a regular basis by Roman entrepreneurs working from the province. Pompey's successes in the eastern Mediterranean in 67 BC in all probability led to considerable increased demand, until Caesar's campaigns totally altered the political geography of the west. The effects of these factors on commercial activity with Gaul and Britain in the period 120–60 will be discussed in detail in the next chapter.

The dynamics of the late Republican economy

In the pages above we have attempted to examine some of the causative factors and directions of change inherent in the complex socio-economic development of the Roman world of the late Republic. But even if all the relevant facts were known and agreed (which they certainly are not), and the space were available, it would be impossible to do justice to such a complex system in the two dimensions of the printed page. Yet a convincing, if generalized, scheme can be offered. In essence the main contentions are these:

(a) In Roman society warfare was endemic, and among the élite status was related to military success. *Intensification* led to a state of continuous warfare after the late third century.

(b) Involvement of a peasant militia in more frequent and longer wars led to a crisis in the countryside, dislocating peasants from their roots and leading to the emergence of a landless rural poor. *Intensification* created a migration of the rural population, to Rome, to long-term military service and to citizen colonies.

(c) The élite, through continuous warfare, acquired wealth to invest. The social and economic systems in Italy were such that land was the only major field for investment. *Intensification* led to the development of increasingly large élite-owned estates.

(d) The only efficient way to work large estates to create a sufficient return on investment was with slaves. *Intensification*: as the estates grew in size so the demand for slaves increased and sources of supply, through warfare, pirate raiding and regular trade with barbarians, had to be developed.

(e) Estates began to produce surpluses of a limited range of products particularly wine which could not easily be disposed of at sufficient profit in the home market. *Intensification*: the need grew to create overseas markets to which bulk commodities could be trans-shipped for profit.

What emerges from all this is that the pressures, tensions and responses inherent in Roman society created the need to develop world-wide trading networks so that raw materials and manpower could be drawn into the core in return for the outflow of manufactured goods and Mediterranean agricultural surpluses. The system of provinces, and the nature of provincial administration which developed, was a direct response to this need. At its very simplest this can be characterized as a core-periphery-beyond model. The *core* is Italy, the *periphery* is the provincial penumbra, while *beyond* are the barbarian regions outside the frontier. Each zone is in a state of symbiotic equilibrium with its neighbour; they are bound together in a web of interdependence. In the same way that Italy developed close economic ties with Transalpina, so Transalpina developed its own systems of interdependence with the barbarians beyond the frontier. These are matters to which we must now turn.

5 Gaul: continuity and change 125–59 BC

Gaul: historical outline 125–59 BC

The events of the years 125–121 BC mark a turning-point in the history of Gaul. Before that, while trading contacts began to build up, Roman military involvement was sporadic, but afterwards Romanization and the organization of the province of Transalpina proceeded apace. Even so, the next 70 years were far from peaceful. The threat from the Cimbri and Teutones between 109 and 101 BC caused widespread disruption and panic, and inspired the Volcae Tectosages to rebel, resulting in the Roman capture of Tolosa (Toulouse) in 106 BC by Caepio. But after the defeat of the barbarian invaders in 101 BC the province settled down to a period of comparative security.

The early organization of the new province is obscure. To begin with, the two Gallic regions, Transalpina and Cisalpina, normally formed part of the single *Provincia Gallia*, but when able governors were in short supply it was customary to attach Transalpina to Hither Spain, echoing the practice of the earlier decades. It was not until the 70s that Transalpina was governed as a single province.[1]

Sporadic border problems required some military action of the governors. In 90 BC we hear of C. Coelius Caldus subduing a revolt among the Saluvii, but it was the events consequent upon the return of Sulla from the east in 83 BC, and the resulting Sertorian revolt in Spain, that were to cause major upheavals in Transalpina.[2] Matters came to a head in 77 BC when M. Aemilius Lepidus raised Cisalpina to revolt and marched on Rome, only to be defeated and forced to flee to Spain. The situation in Transalpina, caught in the middle of the power struggle, must have deteriorated into near anarchy. Towards the end of the year, when Pompey was sent to restore the west, he had to fight his way through the area, later claiming that he had 'recaptured Gaul'. Transalpina now became his base for operations in Spain, and to ensure civil order and stability M. Fonteius was installed as governor.[3] One of his main tasks was to maintain the supply lines and we hear of him restoring the Via Domitia. He was also active in raising food and supplies for Pompey's army by requisition and tribute, actions which caused severe financial problems for the provincials, and brought him under much criticism (as we shall see below, p.82–3). He also found it necessary to campaign against the Vocontii.

The murder of Sertorius in 72 BC marked the end of the rebellion in Spain, and it was probably as part of the reorganization which followed that Pompey provided Transalpina with its legal framework — the *Lex provinciae*. Throughout this period, Rome's relations with Massalia remained cordial. Without the help of the Massaliots, says Cicero, 'Rome could never have triumphed over the Transalpine Gauls', and, in the course of reorganization, land to the west of the Rhône, once belonging to the Volcae and Helvii, was made over to Massalia. To mark his successes, Pompey built a Trophy at the crest of the Pyrenees, close to the Mediterranean coast, which was soon to be recognized as the boundary between Spain and Gaul. Pompey's reorganization evidently adopted convenient physical boundaries rather than respecting the traditional cultural divide which had failed to acknowledge the Pyrenees.

Two themes pervade the 60s in Gaul: exploitation by successive Roman governors and their followers, and discontent among the Allobroges; the two were no doubt linked. One governor after another was charged with malpractice. In 63 BC C. Calpurnius Piso (governor from 67–64 BC) was accused of extortion; we learn from Cicero that his successor, L. Murena, was diligent in debt-collecting, while one of his assistants P. Clodius was accused of forging wills and cheating heirs of their rightful inheritances. Abuses such as these were commonplace in newly-won provinces, and provided a catalyst to fermenting discontent. In 67 BC Piso had to put down a rebellion among the Allobroges of the Rhône valley, but the problem remained and in 63 BC an Allobrogic embassy went to Rome to complain about oppressive treatment, probably at the hands of tax- and debt-collectors. They got nowhere and the situation so deteriorated that C. Pomptinus was sent to Transalpina in 62 BC to stamp out another uprising among the tribe, this time, it seems, with lasting success. The tribes of the Rhône valley and of the rest of Transalpina gave Caesar no trouble when, in 58 BC, he began his ten-year command in Gaul.

The western trading system

In spite of various problems, both internal and external, which Transalpina suffered in the period 125–59 BC, trade flourished. To the west the Aude-Garonne route developed rapidly. There is now ample evidence to show that already, by the first half of the second century BC, Graeco-Italian amphorae were reaching Tolosa in quantity, some of them bearing shippers' marks painted in Iberian script.[4] From here the amphorae, or their contents, were presumably being distributed to the natives of Aquitania and beyond. The use of Iberian script is particularly interesting, suggesting that the middle-men handling the wine, after it was off-loaded at the ports, were locals and not the Romans who did the shipping. This pattern continued and intensified after the foundation of the colony at Narbo in 118 BC, the only significant difference being that, by now, Roman entrepreneurs had moved in.

The siting of the port of Narbo was considerably influenced by the difficult nature of the land forms on this part of the coast (fig 33). Long-shore drift had built sand and gravel banks across the river mouths, diverting them and creating large expanses of marshland behind. Narbo was 20km from the sea, inland from the series of lagoons and marsh — the *Lacus Rubresus* — through which the River Aude found its way to the sea. Goods arriving in sea-going ships had therefore to be off-loaded at an outport at St Martin and trans-shipped to lighters for the journey by canal, lagoon and river to the river port of Narbo.[5]

Although Narbo developed as a complex commercial centre, producing a wide range of goods and serving as a market for food and raw materials to be acquired for export, one of its prime economic activities continued to be the import of Italian wine.[6] A fascinating insight into the mechanisms of the trade in the 70s is provided by Cicero in his defence of the governor Fonteius in *Pro Fonteio*. It appears that Fonteius instructed his clerks to extract a tax — *portoria* — on wine as it passed through inland towns *en route* from Narbo to Tolosa:

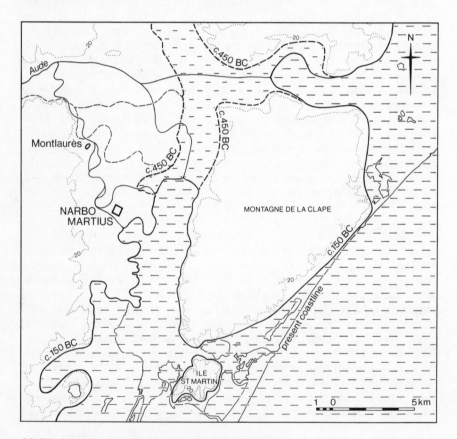

33 *The location of Narbo Martius (Narbonne) and the native* oppidum *of Montlaurès in relation to changing coastal conditions. (Based on Guy 1973, figs. 7–9)*

Titurius extracted at Tolosa four denarii per amphora of wine as transportation tax; Porcius and Munius extracted three victoriati at Crodunum, at Vulchalo Servaeus extracted two victoriati; also in these places the transportation fee was extracted from those who turned aside at Cobiomachus not wishing to go to Tolosa; and they exacted at Elesioduli six denarii on each amphora from those who shipped [the wine] to the enemy.

Although the corrupt text leaves some doubts about exact interpretation, the implication of Cicero's passage is that admittedly *portoria* was charged on the transport of wine, but this was entirely permissible because the increased cost, more than 300 per cent, was being passed on to the native barbarians living beyond the province.[7]

The vast quantities of amphorae found at Tolosa strongly suggest that here was one of the *emporiae*, most likely the principal *emporium* in the west, where the Italian wine was decanted into barrels, brought to the town by the independent Gauls, who preferred this traditional means of transport to carry the wine to their homes. Some such explanation is needed to account for such a colossal number of amphorae discarded at Tolosa. Precisely this was done at Aquileia, at the head of the Adriatic, where the Illyrians came to trade with the Romans, and the use of wooden casks by the natives of the Cahor region, not far from Toulouse, is recorded in the 50s.[8] Not all the wine was decanted in this way: large numbers of amphorae found on native sites in the region, and indeed much further afield, even in Britain, show that the original containers were often used to distribute wine over very considerable distances. The fact that the two methods of transport were used makes it impossible to quantify the consumption of wine or to compare consumption from site to site.

The mechanisms by which wine was distributed to the natives of Transalpina, and to the independent Gauls beyond, were no doubt varied and complex, but a map of the known distribution of Dressel 1A amphorae in the region, incomplete though it must be, gives some idea of the extent of the trade (fig 34). At the risk of over-simplification we might distinguish two mechanisms, one reflecting essentially local trade within the province, the other long-distance trade to the regions beyond.

The local distribution patterns represent the exchange of a range of locally-produced commodities, among which metals seem to have been of outstanding significance. The Montagne Noire, the Corbières and the Rutènes were rich in silver, lead and copper, while gold was to be won in a number of localities, particularly south of Tolosa in the valleys of the Ariège and Arize, both tributaries of the Garonne, and in the Montagne Noire around Salsigne, north of Carcassonne. The discovery of amphorae at a number of mines in this zone, sometimes in considerable quantity, is a clear indication of reciprocal exchange, the ingots of metal, no doubt, finding their way to Narbo for trans-shipment to Italy (fig 35).[9]

Long-distance trade was no doubt organized in a number of ways, but two broad systems may be suggested: (a) an *emporium* could be set up within the province and visited by independent Gauls, exchange taking place under the auspices of Roman authority; or (b) a commodity could be transported in

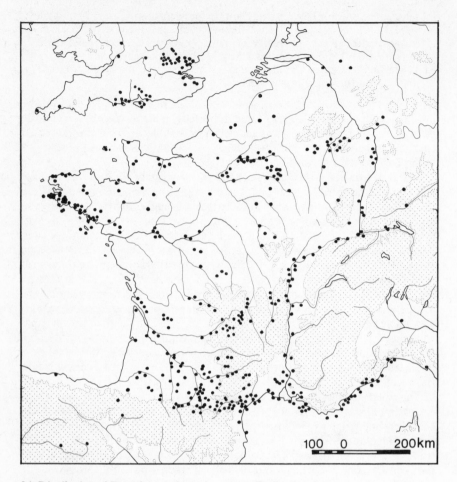

34 *Distribution of Dressel 1 amphorae in western Europe.*
(After Fitzpatrick 1985, fig. 3)

bulk to a native centre outside the province, for redistribution within the local socio-economic system (fig 36).

Tolosa falls into the first category, but it was originally an example of the second, which had been overtaken by the advance of the Roman frontier though retaining its traditional role. The second system is more normal, and along the western axis, which we are considering, two examples, at different extremes of the scale, may be mentioned. The first is the massive native *oppidum* of Montmerlhe at Laissac in the upper Aveyron valley, 20km east of Rodez. The vast size of the defended site, its central position with regard to routes and the general availability of metals, together with the large number of complete or near-complete Dressel 1 amphorae found in casual excavations in the past, single it out as a major *oppidum*, in all probability involved in

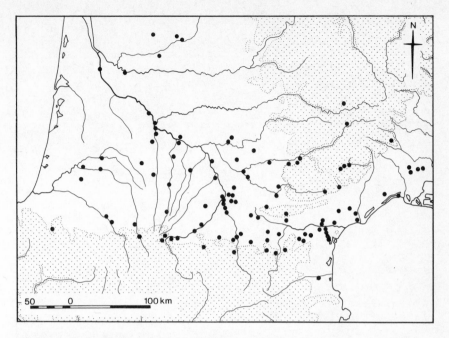

35 The Aude-Garonne route. Above: distribution of Dressel 1 amphorae.
Below: distribution of copper sources.
(After Roman 1983, fig. 53 [amphorae] and Ramin 1974, map
2 [copper])

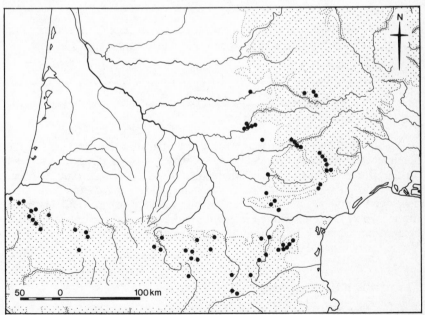

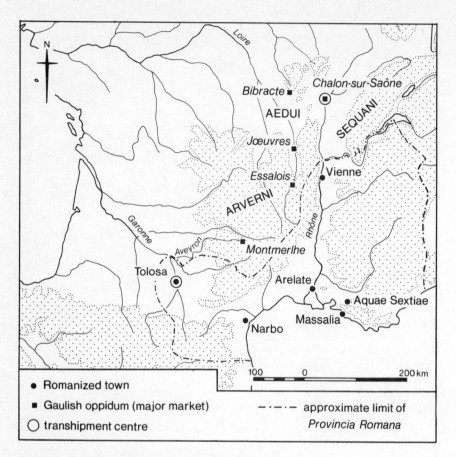

*36 Major Gaulish markets beyond the western boundary of
Provincia Romana in the early first century* BC

large-scale systems of trade and redistribution between the free Gauls of the
north and the Roman province.[10] The second example is Hengistbury Head
on the Dorset coast of Britain where, in the same period, trade in wine,
metals and other commodities is attested (below, p.102–3). Both sites
developed, under the impact of the Romanization of southern Gaul, and both
functioned as locations where exchange could take place, the only difference
being that whereas Montmerlhe was barely 60km from the province,
Hengistbury was 800km away.

The northern trading system

Turning now to the route north along the Rhône, we have seen that the
Roman province extended westwards to the Cevennes, north to the

confluence of the Rhône and Saône and eastwards to Lake Geneva and the Alps. The ancient trading post at Vienne had been incorporated within the Roman sphere, but it may well have continued to perform its function as an *emporium*, much as Tolosa did in the west. The evidence is not yet sufficient to assess its changing role, but the colossal quantities of amphorae found in the Saône at Chalon (p.74) strongly suggest that this was a major entrepôt, significantly sited in the heart of the territory of the pro-Roman Aedui, who clearly encouraged Roman trade and traders. Here, the bulk of the wine, brought up the river by boat, would have been trans-shipped (perhaps some of it decanted into barrels) to be consumed by the Aedui themselves and traded to their neighbours. Little is known of the Aeduan settlement at Chalon (*Cabillonum*), but that it was a thriving trading centre is evident from Caesar's brief reference to the expulsion of 'the Roman merchants who had settled there' in 52 BC by the Aedui, during a brief period of hostility to Rome at the end of the Gallic war.[11]

Three good examples of inland *emporia* are known beyond the western and northern fringes of Roman territory: Essalois and Joeuvres in the territory of the Segusiavi, and Bibracte, the capital of the Aedui (fig 36). All share in common the considerable extent of their defensive systems (12, 75 and 135ha respectively) and the exceptionally large number of Dressel 1 amphorae recovered.

Both Essalois and Joeuvres are situated on the upper Loire, Essalois commanding the spot where the most convenient land route from the Rhône valley reached the valley of the Loire. Joeuvres was some way downstream. Bibracte (Mont Beuvray) was somewhat more remotely situated but within easy reach of the entrepôt at Chalon, and accessible from the Loire valley and the tributaries of the Seine. The archaeological evidence from all three is, sadly, slight and of comparatively limited use, but Joeuvres has produced imported pottery of the fourth and third centuries BC, showing that it was of significance in the earlier period, while Essalois has yielded a collection of 2–300 Gaulish coins from a number of different *pagi* of the Aedui and Sequani and also from Massalia, emphasizing its broad trading links.[12]

It would be wrong to suppose that these were the only first-century sites producing unusual quantities of amphorae. The *ad hoc* nature of archaeological discovery makes it almost certain that more will be recovered, but the distribution of those we can detect at this stage is informative — they lie on an arc stretching through the territory of the Ruteni, Segusiavi and Aedui, all within free Gaulish territory on an interface between two economic systems: that of the Roman province and that of the heart of free Celtic Gaul.

Gaulish society

Something of the exchange process involved can be gleaned from Diodorus Siculus's account of the Gauls:

> They are exceedingly fond of wine and sate themselves with the unmixed wine imported by merchants; their desire makes them drink it greedily and when

they become drunk they fall into a stupor or into a maniacal disposition. And therefore many Italian merchants with their usual love of cash look on the Gallic craving for wine as their treasure. They transport the wine by boat on the navigable rivers and by wagon through the plains and receive in return for it an incredibly high price, for one amphora of wine they get in return a slave — a servant in exchange for a drink.[13]

Diodorus's simple statement puts the archaeological evidence into vivid perspective.

Several points of interest emerge. To begin with, the exchange rate, if that is what it was, seems too high by a factor of 5 or 6 in favour of the Roman traders. Even allowing the cost of transport, the *portoria* and the inflated demand caused by the Gallic love of wine, an amphora of wine was still grossly overpriced. Perhaps Diodorus was indulging in poetic licence. But there is another explanation, and that is that the exchange was not commercial, but was governed by the rules of a 'potlatch'. In such a system a Gaul, offered the gift of an amphora of wine by a Roman merchant, would be socially constrained to reply by giving something of greater worth. The wily Roman, knowing the high esteem of wine in Celtic society, would thus be sure to receive an item of considerable value in return. In such a system, a slave would not be an inappropriate gift.[14] Once within the Gaulish system the wine would be redistributed as gifts or at feasts governed by the same social constraints.

The volume of the Gaulish slave trade has been assessed by Tchernia, who argues for a minimum output of 15,000 per year. Comparing this with his estimate of the volume of wine imported annually he concludes that the slave trade must have accounted for one-tenth to one-third of the goods given in return for Italian wine.[15] Even so, a regular demand for slaves at this level cannot have failed to have had a dramatic effect on the structure of Gaulish society.

The reconstruction of what we might call 'classical' Gaulish society is fraught with difficulty and, indeed, it could be argued that the size and diversity of the country was such that no general model can fairly encompass the regional variety reflected in what is now France and Belgium. Nevertheless the Greco–Roman classical and Irish vernacular literature together combine to allow a generalized view of Celtic social structure to be built up which can serve as a guide to the nature of the communities occupying central Gaul in the period leading up to establishment of the Roman presence in the south.

Two sources are directly relevant. The lost works of the Stoic philosopher Posidonius contained detailed descriptions of Celtic society in Gaul based on observations made in the early first century BC. Scraps of his work are reproduced in later writings, especially those of Athenaeus, Diodorus Siculus and Strabo. A second tradition is that of Julius Caesar, who recorded a range of observations and generalizations in his war commentary *De Bello Gallico*, much of which must have been based on his own first-hand experience. To these two main sources we may add observations on the Celts noted in the works of Polybius (second century BC) and Pliny (first century AD). Much of the general model built up from these classical sources is supported, often in remarkable detail, by the Irish vernacular literature which was not written down until the eighth century AD and later.[16]

What emerges is a picture of 'classical' Celtic society. The basic social unit was the family, several of which constituted the clan, while a number of clans made up a tribe. The families varied in status: some were of little significance, others were aristocratic and there is some evidence to suggest that certain families were singled out as those from which the tribal chieftain would traditionally be drawn.

Caesar goes so far as to say that there were only two classes of people in the Celtic world: the free and powerful, including the knights and the Druids, and the rest who were little better than slaves. This is undoubtedly an over-simplification, but it points to what may be a real distinction between those who were the food producers — the farming families tied to the land — and the nobility, whose status was gauged by their prowess and whose wealth was measured in loot and cattle. The vernacular literature allows us to see how such a system could work in economic terms. The social process adopted was clientage (Caesar also mentions this among the Gauls). An aristocrat would formalize a relationship with a peasant farming family, usually by investing with them a number of his own cattle. They would maintain the herd on their own land and pay a tithe, usually in farm produce. This simple economic system had embedded social relationships within it: on the one hand the aristocrat had a vested interest in the safety of his client, while the client could be called upon to serve his patron when the need arose. Thus an aristocrat with a large number of cattle to invest was able to acquire a considerable surplus of consumables, which he could dispense at feasts, in this way gaining status, while at the same time he could call upon an army of followers whenever he wished to lead an expedition or to stake a claim. The greater his following, the greater his status — and the more chance he had of acquiring further loot in the raid. A socio-economic system such as this ensured a sound subsistence economy. It also allowed the aristocracy a degree of mobility, but since it was a society in which prestige was, to a large extent, gained by prowess in the raid, it meant that warfare, at least on a raiding level, remained endemic.

One of the mechanisms used to maintain a degree of order within the hierarchy was the feast. Posidonius (quoted by Athenaeus) gives a succinct account:

> The Celts sometimes engage in single combat at dinner. Assembling in arms they engage in a mock battle of mutual thrust-and-parry, but sometimes wounds are inflicted, and the irritation caused by this may lead even to the slaying of the opponent unless the bystanders hold them back. And in former times, when the hindquarters were served up, the bravest hero took the thigh piece, and if another man claimed it they stood up and fought in single combat to death.

In this fascinating statement Posidonius is, in fact, telling us how the social order was maintained. The feast was the occasion when the assembled nobility observed the symbolic cutting of the joint and the response of each of their number to the portion he was offered. If the carver offered the hero's portion to one man and another considered himself to be the foremost warrior then he would contest the apportionment. If the contest was resisted, physical violence might ensue until the matter was resolved. The contest was observed by the assembled company, who accepted the outcome as the new order. In this way the hierarchy of the nobility was established until the next occasion.

A man might, however, aspire to improve his status in another way. Through boastfulness at a feast a young man could encourage others to follow him in a raid on the following day. The more followers he could attract the greater his prestige and the greater the chance of success.

Another mechanism for establishing and demonstrating status was by means of conspicuous consumption — what is known anthropologically as the 'potlatch'. An example is detailed by Posidonius (quoted by Athenaeus). It concerns the chieftain Louernius who:

> in an attempt to win popular favour rode in a chariot over the plains distributing pieces of gold and silver to the tens of thousands of Celts who followed him: moreover, he made a square enclosure one and a half miles each way, within which he placed vats filled with expensive liquor and prepared so great a quantity of food that for many days all who wished could enter and enjoy the feast prepared, being served without break by the attendants.

The distribution of largesse, and the provision of a feast on so vast a scale (allowing, of course, for exaggeration), will have assured the pre-eminence of Louernius.

Another aspect of the 'potlatch' was that deeds, such as the feast of Louernius, had to be broadcast to be effective. To this end the nobility employed specialists to compose poems and to present them on public occasions. Posidonius again provides the details:

> The Celts have in their company, even in war, companions whom they call parasites. These men pronounce their praises before the whole assembly and before each of the chieftains in turn as they listen. Their entertainers are called Bards. These are poets who deliver eulogies in song.

It seems that Louernius had arranged for such a man to be present during his feast but the bard arrived late. Having met Louernius, however, he

> composed a song magnifying his greatness and lamenting his own late arrival. Louernius was very pleased and asked for a bag of gold and threw it to the poet who ran beside his chariot. The poet picked it up and sang another song saying that the very tracks made by his chariot on the earth gave gold and largesse to mankind.

Social cohesion was maintained in a variety of ways. We have already considered direct patronage in terms of clientship, and the loose form of binding, essentially the demands of reciprocity, created by the potlatch. These systems were undoubtedly powerful but there were others such as intermarriage and fosterage which established bonds between families. We hear comparatively little of these relationships in the classical literature, but Caesar makes an oblique and obscure reference to fosterage when he says:

> Their children are not allowed to go up to their fathers in public until they are old enough for military service: they regard it as unbecoming for a son who is still a boy to stand in his father's sight in a public place.

A far clearer idea of the widespread nature of fosterage is provided by the Irish vernacular literature which derives dramatic effect from accidental conflict between foster brothers.

The bonds of obligation and the significance of broadcast prowess can be seen in accounts of classical Celtic battles. One will suffice for illustration. Strabo mentions the use of the two-horse chariot in battle, describing how when battle has commenced the knight, having cast his javelin, descends from the chariot to fight hand to hand with sword:

> Some of them so far despise death that they descend to do battle, unclothed except for a girdle. They bring into battle as their attendants, freemen chosen from among the poorer classes, whom they use as charioteers and shield-bearers in battle. When the armies are drawn up in battle- array they are wont to advance before the battle-line and to challenge the bravest of their opponents to single combat, at the same time brandishing before them their arms so as to terrify their foe. And when someone accepts their challenge to battle, they loudly recite the deeds of valour of their ancestors and proclaim their own valorous quality, at the same time abusing and making little of their opponent and generally attempting to rob him beforehand of his fighting spirit.[17]

Sufficient will have been said to show that in classic Celtic society, power lay in personal prowess and the size of the individual's following, but the maintenance of that power required the lavish distribution of gifts in displays of conspicuous consumption. Such extravagance could only be kept up by raiding and looting. Hence warfare on this scale was endemic.

The overall effects of this kind of socio-economic system were to keep society fragmented in a multitude of loosely linked chiefdoms. Alliances could suddenly appear, great war leaders could emerge, but equally quickly they could disintegrate and vanish overnight. In short, the socio-economic system of Celtic Gaul in its classical period, before the first century BC, actively worked against the emergence of large stable confederations. The only force which seems to have had a degree of coercive power transcending local hierarchies was the religious class — the Druids. Caesar, in enumerating the powers of the Druids is quite specific:

> They act as judges in practically all disputes, whether between tribes or between individuals, when any crime is committed. . . . [When] a dispute arises about an inheritance or a boundary they adjudicate the matter and appoint the compensation to be paid. . . . Any individual or tribe failing to accept their award is banned from taking part in sacrifice — the heaviest punishment that can be inflicted upon a Gaul. . . . on a fixed date in each year they hold a session in a consecrated spot in the country of the Carnutes, which is supposed to be the centre of Gaul. Those who are involved in disputes assemble here from all parts, and accept the Druids' judgments and awards.[18]

If Caesar's generalizations are accurate then the Druids through their religious power and their annual assembly were able to exert a degree of control over intertribal behaviour, and even national events, but there is nothing to suggest that they could significantly influence major political decisions.

We have already stressed that there must have been considerable variety in the social structure and economic systems prevalent in Gaul. This much was recognized by Caesar in his famous opening sentence in *De Bello Gallico*, when he writes:

> Gaul is divided into three parts inhabited respectively by the Belgae, the Aquitani and the people who call themselves Celts, though we call them Gauls. All of these have different languages, customs, and laws. The Celts are separated from the Aquitani by the river Garonne, from the Belgae by the Marne and the Seine.

The archaeological evidence allows these broad divisions not only to be recognized, but to be traced back into the first half of the first millennium BC (fig 37). But the accumulation of archaeological data over the years suggests that Caesar's large central region, occupied by the Celts (or Gauls) might also be subdivided into culturally distinct regions — Armorican Gaul, central Gaul and eastern Gaul — though what the differences in material culture and behaviour pattern, dimly reflected in the very inadequate data-base, mean in terms of social organization it is impossible to be sure.[19] It is probably safe to accept, with Caesar, that the whole of central Gaul shared a broadly similar socio-economic system and a degree of ethnic unity.

At present, the archaeological record of the Aquitani, the Belgae and the Gauls, is far too imperfect to allow it to make much of a contribution to our understanding of Celtic society. The aristocracy appear in the record in the form of warrior burials accompanied by weapons and occasionally by vehicles, and the large number of hillforts may reflect the home bases of chieftains, but without more systematic and large-scale excavation the construction of general models from archaeological data is ill-advised, and we must fall back on the documentary sources discussed above.

Social change in central Gaul

Classical Celtic society began to change as Roman influence increased. The causes were many, and too inextricably bound up to allow simple analysis. The rapidly increasing Roman demand for slaves and raw materials would inevitably have caused a major disruption in Gaulish society. Tribes bordering the Roman frontiers no doubt benefited by direct contact with the Roman traders, while, in the zones where slaves were procured beyond them, raiding and looting will have increased. It is likely, too, that with the upsurge in long-distance trade new trading stations will have emerged at significant route nodes, and coinage is likely to have been reorganized to facilitate exchange both within the tribe and between frontier tribes and the Roman province. In parallel with all this, one might expect to find evidence of social

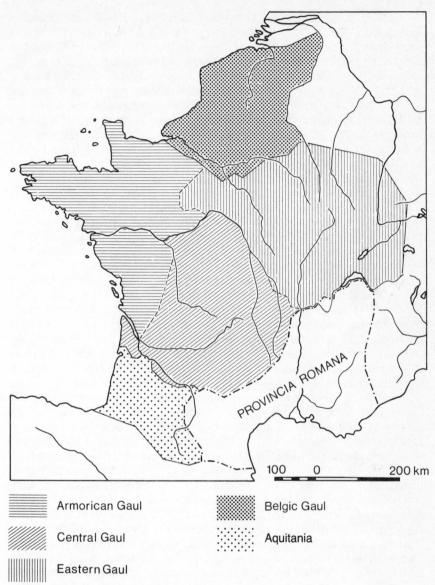

37 *The principal cultural regions of Gaul at the time of Caesar.*
(After Duval 1984, fig. 26)

reorganization, moving away from the fragmented and divisive classical Celtic model towards systems with more centralized control. These theoretical expectations can be compared with the archaeological, numismatic and documentary evidence.

One border tribe, among whom significant socio-political change can be recognized, is the Aedui, occupying Burgundy and the Morvan to the west of the Saône. The Aedui already had a treaty relationship with the Romans as early as 121–20 BC, and it was no doubt under Roman protection, and benefiting from favourable Roman trade incentives, that the tribe became powerful. The Aedui, Caesar tells us, 'had long enjoyed very great prestige and had many satellite tribes' until conflict with the neighbouring Sequani eroded their influence. The Sequani were 'able to bring over to their side a considerable part of the Aeduan dependencies, and to make the Aeduans surrender the sons of their chiefs as hostages'. Eventually, in 61 BC, Diviciacus, an Aeduan noble, went to Rome to ask for help, but without success. One of Caesar's first acts on arriving in Gaul three years later was to restore Aeduan supremacy. Thereafter, until the final stages of the Gallic war, the tribe remained a faithful ally to Rome.[20]

By Caesar's time it is evident that the political structure of the Aedui had developed far from the fragmented, chieftain- dominated, mode of the third and second centuries BC. The affairs of the tribe were now controlled by a chief magistrate — the Vergobretos — who was elected annually and wielded considerable powers. But strict controls were in force to ensure no abuse of power and the orderly transition from one chief magistrate to the next. Election was according to publicly known rules and the Vergobretos held power for only one year. During this time he was forbidden to leave Aeduan territory, thus preventing him from leading raids into neighbouring territories to bolster his own prestige. Another constraint of significance was that during the lifetime of a Vergobretos no member of his family could hold the office or even be elected to senate. The intention, clearly, was to ensure that high office could not be used to enhance dynastic power. All the constraints, then, were designed to prevent the state from being used by individual nobles to build up their own power and that of their lineage groups. The new constitution, for that is what it was, owed much to that of Republican Rome, whence the concepts are likely to have been derived.

In the early years, the preservation of these fragile constitutional oligarchies must have been difficult, and the new state systems were accordingly precarious. Great efforts were made to halt abuses, and anyone who aspired to kingship, that is tried to overthrow the state, could expect to be punished by death. In 58 BC, for example, Orgetorix, leader of the Helvetii, entered into a conspiracy with Casticus of the Sequani and Dumnorix of the Aedui. 'They were won over by his persuasion', writes Caesar, 'and the three exchanged an oath of loyalty, hoping that when each had seized royal power they would be able to get control of the whole of Gaul'. The conspiracy was reported to the Helvetii and 'following their custom, they compelled Orgetorix to stand trial in chains. If he were found guilty the automatic punishment would be death by burning'. Orgetorix attempted to sway events by calling together his vast following of relatives and clients, and managed to escape trial. This provoked the people, and the magistrates were busy raising a military force when Orgetorix died, possibly by his own hand. The incident is fascinating in that it shows the newly emerging state system triumphant over the traditional power structure of classical Celtic society.[21]

A similar incident is reported by Caesar among the Arverni. Writing of the war leader Vercingetorix, in 52 BC, he tells us that 'his father, Celtillus, had once been the most powerful man in the whole of Gaul and had been killed by his fellow tribesmen because he wanted to become king'. Vercingetorix evidently shared his father's aspirations and, wearing the mantle of resistance fighter against the Romans, he behaved in a traditional Celtic way: he 'called his dependants together and had no difficulty in rousing their passions. When it was known what Vercingetorix intended to do, there was a rush of armed men to join him'. This was seen by many as a potential bid for kingship, and his uncle and other senior Arvernians tried to restrain him; he was eventually expelled from the *oppidum* at Gergovia.[22]

From the brief discussion above it is clear that by Caesar's time a number of the tribes of central Gaul had adopted a system of government similar to that of the archaic state (fig 38). The certain examples form a broad arc

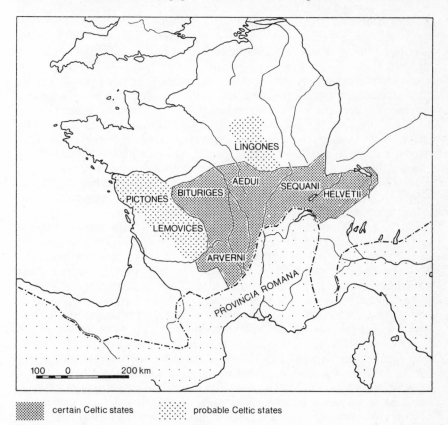

certain Celtic states   probable Celtic states

38 State development in barbarian Gaul. (After Nash 1978, fig. 1)

around the fringe of the Roman province — the Helvetii, the Sequani, the Aedui, the Bituriges and the Arverni. Beyond them the more distant Lingones, Lemovices and Pictones were probably developing similar systems. There can be little reasonable doubt that these far-reaching changes were initiated by the proximity with the Roman world.[23]

The numismatic evidence from central Gaul reflects the changes which were coming about at this time. Native coinage had been in existence in these areas from the third century BC. The coinage of the third and second centuries BC was characterized by comparatively limited issues, minted from time to time by a multitude of minor authorities. The function of coinage in classical Celtic society was not to facilitate regular trade, but to enable the petty chieftains to discharge their obligations through gifts and payments. Thus, issues would be small, localized and minted only sporadically, as need arose.

In the late second and early first centuries BC a dramatic change can be recognized. Precious metal coinages were now restricted in number to one or two in each tribal area; the volumes issued were greatly increased while, in style, a deliberate break with the past can often be recognized. Together, these changes reflect the emergence of individual central Gaulish states (*civitas*). Coins were now being issued to serve the needs of the *civitas* and not the individual, and their distribution patterns tend to respect tribal boundaries. Another innovation of the late second or early first century BC was the minting of small fractional coins, first in silver and later in bronze. These low value issues, like those in use in the Mediterranean, were designed to facilitate payments for subsistence or service of the kind which would be incurred by a state system, especially in urban contexts. Significantly, it is within the *oppida* that this type of coin is most frequently found. These changes probably took place at different times in different regions. The earliest that can be recognized is among the Aedui, dating to about 120 BC. In view of the politically advanced nature of the tribe and their early treaty relationship with Rome, this is hardly surprising.[24]

The archaeological evidence for settlement pattern also demonstrates a major change beginning in the late second century BC with the emergence of large *oppida*, not the ports of exchange discussed above, but large settlement areas usually incorporating a defensive element and invariably centrally sited to command the major communication lines. These must have been the seats of administrative power within the *civitas*.[25] Bibracte, capital of the Aedui, provides an example. Caesar describes it as 'by far the largest and richest *oppidum* of the Aedui'. It was sufficiently prestigious for a council of all the Gauls to be held there in 52 BC, and at the end of the year Caesar decided to over-winter there himself. The location of the *oppidum* is impressive, sited on the top of Mont Beuvray, over 800m high, it dominates the Morvan and is admirably sited in relation to routes. The entire plateau, an area of 135ha is enclosed by a rampart of stone, laced with timber (fig 50). The nineteenth- and early twentieth-century excavations have shown the site to have been occupied from La Téne III times (beginning c. 120 BC) and to have been abandoned some time around 5 BC, when the Roman town of Autun was founded. However, the work lacked the stratigraphical control needed to identify the phased development of the site, and it is therefore impossible to provide any clear idea of its internal arrangement in the period before the Caesarian conquest.

Of the other *oppida* mentioned by Caesar very little is known archaeologically. But at Cenabum (Orléans), the major *oppidum* of the Carnutes, we learn that Roman traders had already settled there by 52 BC, for in the uprising of that year they were attacked and killed. Caesar mentions its narrow streets and its multiplicity of gates, as well as the nearby bridge across the Loire. The *oppidum* of Avaricum (Bourges), described by Caesar as 'the most beautiful town in the whole of Gaul', was only one of 20 towns in the territory of the Bituriges, but it was clearly of considerable size, for when it was besieged by Caesar 40,000 Gauls took refuge within its defences. The river provided protection on three sides, but it was enclosed by a wall as well — a typical *murus Gallicus* — built of stone strengthened with a box-like timber lacing of beams, fastened together with long, iron nails. 'It is a very useful structure, ideally suited for the defence of towns. The stonework protects against fire and the timber against battering rams: for rams cannot pierce or shake to bits such a structure, secured as it is on the inside by continuous timbers up to 40 feet long'. This type of defence was common in Gaul in the mid first century BC.[26]

The Bituriges were by no means exceptional in having a number of towns within their territory. Such a pattern was typical of the *civitates* of central Gaul and reflects the growing complexity of the socio-economic system. Each tribe will have had its capital, but each *civitas* was divided into a number of units or *pagi*, all of which will also have had at least one *oppidum*. This system of administration, complete with its urban centres, was taken over virtually unchanged when Romanization began in the decades following Caesar's conquest.

The documentary, numismatic and archaeological evidence, taken together, shows that the tribes of central Gaul underwent a profound change in the period *c.* 120–60 BC, during which time the old order — the classical Celtic system — was replaced with a new centralized system of government, involving changes in the minting of coins and the development of *oppida*. To a large extent these changes can be ascribed directly to the proximity of the rapidly developing Roman province of Transalpina. The tribes of central Gaul were now becoming a contact zone with the Roman world. Through them much of the trade was articulated, and those tribes who, like the Aedui, were prepared to accept the situation, grew rich. Stability and centralization, institutionalized in a new system of government, enabled the benefits of the proximity of Rome to accrue.

The *civitates* of central Gaul became, albeit briefly, the new middle-men in the trading system. Roman traders were now well established in the major *oppida*, organizing the through-put of raw materials and slaves derived from the territories beyond, essentially Armorica, Belgica and Britain, and it is to these areas that we must now turn.

The Gaulish and British periphery

A recent comprehensive survey of Armorica has shown that amphorae of Dressel 1 type, and particularly the early (1A) variety, are found on a number of sites, frequently in reasonable quantity, and particularly along the south coast of Brittany (fig 39).[27] Three concentrations stand out: on the Quiberon peninsula; in the neighbourhood of Quimper; and at St Servan, a peninsula in the estuary of the river Rance, near St Malo on the north coast. All three can be considered as potential entrepôts, developing at a time when the Roman entrepreneurs, or their middle-men, were probing the possibilities of the north (fig 40). Quiberon was evidently the centre of Venetic maritime power, and it was in the bay that Caesar fought his famous sea battle with the Venetic fleet. The Quiberon peninsula, joined to the mainland by a narrow neck of land, is just the kind of site that traders had been selecting as

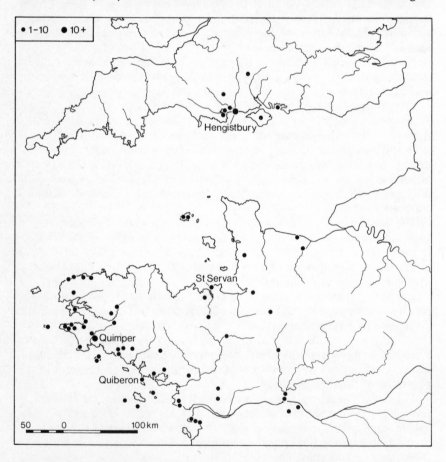

39 Distribution of Dressel 1A amphorae. (Based on Galliou 1982, planche XXIII)

ports-of-trade for hundreds of years, and the concentration of Iron Age finds, including amphorae, here is suggestive of a site of some significance. The existing records, however, are too imperfect to allow more to be said at this stage.

Quimper is altogether different (fig 40). It lies 10km inland, at the head of the navigable stretch of the river Odet, and was later to develop as a Roman settlement. The region has produced considerable evidence of Late Iron Age occupation, including traces of large-scale ironworking. Although the density of discovery is largely the result of active local archaeological research, the apparent concentration could reflect an intensification of activity consequent upon the development of long-distance trade contacts.[28]

The third site, St Servan, later to develop as the Gallo–Roman Alet, is known from a recent series of excavations. Sited on a promontory commanding excellent harbour facilities, together with the River Rance route leading to the interior of Brittany, the location is that of a classic port-of-trade. Excavation bears out its importance, producing, in addition to Dressel amphorae, imported wares from central France and evidence of industrial activity including the smelting of copper-silver alloy, cupellation (the extraction of silver from lead alloys), ironworking and some evidence which may suggest the minting of coins. A similar range of metallurgical activities is evidenced at Hengistbury, due north of St Servan on the Dorset coast of Britain (below, p.103).[29]

In addition to the three potential ports-of-trade, several large *oppida* are known, the location and distribution of which may suggest that they were the tribal centres (fig 41): Camp d'Artus (Osismii), Guégon (?Veneti), Poulailler (Redones), Le Petit Celland (Abrincatui), Grand Moncastre (Venelli), Castillon (Baiocasses), and St Désire (Lexovii). Excavations at two of these, Camp d'Artus and Le Petit Celland, have shown them to have been occupied in the Late Iron Age.[30] The existence of large tribal *oppida* of this kind suggests that a degree of centralized administration was already in operation by Caesar's time, but his accounts of his battle with the Veneti give no indication of social structure. However, the mention of elders (all of whom he put to death) and the absence of any specific reference to a king or war leader hint that some degree of state organization may already have begun. The Venelli of the Cotentin, however, were led by a single commander Viridovix, but he may have been appointed to his position to deal with the emergency.

Stories of the tin-rich lands of the north-west would have been well known to the Roman entrepreneurs, who were evidently eager to obtain detailed information. Strabo records that Scipio (about 140 BC) questioned the Massaliots and people from Narbo and Corbilo about Britain, but no one could 'tell anything worth recording'. This could be taken to mean that they knew nothing because trade was in the hands of middle-men, or that they preferred to keep their secrets. Some time after this, however, Publius Crassus learned the route and 'crossed over to these people and saw that the metals were being dug from only a slight depth and that the men there were peaceable; he forthwith laid abundant information before all who wished to traffic over this sea'.[31] The reference strongly suggests a deliberate

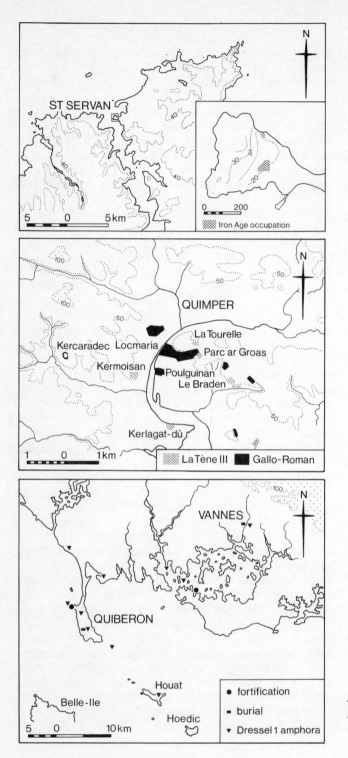

40 *Potential late Iron Age ports-of-trade in Armorica*

41 The major tribes and oppida *of Armorica at the time of the Caesarian conquest. (Based on Wheeler & Richardson 1957, pl. 1 with additions)*

opening-up of the Atlantic routes to Roman entrepreneurs and their agents. It is in this context that the developments in Armorica must be seen.

There is no reason to suppose that Roman ships sailing from the Garonne went far beyond the southern Breton coast. In all probability, cargoes were trans-shipped in the ports of southern Armorica. This much is implied by Caesar's description of the Veneti:

> They have a great many ships and regularly sail to and from Britain. When it comes to knowledge and experience of navigation they leave all the other tribes standing. . . . Since the Veneti control (these seas) they are able to exact tolls from almost all who regularly use these waters.[32]

This emphasis on the Veneti is most likely to be an overstatement, for, as we shall see, the archaeological evidence shows that the principal tribe engaged in trade with Britain, in the first century BC, was the Coriosolites, whose main port was St Servan. But it is understandable if we assume that the principal receivers of the goods shipped along the Atlantic coast of France were the Veneti, who arranged transport for the next stage, either across the peninsula or around the coasts. In other words, the Veneti were the true middle-men. By destroying their power in 56 BC, Caesar effectively took control of trade.[33]

The final leg of the Atlantic trading system was to Britain. Traditionally it had been the tin of the south-western peninsula that was the desired commodity, but the demands of the Roman world were more sophisticated. By the end of the first century BC Strabo listed as the prime exports of Britain, gold, iron and other metals, corn, hides, slaves and hunting dogs. Tin is not specifically mentioned and it could well be that sufficient tin was now being supplied by the Iberian mines to make far-flung sources uncommercial.

The principal British port which developed at this time was Hengistbury Head, on the Dorset coast.[34] The site is admirably sited to be a port-of-trade: it is a landmark easy to navigate towards; it has a fine haven as well as a protected harbour; and it commands river routes to the productive heart of Wessex, the Stour leading into Dorset, and the Avon penetrating the chalklands of Wiltshire and Hampshire (fig 42).

The archaeological evidence shows that the headland was the scene of active trading in the first century BC. A hard was created so that ships could be beached in what was evidently a heavily built-up port complex. Among

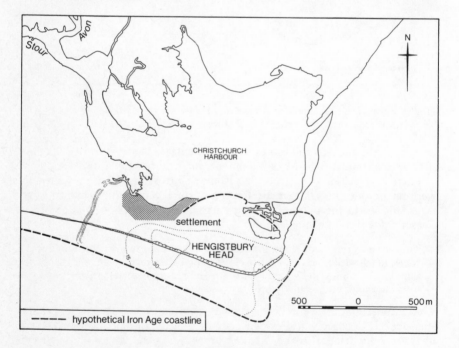

42 Hengistbury Head, Dorset: a late Iron Age port-of-trade

the imports we have evidence of quantities of wine (in Dressel 1A and 1B amphorae), ingots of yellow and purple glass, and figs. To this may be added a range of north-western French pottery imported largely, one suspects, for their contents rather than their intrinsic value.

The activities undertaken in the port point to the exports. Corn was being imported from outside the region, from the chalklands to the north, while exceptional proportions of cattle bones and the occurrence of salt containers hint that cattle may have been brought in and slaughtered on the site, the salt being used to cure their hides. Metalworking was also extensive: iron was extracted from local iron ore, bronzeworking was widespread, silver was refined from argentiferous copper and lead, while some gold scrap was accumulated. Thinking of Strabo's list, the only commodities not accounted for are slaves and hunting dogs, both of which are very difficult to detect archaeologically.

In a British context, Hengistbury seems to have been the prime port-of-trade, calling upon products from the entire south-west of Britain (fig 43) and feeding them into the Atlantic trading system. The presence of quantities of north-western French pottery, together with a preponderance of coins of the Coriosolites, strongly suggests that the ships reaching Hengistbury from the south came from the Coriosolitian port of St Servan. It may well be that the last leg of the Atlantic route was a short-haul trade between the two ports: the locals at Hengistbury may never have seen a Roman merchant. It is even possible that they were a band of Coriosolites.[35]

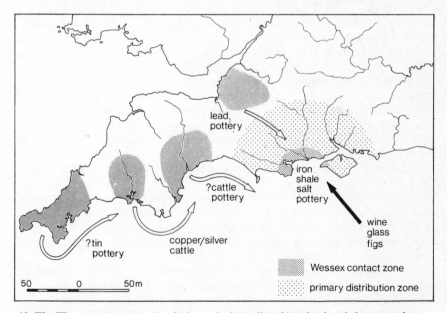

43 The Wessex contact zone in relation to its immediate hinterland and the external sources of the various products brought to it for exchange.
(Based on Cunliffe 1982, fig. 14)

In southern Britain, at the time of the intensified contact, the socio-economic system had evolved over several centuries, giving rise to a hillfort-dominated landscape. The regularly spaced, well-defended hillforts are best interpreted as the seats of warrior aristocracies, of a classic Celtic type, maintained by a land-based peasantry living in farmsteads densely scattered throughout the landscape. This system collapsed in the first century BC. Its demise was quite possibly initiated by the development of long-distance trade through Hengistbury. The sudden creation of a demand for surplus products, especially slaves, cannot have failed to dislocate the economic systems of southern Britain, creating social tensions which the already unstable warrior society was unable to bear. In such a context, the abandonment of the hillforts — the centres of traditional power — becomes intelligible. But trade was only one factor involved in the changes which were taking place at this time; the situation was complex, and will be considered in more detail in Chapter 8.

The Belgae of northern Gaul

In northern Gaul, the area which Caesar tells us was occupied by Belgic tribes, the archaeological evidence is not yet well focused (fig 44). One feature of some interest, however, is the appearance of a group of vehicle burials dating from Late La Tène II and Early La Tène III (roughly 150–80 BC) stretching from the Seine northwards into Belgium.[36] It is tempting to see the resurgence of this tradition, after a gap of nearly three centuries, in terms of the emergence of similar socio-economic conditions. If the tribes of central Gaul formed a loosely-knit core zone, directly serving the needs of the adjacent Roman market, then the Belgic area becomes a peripheral zone, from which and through which commodities were procured. In such a circumstance one might expect the aristocracy controlling the supply to acquire wealth and to display status through burial ritual. It may also be significant that it is in the same area that Dressel 1A amphorae concentrate.[37] Insofar as a focus can be recognized in the varied (and potentially misleading) archaeological distribution map, it seems to be the Aisne valley. It may not be entirely coincidental that, by the time of Caesar's conquest in the middle of the first century BC, the principal tribe of this area, the Remi, had developed a pro-Roman attitude.

There is little in the settlement pattern of the Belgic region to suggest the emergence of large, central, tribal *oppida* like those of Armorica. Many hillforts are known, most of them concentrated on the major river valleys or the coast, but since the majority are totally undated it is impossible to speculate about the emergence of urban centres.[38]

Standing back from the mass of disparate data, so briefly summarized above, we may tentatively divide free Gaul, outside the Roman province of Transalpina, into two broad zones — the core area of the central Gaulish *civitates*, and a periphery comprising roughly Armorica and Belgica. In the core zone, in the period 125–58 BC, there is evidence of rapid social change leading to the adoption of state systems of government by some of the more

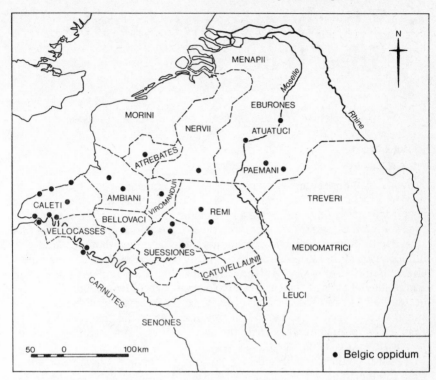

44 *The major tribes and* oppida *of Normandy at the time
of the Caesarian conquest. (Based on Wheeler & Richardson 1957,
pl. 1 with additions)*

forward tribes and the development of tribal coinages designed to aid trade.
Roman merchants were at work deep in these territories, but much trade
seems to have been articulated through 'gateway' ports like Toulouse and
Chalon, and through *oppida*, providing internal markets, sited on major route
nodes close to the Roman frontiers.

The peripheral zone was exploited in a variety of ways. In the Belgic
region, intertribal exchange with the tribes of the core zone seems to have
created a social system which may have been a dim reflection of a prestige
goods economy. Armorica developed differently. Direct maritime trade from
the Garonne will have brought Roman entrepreneurs or their agents to the
ports of southern Brittany. Some of the Armorican tribes, especially the
Veneti and the Coriosolites, developed skills as maritime traders, and it is
quite possible that an enclave of Coriosolites was established in Britain at
Hengistbury, to exploit the British market.

The picture sketched out here is deceptively simple: it is ill-focused in its
detail, and takes little note of development within the 60 years of the period
under discussion, but the archaeological evidence is not yet sufficient to
support a more profound model.

6 The battle for Gaul: 58–50 BC

Julius Caesar

Until the middle of the first century BC the Roman impact on Gaul, beyond the Province, had been comparatively undramatic. Campaigns against recalcitrant border tribes, treaty relationships with carefully selected allies and the penetration of traders, had gradually brought most of the tribes of Gaul and even southern Britain into contact with the Roman world, but for much of that area, Mediterranean influence was indirect, though not without a cumulative influence on native social structure. All this changed in 58 BC, when Julius Caesar began a series of eight annual campaigns which brought the Roman armies into all parts of Gaul and even to distant parts of Britain and Germany, beyond the Thames and the Rhine. By 50 BC Gaul was under Roman control and the equilibrium, established in the first half of the century, had been completely upset: almost overnight the socio-economic systems of much of the barbarian west were shattered.

Whilst it could reasonably be argued that the changes which came about were the inevitable result of long-established Mediterranean systems — the need of the Roman state to expand and to acquire the manpower and raw materials necessary for its survival, the demands made by Roman society for military success as an essential to political advancement, and so on, combined with the innate inability of Celtic peoples to unite in lasting confederations and the population pressures emanating from the heartland of Germany — the pace of change in the midfirst century must nonetheless be ascribed to the particular military genius of one man: Gaius Julius Caesar. Caesar saw Gaul as an opportunity, and he took it.

Caesar was born an aristocrat, yet like some other ambitious young patricians of his day he championed the popular cause, and by the time he was elected praetor, in 62 BC, he had acquired a reputation for being a dangerously able radical — a man feared by the conservative oligarchy. They prevented him from receiving a military triumph after his campaigns in Spain in 61–60 C and then tried, unsuccessfully, to block his election as consul in 59. At this stage Caesar relied on the support of Cnaeus Pompeius (Pompey the Great), who had earned his nickname from his military successes in the east. The three triumphs he had been awarded singled him out as a man of exceptional ability. Caesar's ambition was such that he had to outshine Pompey; to do so he needed to create for himself an opportunity for unlimited military conquest.[1]

In 59 BC, as consul, he forced through a special law which gave him a five-year command in the provinces of Cisalpine Gaul and Illyricum, and in 55

BC he was able to extend it for a further five-year period. This exceptional brief provided him with the power to raise and maintain an army, and to use it more or less as he wished in the interests of the Roman state. The area of command was well chosen. On the eastern flank, the Dacians (of Romania) led by Burebista were beginning to pose a threat to Roman interests, while to the west the Germans were establishing themselves in lands belonging to the Celtic tribes of north-eastern Gaul. In both regions Caesar could legitimately wage war. Of the two threats, the most worrying to Rome was the prospect of the southerly spread of the Germans. The memory of the marauding Cimbri and Teutones, who had come so close to Italy only forty years before, was still fresh. Caesar traded on these fears and the senate were only too prepared to add Transalpina to his area of command, giving Caesar virtually the whole of western Europe as the theatre in which he could display his skills.

But Caesar's power base in Rome was dangerously unstable. His enemies were many and he could not afford to be out of the public eye for long lest his popular support should wane. This would be a dilemma for any ambitious military commander involved in campaigning in distant provinces. Here, his sense of audience and his fine literary skills combined to provide a solution. It was customary for a commander to send regular dispatches to the senate, and it often happened that campaigns were later written up by historians, but this was not good enough for Caesar's purposes: what he needed was a form of rapid communication direct to the public. The method he chose was to send back, at the end of each campaigning season, a *commentarius* — essentially narrative notes from which a full history could be written. These would be copied and rapidly distributed, and were no doubt widely read and proclaimed. The simplicity of the style required of this literary form added to their accessibility, and thus to the immediacy of the message. Cicero was unstinting with his praise:

> The Commentaries are splendid: bare, straight and handsome, stripped of rhetorical ornament like an athlete of his clothes. . . . There is nothing in a history more attractive than clean lucid brevity.

Caesar wrote seven *Commentaries*, one for each of the campaigns from 58 to 52 BC (the eighth, covering the years 51–50, was compiled after Caesar's death in 44, by Aulus Hirtius). Their purpose was, essentially, self-aggrandizement, though no doubt the facts are basically accurate. The ethnographic detail they contain is greatly over-simplified for the benefit of the audience, partially derivative and certainly, in areas, misunderstood. Nevertheless, carefully used, it can provide a useful insight into Gaulish, German and British social structure. But there is much, too, to be learnt from the progress of the campaigns, the shifts of allegiance and, indeed, the subjects which Caesar chose to leave unsaid. Without access to the *Commentaries* our appreciation of our theme would be much the poorer.

It is not the purpose of the present chapter to give a detailed account of the Gallic war — for this the reader needs only to refer to Caesar's masterpiece — but to select from it certain aspects which enliven our understanding of Gaulish society and economy in this crucial period of transition. As a preliminary, however, it is necessary to give a brief outline of the progress of the war.[2]

Caesar's campaigns in Gaul (figs 45–7)

Caesar's excuse for entering into conflict beyond the frontier of Transalpina in 58 BC was that a Roman ally, the Aedui, was under threat from a Germanic tribe from across the Rhine, led by Ariovistus, while the Helvetii, planning a mass migration to the Atlantic coast, intended to pass through Roman-held territory to the south of Lake Geneva. Spring and early summer were taken up with intercepting the Helvetii, engaging them in battle and driving the remnant back to their original home territory in Switzerland. By the early autumn the situation had been contained and Caesar could turn his attention to Ariovistus, whose army he routed in a single set-piece battle. The

45 Gaul at the time of Caesar

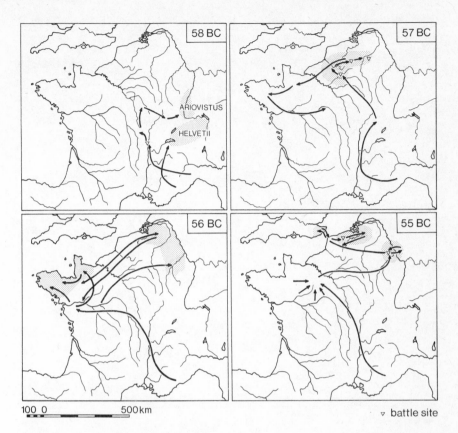

46 *Caesar's principal campaigns 58–55 BC.*
The major areas of conflict are stippled

achievement was considerable, and Caesar could laconically conclude his first
Commentary with the nice understatement, 'in the space of a single summer I
had completed two important campaigns'.

The next year's campaign, in 57 BC, showed Caesar's complete command
of the geography of Gaul; his action also showed that he had, by now,
decided on complete conquest. In a single quick thrust he was among the
Belgic tribes living between the Seine and the Rhine. The audacity of the
advance relied heavily upon the pro-Roman attitudes of the Remi. The
Bellovaci, Nervii and Aduatuci were defeated in succession. Meanwhile, his
legate, Publius Crassus, was sent with a single legion to deal with the
Armorican tribes whose submission he apparently received without significant trouble. The boldness of the campaign cannot fail to impress: in a single
season Caesar had driven a firm wedge between the potentially troublesome
Germans and the rest of central Gaul, and in dealing so decisively with the
tough Belgae he had amply demonstrated the strength of the Roman army to

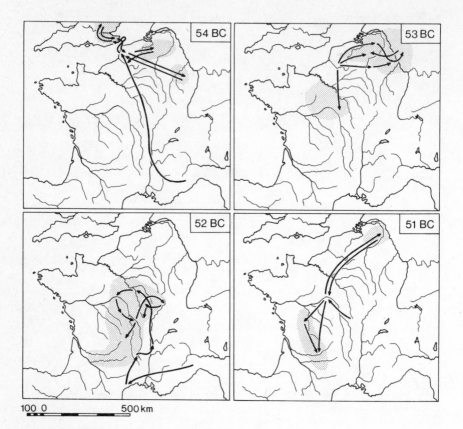

47 *Caesar's principal campaigns 54–51 BC.*
The major areas of conflict are stippled

any tribe who might have considered opposing him. It is hardly surprising that the Armorican tribes capitulated so readily. Even so, Caesar recognized the potential instability of his rapid conquest and left most of the legions in winter quarters in the newly-conquered region. Significantly, some were spread along the north bank of the Loire, in territories of the Carnutes, Andes and Turones, evidently in an attempt to create a Roman presence and prevent the Armorican tribes from joining those of the so far unsubdued regions of central Gaul.

In 56 BC the anticipated rebellion broke out, centred on the Veneti of southern Brittany, and soon much of Armorica was in revolt. Clearly, the submission of the previous year was a nominal affair and the proximity of Roman legions throughout the winter brought matters to a head. Caesar's response to the news was decisive: first the revolt had to be contained, and then dealt with. Orders were issued for ships to be built on the Loire in preparation for battle, while a part of the available force was dispersed to deal with potential trouble-spots.

Labienus was sent to the territory of the Treveri to keep the Belgae loyal and to watch for any aggressive activity among the Germans; Crassus was sent to Aquitania to 'stop reinforcements being sent from those tribes to Gaul and to prevent such powerful peoples joining forces',[3] while Sabinus was sent to the territory of the Venelli, Coriosolites and Lexovii (Lower Normandy and north-eastern Brittany) 'to make sure that that group was kept separate from the rest'.[4] This left Caesar free to join his fleet on the Loire, and move on against the Veneti and their allies. The campaign, fought in early summer, brought the rebels to heel. Sufficient time remained for an inconclusive strike against the Morini and Menapii, who had refused to send envoys the previous year. At best it was little more than a show of strength, but one of the reasons behind the thrust may have been Caesar's curiosity to see for himself this stretch of the Channel coast. He would have been made well aware of Britain through the regular contact of the British tribes with Armorica. By this stage the idea of crossing the Channel must have formed in his mind, and the shortest crossing, he would have been told, was from the territory of the Morini.

In the next year, 55 BC, Caesar's activities were spectacular. He took frightening risks, all largely, one suspects, in the interests of the impact he would have made at home. He began by crossing the Rhine to confront the German tribes on the east bank, and then, in late summer, went on to cross the Channel to campaign briefly in Kent. Both adventures were justified by Caesar in terms of the potential threat posed by Germanic and British involvement in Gaulish affairs, but such an excuse was special pleading. In reality, we see here Caesar pitting himself against two physical barriers — the Rhine and the Channel: both were emotive. In the eyes of his public, Caesar was leading Rome into separate and uncharted worlds. His exploits must have electrified his public in a way not unlike the American moon landing, but in reality the German campaign was of no great consequence, while the invasion of Britain ended in near disaster. Moreover, in the autumn, on his return, Caesar was faced with further problems among the Morini requiring his presence. The campaigns of 55 BC had been a gamble, but in the end they paid off.

The British adventure appealed to Caesar and to the Roman public, and in the next year, 54 BC, a much larger force was amassed. While the preparations were in hand, news reached Caesar of trouble among the Treveri, requiring his attention, but eventually he was able to set sail with five legions and 2000 cavalry. The invasion armada amounted to 800 vessels!

From a propaganda point of view, the British campaign was a success. The Thames had been crossed and a number of tribes had made formal submission to Rome, agreeing to pay tribute. But from a military stance the campaign was ill-judged, and while the bulk of the army was in Britain a crisis was brewing in the Belgic area. To this Caesar returned in the autumn of 54 BC. The Belgic rebellion was a serious affair: a legion commanded by Sabinus was cut to pieces by the Eburones and the situation became extremely tense. A legion had to be sent to the Carnutes, south-west of the Seine, to ensure their allegiance, while another, based among the Lexovii, had to patrol Lower Normandy and northern Brittany to maintain order. A series of brilliantly managed campaigns, masterminded by Caesar, saved the day, but it was a close run thing and had Caesar not allowed himself the British indulgence, the Belgic revolt could probably have been prevented. The events of the autumn of 54 must have been a salutary reminder to Caesar that Gaul was by no means conquered. Indeed, with hindsight Caesar began his sixth *Commentary*, in the year 53 BC, by saying that he had many reasons for expecting a more serious disturbance in Gaul before long. For this reason a fresh levy of troops was raised: 'I wanted to impress public opinion in Gaul not only for the present but for the future as well'.[5]

The troubled area was the northern part of the Belgic area, and it was the tribes of this region, the Nervii, Aduatuci, Eburones, Menapii and Treveri who felt the full force of Caesar's attack. Resistance was crushed, land was laid waste and the Rhine was crossed once more. So thorough was Caesar's action that in the next year, when a general revolt flared up in central Gaul, the Belgic region remained quiet, unable to raise itself above the devastation wrought in 53.

For Caesar an even more worrying turn of events was the growing dissatisfaction of the Carnutes and Senones south of the Seine: 'The Senones refused to come at my command and were intriguing with the Carnutes and other neighbouring tribes'.[6] A rapid march into Senonian territory in the spring had caught the tribe off guard and a temporary peace was established, but at the end of the campaigning season Caesar saw fit to institute an enquiry into the conspiracy, as the result of which its leader, Acco, was condemned and executed. Caesar's assessment of the seriousness of the situation is shown by his choice of location for the troops' winter quarters: two legions were placed on the Treverian frontier, six were concentrated at Agedincum in the territory of the Senones and two more were located among the Lingones — a tribe living between the Senones and the friendly Aedui. The intention here seems to have been to protect the Roman supply line, to ensure easy access to the potential trouble spot.

During six years of campaigning, central Gaul had been left untouched. The implication must be that Caesar judged the socio-political situation there to have been stable and favourable to Roman interests. However, lack of Roman military presence seems to have allowed discontent to ferment, and in 52 BC much of the region burst into rebellion. 'Meetings were arranged in remote places in the forests . . . they lamented the condition of their whole country and promised all kinds of rewards to any who would make the first moves in a war and be prepared to risk their own lives to set Gaul free.'[7] The Carnutes took the lead, and the rebellion opened with the massacre of Roman traders who had settled in Cenabum. Soon other tribes joined in and overall leadership passed to the young Arvernian noble Vercingetorix.

Many of the tribes on the borders of Transalpina, including the Ruteni, Nitiobriges and the Gabali, joined the revolt, threatening the towns of Languedoc, in particular Narbo. The seriousness of the threat was such that

Caesar's first move was to reassure the inhabitants of southern Gaul, establish garrisons and then to march north through the Cevennes to the territory of the Arverni to make a rapid show of strength. Leaving some troops there, he then left and, bypassing the rebellious tribes via Vienne and the Aedui, he made for the main troop concentration at Agedincum and from there began to contain the rebellion with a series of marches, sieges and set-piece battles, culminating in the siege of Alesia, where Vercingetorix was cornered (fig 48). From the size and composition of the relieving force, amassed under the command of the rebel leader Commius, it is clear that the greater part of central and northern Gaul was now in open revolt, including the Aedui who hitherto had been strongly pro-Roman.

The culmination came when the Gaulish relief force met the Roman army and was routed in full sight of the defenders in Alesia. The next day, Alesia capitulated and Vercingetorix was surrendered to Caesar. In the aftermath Caesar was very careful, through acts of clemency, to win back the support of the Aedui and the Arverni, who formed an important buffer along the western boundary of Transalpina, and to send two legions to the pro-Roman Remi to protect them from recriminations. The other legions he dispersed at strategic places. The seriousness of the events of 52, and the need for intense political activity to re-establish stability, is demonstrated by Caesar's decision to stay in Gaul through the winter, setting up his base at the Aeduian capital of Bibracte.

Although Hirtius could begin the eighth book with the words, 'The whole of Gaul was now conquered', this was evidently not so and in several parts of

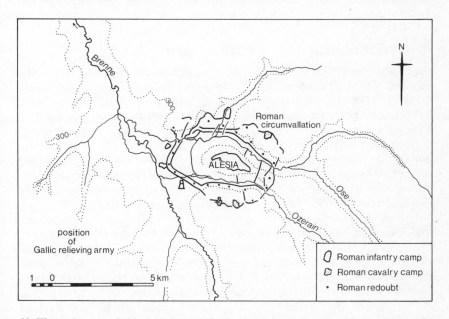

48 The native stronghold of Alesia and the Roman siege works. (Based on a plan commissioned by Napoléon III 1865)

the north and west there remained significant pockets of resistance to be put down. Even during the severe winter of 51–50 BC Caesar had to deal with troubles first among the Bituriges and then the Carnutes, and when spring came it was necessary for him to return to the Belgic region where the Bellovaci were stirring up trouble. The recalcitrant tribes listed as allies of the Bellovaci — the Ambiani, Aulerci, Caleti, Vellocasses and Atrebates — show that the whole of the western part of Belgica up to the Channel coast was in revolt and Commius, of the Atrebates, had gone to get help from the Germans. Swift action by Caesar brought the revolt to an end, but it was far from a minor affair. Labienus was sent to mop up further pockets of resistance in Treverian territory and Ambiorix of the Eburones was still at large defying Roman authority. But the problem was quickly dealt with: 'detachments of legionary or auxiliary troops were sent out all over Ambiorix's territory, killing, burning and pillaging: everything was destroyed and great numbers of people were either killed or taken prisoner.'

The western tribes were also posing a problem. One faction of the Pictones led a successful resistance for a brief period, while guerrilla groups among the Senones were attacking convoys. The dissidents eventually gravitated to the native fortress of Uxellodunum which was besieged and fell to the Roman troops. Caesar, evidently concerned at the continuing pockets of Gaulish resistance, decided to make a demonstration of Roman determination to subdue Gaul. The defenders of Uxellodunum were amassed and all those who had carried weapons had their hands cut off. They were then sent away so that all could see how rebellion was punished. In this way the Gallic war petered out.

Ethnic movements at the time of the conquest

Embedded in Caesar's narratives is a wealth of detail reflecting on the structure of Gaulish society and the devastating effect of Roman militarism on it. Some aspects of social structure, in particular the regional variation apparent by the mid first century BC, have already been considered in Chapter 5. Here we will concentrate on the rather broader issues raised.

From the fourth century BC there had been a succession of folk movements among the Celts, often involving populations of considerable size. These had died down by the first century BC, but in 58 BC Caesar encountered one of the last — the migration of the Helvetii — and his account enables the mechanisms of a folk movement to be examined in rare detail.

One of the reasons given for the desire of the Helvetians to migrate was that their land was too small. Hemmed in by natural barriers like the Rhine, the Jura range and the Rhône, they had no room to expand: 'They considered that the territory they had did not match the size of their population or its reputation for bravery in war'.[8] The charismatic leadership of Orgetorix persuaded the tribe to prepare for migration, which they did by buying up as many draught animals and vehicles as they could and sowing the land intensively to provide enough grain for the journey, estimating that it would take two harvests to achieve this. They also began to pave the way politically by establishing good relations with neighbouring tribes, and it was presumably as part of this diplomatic initiative that they came to an agreement with the Santones of the Atlantic coast in whose territory they wished to settle.

When the preparations had been completed they set fire to their twelve or so *oppida*, 400 villages and isolated houses, and burnt any surplus grain so that all would be compelled to leave and there would be a disincentive for the faint-hearted, who might have been otherwise inclined to return home. Each person was ordered to carry with him three months' supply of flour. This seems rather little: it would have covered the journey but hardly the time needed to raise a crop in the new territory. The implication would seem to be that additional supplies would be acquired through raiding.

Several other tribes, probably dependent peoples, were persuaded to join in together with the Boii who had been moving through Europe since they had been ousted from their homeland in the Po valley 150 years before. According to Caesar the migrants provided a list, written in Greek, of all those on the move, categorizing the population as fighting men, old men, women, and children. The documents, which he claims were brought to him, listed 368,000 people: 263,000 Helvetii, 36,000 Tulingi, 14,000 Latovici, 23,000 Raurici and 32,000 Boii. Of the total, 92,000 — that is, a quarter — were capable of bearing arms. If these figures and those which Caesar gives for the size of Helvetian territory are taken on their face value, they indicate a population density of 6–7 people per square mile which, given the terrain, is surprisingly dense. If the bulk of this population lived in the 12 *oppida* and 400 villages the settlements must have been of considerable size. Caesar's figures may be exaggerated but there is no reason why he should have falsified them and the way in which he presents them has a ring of authenticity.

The movement of such a large force inevitably caused disruption in the territories through which it passed. The Aedui complained to Caesar that their land and settlements were being pillaged and their children carried off. Much the same fate fell to the Ambarri and the Allobroges. There seems to have been traditional Celtic raiding, providing not only the food for the march but booty and captives for subsequent sale to the slave-traders.

It is not clear whether the entire force moved all the time in concert. Almost certainly it did not, and this much is implied by Caesar's account of an engagement on the Saône, where he encountered only the Tigurini — people from one of the four cantons into which Helvetia was divided. But by the time they were marching through Aeduian territory the force seems to have come together. After the battle near Bibracte, at which the Boii and Tulingi were certainly present, Caesar records that 130,000 survived and marched without stopping to the territory of the Lingones.

In the battle, the Helvetii had probably lost most of their supplies, and Caesar's instructions to the Lingones not to supply the migrants brought them to their knees. While surrender terms were being negotiated, 6000 men from one of the cantons of Helvetii, called Verbigenus, moved off by themselves to join the Germans across the Rhine, but Caesar had them rounded up and returned.

In the settlement which followed, the Helvetii, Tulingi and Latovici were provided with corn and told to return to their original territory. The Helvetii were ordered to rebuild their *oppida* and villages. The small group of Boii were allowed to settle on the borders of the Aedui as dependants of the tribe, quite possibly to provide a friendly buffer against hostile neighbours. Altogether, of the 368,000 who had set out on the migration, only 110,000 returned home.

The migration of 58 BC must have been like many that had preceded it. It echoes the mobility of the archaic Celtic world, which had now, for the most part, become sedentary, but the less-developed Germanic peoples to the north still retained a high degree of mobility, and it was they whom the Romans feared most.

Caesar presents a simple picture of the Germans: they were warlike and hardy, untouched by enervating luxuries. Their social organization and economy differed from that of the Celts, and the River Rhine formed their western boundary. Moreover they were a people on the move. Ariovistus, king of the Germans, a Suebian by birth, had already led 120,000 Germans into Gaulish territory and many more were ready to follow. If Gaul was left unprotected by Rome the Germans would overrun it. It was a clear picture, easy for the Roman reader to comprehend and immediately frightening in its implications. To what extent Caesar was deliberately simplifying for effect it is impossible to say, but later in the *Commentaries* something of the true complexity of the situation can begin to be appreciated, and the archaeological and linguistic evidence combine to show that no clear ethnic divide existed at the time.[9]

It is notoriously difficult to link material culture, represented in the archaeological record, to ethnic grouping, but if the type-fossils of 'Celtic culture' are plotted — settled communities represented by *oppida*, wheel-turned pottery, coinage, rectangular religious enclosures and adherence to a distinctive art style — then the northern limit of the Celts lies far beyond the Rhine, and reaches almost to the river Lippe. But similarly, if assemblages of Germanic artefacts, like those found north-east of the Elbe, are mapped there is a broad zone of overlap stretching westwards to the Rhine, suggesting a culture-mix over a considerable area. This is not to say that the two distributions are exactly contemporary. Where a chronological sequence can be established there is some evidence for progressive Germanization, for example, in Bohemia, Moravia and the Main valley, where Celtic 'culture' is overtaken by Germanic 'culture' roughly in the Augustan period. The archaeological evidence, then, strongly suggests that both sides of the Rhine showed a broadly similar material culture, which we can characterize as Celtic at the time of the Gallic wars.

Caesar's model of the Rhine dividing Celt from German was too simple, yet it is clear from his description of social structure and warfare that the people of northern Gaul and the east bank of the Rhine were markedly different from the Celts of central Gaul. The simplest explanation is that we are dealing with a gradation from the complex state system of the Celtic groups south of the Seine to the far simpler village economy of the Germans east of the Elbe. Caesar's ethnographic descriptions of the Gauls and of the Germans are idealized accounts, designed to emphasize the differences of the two extremes.

Later on, in his description of his Gallic campaigns, Caesar admits to a cultural blurring. The Boii and Volcae Tectosages, both Celtic tribes lived east of the Rhine, while tribes to the west were of Germanic ancestry. Of the Belgae, for example, Caesar writes that most 'were of German origin; they had crossed the Rhine long ago, driven out the Gauls they found living there and settled in that part of Gaul because the soil was fertile'. A little later he refers to the west bank tribes, the Condrusi, Eburones, Caeroesi and Paemani, as 'the so-called German tribes', and of the Aduatuci he tells us that they were descendants of the Cimbri and Teutones who had remained behind during the migration 50 years before. The Treveri, too, were of Germanic origin and looked to Germany for help against Caesar.

Close relations evidently existed between tribes on both sides of the river. Two tribes from the 'German' side, the Usipetes and Tencteri, were invited to settle among the Condrusi and Eburones, hinting at a degree of kinship. Even more impressive is the reference to the Menapii who 'had lands, buildings and villages on both banks of the river'.[10]

Thus, a detailed reading of Caesar tends to support the archaeological evidence in suggesting that the Rhine at this time was not a significant cultural barrier. On the east bank was a swathe of tribes who shared a common heritage with the Belgic tribes to the south, and had a material culture that was similar to much of central Gaul.

The real difference lay between this northern group and the Suebi who lived beyond them to the east, 'by far the largest and most warlike of all the German tribes'. It was Suebian pressure on the east bank tribes that caused the Usipetes and Tencteri to cross the Rhine: 'Their reason for crossing was that for several years they had been harassed by attacks from the Suebi and prevented from cultivating their own land'. Caesar's description strongly suggests that the Suebi conformed far more to his generalized picture of the Germans than did the east bank tribes, and it was here that the real cultural division lay.[11]

When Caesar entered Gaul the situation was fluid. Germanic pressure from the Suebi and beyond was clearly building up and thrusting into Gaul (remembering that Ariovistus was of Suebian ancestry) but the Rhine was not a significant divide. It was made such by Caesar, largely for military reasons. Once the Roman presence was firmly established on the west bank, the communities of the east bank soon succumbed to the more Germanic peoples pressing in from the east, and what had once been a broad zone of cultural mix became a hard line of division. The Rhine divide began as a literary over-simplification, but soon became a reality.

Allegiances

Caesar's *Commentaries* throw considerable light on the complex politics of Gaul in the middle of the first century BC. One theme that deserves consideration is the use that Caesar made of allies, particularly the Aedui and the Remi. Together with their dependent tribes they provided him with a safe corridor into the heart of northern Gaul, and this explains the progress of the campaign of 57 BC, in which we see the Roman armies thrusting deep into the territory of the Belgae before fanning out east and west to mop up resistance in Belgica and Armorica. So sure was the advance that Caesar must have been certain of Remic support. As he approached, the two leading men of the tribe came to meet him, to place their tribe under Rome's protection. It was one of the few allegiances which were to last throughout the war. The Remi benefited from Caesar's protection and very soon became dominant in the region, acquiring other tribes as dependants, including those who could not bring themselves to align with the other pro-Roman tribe, the Aedui. One of the dependants of the Remi was probably the Lingones tribe. Together they had boycotted Vercingetorix's war council at Bibracte in 52 BC, and both tribes provided Caesar with cavalry the next year. By virtue of their location, the Lingones could well have been one of the dependent tribes who deserted the Sequani when Caesar began to restore the Aedui, and who, because of old feuds with the Aedui, joined Caesar's other allies, the Remi, instead.

Caesar was evidently concerned to protect the Remi. The troop dispositions in the difficult winter of 54 BC created a protective zone around the tribe, and in the winter of 52–1 BC, in the aftermath of the Vercingetorix uprising, two legions were stationed in their territory 'to prevent them suffering harm at the hands of their neighbours the Bellovaci'. In the following year, when the Remi sent envoys to Caesar, reporting that the hostile Bellovaci were planning to attack the Suessiones (now dependants of the Remi), Caesar again felt constrained to help: 'The Remi were allies who had served Rome well and Caesar considered that his honour, as well as his interests, demanded that they should not come to harm.'[12]

The establishment and maintenance of allegiances with native tribes was crucial to Caesar's success, and nowhere is this better illustrated than in his relationship with the Aedui. Early in the first century BC the two most powerful tribes, leading opposed factions, were the Aedui and the Arverni. For years they struggled for supremacy until the Arverni, in concert with the Sequani, employed 15,000 'Germanic' mercenaries against them. A series of conflicts ensued, during which the Aedui and their dependants were seriously weakened. After an appeal for Roman help failed, they seem to have become dependants of the Sequani and, as the Sequani were swamped by increasing inpourings of Germans, so the Aedui had to face the depredations of the incomers. Caesar quickly grasped the situation and, reinvoking the old alliance, gave support to the Aedui. The immediate result was that the Sequani were forced to return hostages to the Aedui and 'their former dependent tribes were restored and with my help new ones were acquired'. (Among those later listed were the Segusiavi, Ambivareti, Aulerci Brannovices and Blannovii.) '. . . In other respects too the influence and prestige of the Aedui were increased.' Caesar's action quickly re-established the tribe, and ensured a comparatively safe foothold for the Roman forces deep in Gaulish territory.[13]

In the next year's campaigns against the Belgae, Caesar used his new allies, persuading them to send their armies against the Bellovaci to draw fire from his own forces. This was all the more remarkable because the Bellovaci were, traditionally, friends and clients of the Aedui, and, at the end of the campaigns, Diviciacus, leader of the Aedui, interceded on behalf of the defeated Bellovaci to persuade Caesar to take a lenient attitude.[14]

Like most tribes, the Aedui was split into factions, centring around family rivalries, each led by charismatic figures. When Caesar arrived in Gaul the chief magistrate was Diviciacus, who took a firm pro-Roman attitude and was rewarded for this with Caesar's support. His brother Dumnorix was an ambitious and powerful man, but frustrated in that, by Aeduian law, he could not aspire to high office during his brother's lifetime. His behaviour, as depicted by Caesar, was that of a typical Celt of the old order. He established his intertribal power on a network of intermarriages: he himself married the daughter of the Helvetian chief Orgetorix, and he arranged for his own mother to marry a Biturigan noble; his half sister and other female relations were married into other tribes. At home he maintained a large following of mounted warriors, and through massive generosity he established a substantial body of clients. As Caesar said, 'He was eager for political change and wanted to have as many tribes as possible bound to him by ties of gratitude'.[15]

Such men were dangerous, and already in 58 BC Dumnorix seems to have been fermenting trouble for the Romans by stirring up discontent among his own tribe. Caesar learnt of this, but decided that it was politic to avoid precipitate action. To react would have been to upset his delicate alliance with the Aedui, which he could not afford to do. Dumnorix was warned, and kept under surveillance.

No doubt there were many powerful men of this kind in Gaul at the time who had to be carefully watched. Caesar's approach was to keep them about himself, allowing them to command their own cavalry detachments. So it was in the spring of 54 BC when preparations for the invasion of Britain were in progress:

> Four thousand cavalry from all parts of Gaul, and leading men from all the tribes assembled there too. I had decided to leave behind just a few of these men, whose loyalty to me had been proved, and to take the rest with me as hostages because I was afraid there might be a rising in Gaul while I was away in Britain.

Dumnorix, with his entourage of cavalry, was present at the gathering, but in spite of Caesar's commands he decided to remain in Gaul, and made off. Caesar was faced with no alternative: troops were sent after him and Dumnorix was killed.[16]

It may well have been this act that cost Caesar the allegiance of the Aedui. He was unsure of their reliability in the early stages of the rebellion of Vercingetorix, and a little later was called to intervene when a factional dispute broke out among the tribe over the election of the chief magistrate. At this stage Caesar was still looking to them for military support, asking them to send all their cavalry and 10,000 infantry to him to patrol his supply routes. But events moved quickly and the commander of the Aeduian force, Litaviccus, engineered an uprising among the troops. It was a muddled affair, but the news of it which reached the Aedui was enough to pitch the already discontented nobility against Rome, and a full-scale rebellion broke out:

> They plundered Roman citizens of their property, killing some and dragging others off into slavery. Convictolitavis (the chief magistrate) helped the movement along, goading the people on to frenzy, so that once they had committed serious crime they would be too ashamed to return to their senses.

An even more serious blow was to follow when the Aeduian force, led by Eporedorix and Viridomarus, took the *oppida* of Noviodunum on the Loire, where Caesar had concentrated his baggage, funds, grain and Gallic hostages. This was an extremely serious set-back for the Romans — much more so than Caesar admitted. The acquisition of the hostages gave the Aedui considerable bargaining power with the rebel leader Vercingetorix, and they played an active part in the revolt, contributing 35,000 troops to the rebel cause.[17]

When the fighting was over and Vercingetorix had surrendered, Caesar had to decide how to deal with the Aedui. It is indicative of the importance he attached to their friendship that he singled out the 20,000 Aeduian and Arvernian prisoners for special treatment (the rest were distributed to the soldiers as booty) and having received the submission of the tribes, returned them to their people. This act of friendship allowed the allegiance to be rebuilt. It was, no doubt, in the interests of re-establishing a pro-Roman political balance among the tribe that Caesar chose to spend the winter in the chief Aeduian *oppidum* at Bibracte.[18]

The behaviour and treatment of the two principal Roman allies, the Remi and Aedui, provide an insight into the nature of Celtic society at this time — split by factions, volatile and entirely subject to the will of powerful men. It is to the question of the power of the individual that we must now turn.

Gaulish leadership

Although there was little cohesive political structure above the tribal level in Gaul, national assemblies could be called, at which decisions affecting many tribes could be taken. Once agreement had been reached it was binding. Thus, through meetings of this kind, supratribal responsibility could be vested in a single individual who would then wield massive coercive powers.

The emergence of Vercingetorix is instructive. Vercingetorix was an ambitious young Arvernian whose father, Celtillus, had been assassinated for aspiring to kingship. Significantly, Vercingetorix's first act was to follow in his father's footsteps and make a bid for supreme power, using the traditional Celtic stratagem of calling his dependants together and inspiring them to join him in his enterprise against the Romans. This bid for power was against tribal laws, and the elders, including his uncle, tried to restrain him but without success. Eventually he was expelled from the *oppidum* of Gergovia, but such was his charisma that he was able to win a majority following and was proclaimed king, thus overturning the socio-political system within the tribe and reverting to the earlier system. That this could happen is in part a reflection of the inherent instability of the new order, and in part a response to the extraordinary situation created by the Roman presence.[19]

Vercingetorix's next act was probably to call an assembly. Though this is not explicitly recorded, Caesar says that he won the support of the Senones, Parisii, Pictones, Cadurci, Turones, Aulerci, Lemovices, Andes and all the other tribes of the Atlantic coast. By general consent he was given supreme command. In other words, he was building a massive confederation of all the tribes of central Gaul, from the river Allier and the upper Seine to the Atlantic, and from the lower Loire to the Garonne. The confederation was stiffened in the usual way by each tribe providing hostages.

After initial Roman successes, another council was held at which Vercingetorix proposed to destroy everything in the Roman line of advance — all buildings, villages and ill-defended *oppida*. 'This proposal was approved unanimously, and in a single day more than 20 towns of the Bituriges were set on fire. The same thing was done in the other tribal regions, and fires could be seen in every direction.' The severity of the measure, and its successful execution, is a reflection of the coercive power wielded at the time. The success of the rebels encouraged other tribes to join them. The Nitiobriges and Aedui, who had both been 'friends and allies' of Rome, came over, after which the war was stepped up. The Aedui now contested the leadership of the rebellion and in consequence a general council was summoned at Bibracte. Gauls came from all over the country (all except the Remi, Lingones and Treveri, according to Caesar); the matter was fully debated and Vercingetorix was confirmed unanimously as supreme war leader, to the chagrin of the Aedui.[20]

The culmination of the rebellion came when Vercingetorix withdrew his forces to Alesia, an *oppidum* in the territory of the Mandubii, and this gave Caesar the opportunity to envelop the entire Gaulish enclosure in siege works (fig 48). The situation was potentially serious for the rebels, who now, without Vercingetorix, summoned another council (where we are not told). On this occasion they decided to demand a levy of troops from all the tribes to constitute a relieving force. Numbers were fixed, the total being 281,000. When most of them were assembled in Aeduian territory, the command structure was agreed. Four joint supreme commanders were appointed: Commius, an Atrebatian, the Aeduians Viromarus and Eporedorix and an Arvernian, Vercassivellaunus, a cousin of Vercingetorix. Tribal representatives liaised with each of the four commanders, acting as advisers. It was a careful balance of command, involving a representative of the Belgic tribes and giving due power to the Aedui, while at the same time maintaining a direct link with Vercingetorix himself.[21]

When the vast relief force arrived at Alesia and camped only a mile outside Caesar's outer line of circumvallation the spirits of Vercingetorix and the defenders in Alesia were raised, but after a two-day battle the Gaulish force was routed and fled in disarray. In the aftermath Vercingetorix called a council and put himself in the hands of the elders. He had failed as a war leader and therefore had no option but to give up power. Envoys were sent to discuss surrender terms with Caesar. They agreed to lay down arms and hand over all the tribal chiefs, including Vercingetorix, to Caesar. Apart from the captured Aedui and Arverni, who Caesar retained, hoping to use them to regain the loyalty of the tribes, the rest of the defenders were distributed as booty among the soldiers.[22]

A rather different example of Celtic leadership is provided by Commius, who Caesar had appointed as king of the Atrebates, presumably choosing him from the ranks of the Atrebatian aristocracy because of his pro-Roman attitudes. He appears to have been a man of influence, and Caesar used him on several missions. In 55 BC he was sent to Britain, where he was greatly respected, to persuade the native chieftains to submit to Rome, but his mission was not altogether a success and he was taken captive by the British, only to be returned, with apologies, after Caesar had landed. Commius returned to Britain with Caesar in the following year and acted as an intermediary in negotiations with the native king Cassivellaunus. The next year, 53 BC, we hear of him commanding a detachment of cavalry deployed to keep watch on the Menapii. In return for his faithful service, Caesar ordered that his tribe should be given its independence and should be exempted from taxes; he was also given control over the Morini. However, in the general uprising of 52 BC, Commius, like so many of his kind, turned against Rome, no doubt in the firm expectation that Caesar would be driven from Gaul. In the general levy raised at the time the Atrebates provided 4000 troops to the rebel cause, and it seems that Commius was now active among the Belgae, helping to organize the rebel forces. His status was such that after the vast relieving force had assembled, he was appointed one of the four commanders.[23]

In the aftermath of Gaulish defeat at Alesia, the rebel leaders who had escaped were in a difficult position, not least those who had deserted the Romans. But the Romans had reason to fear powerful men like Commius, and during the winter of 52–1 BC, in the guise of a meeting, a party of Roman centurions attacked and severely wounded him. He managed to escape, but swore that he would never again enter the presence of a Roman.

In the following year, 51 BC, the focus of resistance moved to the Belgic region, where Commius was now actively mustering troops and negotiating with the Germans, in concert with the Bellovaci led by Correus, who seems to have been the supreme commander. When the revolt collapsed, Commius fled rather than submit to the Romans, from whom he could have expected no mercy, but he remained active for some time, leading guerrilla attacks against Rome — more as a personal vendetta than as organized resistance. The Atrebates were, on the whole, obedient to Rome, but 'Commius and his band of horsemen were supporting themselves by brigandage. They planted ambushes along the roads and intercepted several of the convoys on their way to the Roman winter quarters.' Eventually, waning support caused Commius to negotiate an uneasy peace with the Roman commander Mark Anthony, which enabled him to retain his freedom but little else. That was in the winter of 51–50 BC.

Soon after this, Commius decided to leave Gaul for Britain, where, as we have seen, he had political connections. To the last he was pursued by the Romans and, arriving at the beach ahead of them, found his ships high and dry at low tide. Not to be beaten he raised the sails and when his pursuers saw this in the distance they turned away thinking that he had escaped. Commius eventually reached Britain to 'join his people already there'. He appears to have settled in the Hampshire region, and soon reappeared as head of a dynasty, issuing his own coins, followed by a succession of rulers who styled themselves 'son of Commius'.[24]

The story of Commius offers a particularly valuable insight into the powers of the individual in Celtic society. An aristocrat showing valour and leadership could change allegiance without difficulty, still retaining credibility, and a man with suitable connections and charisma could establish his authority in widely-flung territories.

The fate of the conquered Gauls

A final area to be explored here is the Roman treatment of native tribes during a conflict such as the Gallic war. Sufficient will have been said to show that Caesar was at pains to nurture allies, and through Roman patronage such people could grow rapidly in power, with a return in benefit to Rome. The treatment of the Remi and Aedui are clear examples of such a policy in action, and even though the Aedui eventually rebelled they were surprisingly gently treated. This is far more likely to have been a policy dictated by necessity than one tempered by sentiment. Caesar needed a safe axis through the heart of Gaul, and he sought, through patronage and clemency, to maintain it.

Caesar's attitude to other tribes varied considerably according to circumstance. In the campaign against the Nervii in 57 BC Caesar came up against a fierce, courageous people who refused to send envoys or discuss peace terms. The fighting was bitter and for the Romans, extremely testing. Caesar was evidently much impressed by the great fighting spirit he encountered and overcame. After the final battle he realized that the tribe, and even their name, had been virtually wiped out. Of the council of 600 only three remained; of the fighting force of 60,000 barely 500 survived. Caesar's settlement was deliberate. All the old men, women and children who had been sent away to the creeks and marshes for safety were given back their land and their *oppida*, and orders were given that the neighbouring tribes must refrain from doing damage and injury, and offer instead protection.[25] In such a case Caesar could afford to show compassion. It was not so with the Veneti, who rebelled in 56 BC. The sea battle in Quiberon Bay had been decisive, but casualties were not high (at least they are not recorded) and it must have been clear to Caesar that these isolated people sitting astride an important trade route could soon regroup and rearm; they were potentially dangerous. His solution was briefly recorded: 'I put all their elders to death and sold the rest into slavery.'[26]

Another tribe Caesar treated harshly was the Aduatuci, living close to the Rhine. Caesar had besieged their *oppidum* and agreed terms with their envoys, but the tribe tried to trick him by attempting to burst out and escape at night. In the onslaught 4000 natives were killed. On the next day Caesar's troops smashed down the gates. 'I sold all I found inside by auction in one lot. It was reported to me by the purchasers that the number of people sold in the auction was 53,000.' No doubt they soon found their way to the Roman slave market.[27]

Caesar's attitudes to defenders in besieged *oppida* varied considerably, largely in response to severity and duration of the action. He had been prepared to show mercy to the Aduatuci until they tried to trick him; then there was no mercy. At Vellaunodunum, when the Senones sued for peace after only three days, Caesar required them simply to surrender their arms, their pack animals and 600 hostages, but then he was in a hurry and wanted to win over the tribe.[28] The siege of Cenabum, which took place a few days later was altogether different. The Carnutes had slaughtered the Roman traders in the town some time before, and the *oppidum* was now fiercely contested. When eventually it fell, the Roman troops showed no mercy. Old men, women and children were slaughtered. Of the entire population of 40,000 barely 800 escaped.[29]

The last of the sieges of the war was the long, drawn out and bitterly contested siege of Uxellodunum in the Dordogne. The defenders held out doggedly until the Roman engineers managed to tap their water supply, and the springs inside the fortifications dried up. Believing it to be an act of the gods, the occupants surrendered. Caesar's response was considered. He realized that if revolts continued to break out in other parts of the country he would never successfully conclude the war, so he decided to make an example of the defenders. 'All those who had carried weapons had their hands cut off but their lives were spared so that everyone might see how evil-doers were punished'.[30]

The Gallic war had dragged on for eight years. During that time an unending supply of Roman military manpower had been brought into the war zone. By simple attrition, the strength of the Gauls and their desire to resist were worn away: hundreds of thousands were killed, hundreds of thousands were carried away to be sold in slavery and incalculable numbers were maimed. The countryside in 50 BC must have looked very different from the countryside ten years earlier. The population was decimated, the land ravaged and the old social and economic systems were in ruins. More to the point, the desire to resist had gone. It is difficult now to appreciate the magnitude of the Gallic war, but that it was a major dislocation to Gallic society there can be no doubt. What followed in Gaul and beyond involved massive rebuilding using new bricks.

7 The creation of the three Gauls

Caesar's military involvement in Gaul ended in 50 BC. Gaul had served its purpose: it had provided him with a theatre in which to enact spectacular deeds and to create a reputation rivalling that of Pompey. Now the real struggle for power could begin.

In 49 BC Caesar led his army across the Rubicon, in direct challenge to the established authority of the conservative senators. His deliberate defiance of time-honoured rules plunged the Roman world into a civil war which was to last for four years, until the two protagonists, Caesar and Pompey, met on the Spanish plain of Munda. Triumphant, Caesar returned to Rome; a year later, on the Ides of March 44 BC, he was stabbed to death at the base of Pompey's statue. The orgy of blood-letting which followed lasted for 15 years.

In 31 BC, at the great sea battle of Actium, Octavian emerged triumphant. Four years later, in 27 BC, he had so established himself that he could assume the name Augustus and the title *Princeps* ('first among equals'), thus initiating a style of government — the Principate — that was to continue for a quarter of a millennium. One of his first acts as Princeps, in 27 BC, was to look to the organization of Gaul, now, after a full generation, beginning to recover from the trauma of the Gallic war.

The organization of Gaul: 50–12 BC (fig 49)

Caesar's settlement of Gaul had been minimal: the land and its people — those who survived — were exhausted. Little appears to have been done, and once the old allegiances had been reinforced, the country was left to recover at its own pace, supported by the institution of Roman patronage. But Rome necessarily made a number of demands on its newly-annexed territories. Communications had to be improved and kept open, land had to be found for veteran colonies and the new territory had to be 'harvested' to provide a regular supply of auxiliary troops and a constant tariff in the form of tax in cash or in kind.[1]

The first two needs could be met by the creation of full citizen colonies. At least four were established in the old province of Transalpina, at Narbo (Narbonne), Arelate (Arles), Forum Julii (Fréjus) and Baeterrae (Béziers).[2] All were sited on densely populated, fertile land at important route nodes. These Roman implants, together with the continued influx of Italian immigrants into the ancient towns of the south, and the deliberate, and rapid, advancement of natives by the grant of citizenship, ensured that Transalpina was soon transformed into a thoroughly urbanized extension of Italy.

49 The principal routes in Gaul in the Augustan period

Outside the old province, in Gallia Comata — barbarian Gaul - there was very little attempt to accelerate the process of Romanization. Only three colonies were founded and each was placed for strictly strategic reasons, to protect the major lines of communication from Italy to the Rhine and around the western fringes of the Alps. Noviodunum (Nyon) lay in Helvetian territory on the shores of Lake Léman, Lugdunum (Lyon) developed at the confluence of the Rhône and Saône, while Raurica (Augst) was positioned on the Rhine, commanding the gap leading away from the Rhône–Saône valley, via the upper Doubs.[3] This newly- defended axis was essentially an extension of northern Transalpina, carefully shielded along its western fringe by a pro-Roman buffer composed of the Aedui, the Arverni and their dependants.

Rome also needed a constant supply of auxiliary troops, and Gaul provided a ready base for recruitment. Caesar had already made good use of Gaulish and German cavalry detachments in his Gallic campaigns, and the newly-won territory continued to supply recruits of high calibre, in particular cavalry. Bands of rampaging horsemen led by young aristocrats had long been a feature of Celtic society; it was a simple matter for them to turn their allegiance to Roman commanders under whom their desire for adventure and loot could easily be satisfied. The recruitment of such bands into the ranks of the auxiliaries provided a very valuable safety valve. The high spirited could use up their energy in the service of Rome and, if they survived, would return home as ambassadors of the Roman way of life, using the tastes and patronage they had acquired to enhance their superior status in the local community. In this way the Roman administration took the Celtic institution of the élite retinue and adopted it to suit Roman needs. In doing so, the potentially dangerous Celtic spirit was channelled into a positive force for Romanization. The process could occasionally misfire and young Gallic cavalry officers returning home could ferment discontent, but all in all the system worked to Rome's advantage.[4]

The first two decades following the end of the Gallic war were comparatively peaceful, but there were minor upsets. In 46 BC the governor had to put down a revolt among the Bellovaci, and in 44–3 L. Munatius Plancus found it necessary to campaign among the Raeti. It was as the result of this that the colonies were founded at Lugdunum and Raurica.[5]

In 39 BC Octavian visited Gaul for the first time, in the same year appointing the highly competent M. Vipsanius Agrippa as governor. Agrippa's appointment seems to mark the beginning of a new interest in the conquered territory.[6] Gaul was still very much a frontier region: to the north, beyond the Belgae, lay the unsubdued and troublesome regions of Germany, while to the south-west, next to Aquitania, were the unconquered tribes of north-western Iberia. Both areas were potentially unstable and had therefore to be garrisoned at strength. Unrest was inevitable and seems to have continued to ferment for some time. In 30–29 BC troops were campaigning among the rebellious Morini and their neighbours in western Belgica: in 29 BC the Treveri were in revolt, and in the next year we learn that the governor won a major victory against the Aquitani.[7]

In the wake of these troubles, Octavian, now Augustus, paid his second visit to Gaul, in 27 BC, to observe the organization of the first national census, designed to facilitate the more efficient taxing of the province.[8] The census was a thorough piece of bureaucratic reorganization, listing not only the population but also the value of all landed property, the acreage of arable and pasture, the number of fruit trees, olives and vines and the size of flocks and herds. Its instigation marks the beginning of the process by which Gaul was integrated into the Roman empire.

For ease of government the country was divided into administrative units. The old Transalpina was designated a separate province, now known as Narbonensis, while Gallia Comata was divided into three: Belgica, Aquitania and Lugdunensis. Belgica broadly reflected the ethnic entity noted by Caesar but the division between Aquitania and Lugdunensis, drawn along the Loire, was arbitrary and had no basis in traditional ethnic groupings. At first, all four provinces were governed by the emperor through legates, but in 22 BC Narbonensis was returned to senatorial control and administered by a proconsul.[9]

The provincial reorganization and the census were designed to make administration, and in particular the collection of taxes, easier. As part of the same process, *civitas* boundaries were redrawn to create local units of more regular size, and where necessary, new towns were created to serve as administrative centres. Augustodunum Aeduorum (Autun) was founded in 12 BC, 20km from the old Aeduian capital of Bibracte, in a far more accessible spot, convenient in relation to the new communications system. Augusta Treverorum (Trier) was a new foundation on the Moselle providing an urban focus for the recalcitrant Treveri, while the Andes were given a new urban centre at Juliomagus Andecavorum (Angers) placed, conveniently, on the Loire.

The period of the Augustan reorganization of Gaul, 27–12 BC, was accompanied by campaigning on the frontiers designed largely to enable the troop commitment in Gaul to be cut. The subjugation of northern Spain (28–13 BC) effectively ended Aquitanian unrest, while the difficult mountain tribes of the Alps Maritime were finally brought to heel in a brief campaign in 27–25 BC, after which the coast route from Italy to Narbonensis was made safe — a fact proclaimed by the Tropaeum erected by Augustus at La Turbie, in the hills above Monte Carlo. It records the names of the forty-four Alpine tribes who had been subdued.[10]

It had taken Augustus 15 years to complete the reorganization of Gaul and to stabilize its frontiers. In 12 BC the end of the process was commemorated with the inauguration of an altar dedicated to Rome and Augustus, set up at Lugdunum at the confluence of the Rhône and Saône. The ceremony was conducted by Augustus' stepson Drusus on 1 August in the presence of representatives from the sixty tribes of the three Gauls, and was stage-managed to symbolize the integration of Gaul into the Roman world. The date chosen, in addition to being the Celtic feast of Lugnasad, was also the birthday of Augustus — a coincidence that would not have been allowed to pass without some careful emphasis.[11]

The ceremony also provided the occasion for the formal reconstitution of the ancient annual meeting of the Gauls, the *Concilium Galliarum*. At this inaugural meeting it was presided over by the leading Aeduian, a deliberate reminder to all present of the rewards of being faithful to Rome. Henceforth the council would assemble annually in its new Gallo-Roman guise.[12]

The German frontier

Before we turn to consider the changes brought about in Gaulish society, and the development of new patterns of production and trade, it is necessary to say something, in outline, of the Roman attitude to the German frontier and to free Germany beyond. Caesar's crossing of the Rhine had been little more than a deliberately calculated act of bravado, designed to impress Germans, Gauls and Romans alike. There had been no intent to conquer, but the campaign had captured the public's imagination, and others were to follow with more ambitious intent.

With the consolidation of Gaul nearing completion, Augustus began to look to free Germany, and in 16 BC he returned to Gaul for the third time, to draw up plans for a massive military thrust across the Rhine and Danube. The intention was to annex the territory up to the Elbe or even beyond, thus creating a short land frontier from the Baltic to the Black Sea along the Elbe and Danube. Once Gaul had been consolidated, the campaign could begin. Thus it was, in 12 BC, that Drusus led his army across the Rhine. Then followed advances, setbacks, hesitations, further advances and finally, in AD 16, the decision to abandon Germany altogether and return once more to the Rhine. After nearly thirty years of hostilities and costly warfare the frontier was no further advanced.[13]

Social and economic change in Gaul

The administrative and military background provides the essential framework for understanding the enormous social and political upheaval which the Gallic communities experienced. The first decade after Caesar, 50–39 BC, was a time of little deliberate action on the part of Rome. Then followed a period of consolidation, 39–27 BC, during which the frontiers and communications system were organized. The third phase, 27–12 BC, was one of extensive administrative reorganization, and this was followed by a fourth phase, 12 BC to AD 16, during which Gaul was required to provide the back-up for the German adventure. Thereafter, the provinces could settle down to a period of peaceful development as a fully integrated constituent of the empire. Against this background we can now begin to examine the development of Gaulish society in the two generations or so following Caesar's conquest.[14]

Caesar's army had been present in Gaul for eight years, its energies geared entirely towards conquest. During that time it had been supplied with corn and the other necessities of life almost entirely from the countryside it was attempting to conquer. Friendly tribes like the Aedui were expected to supply food willingly in return for Roman patronage and protection, while those who were defeated were forced to make reparation in foodstuffs. During the winter, grain was requisitioned. It could never have been easy for a people unused to producing grain surpluses to provide sufficient for themselves and the troops — particularly in times of war. In the winter of 57/56 BC, grain shortage and Roman requisition methods sparked off the unrest which led to the Armorican revolt. Later, in the winter of 54/53 BC, an exceptionally poor grain harvest, following a drought, was a sufficiently serious constraint to force Caesar to distribute his legions widely among the Belgic tribes rather than to concentrate them as he would have wished.[15]

After 50 BC the garrisons in Gaul would have been reduced, but so too was the productive capacity of the people and their devastated landscape. Provisions for the standing army must have been drawn from Gaul for years after the formal end of the war. Allowing for a garrison of 40–50,000 men, the burden on the hard-pressed Gauls must have been considerable.

Another aspect of production was the need to generate, and to cull, surplus manpower. All the time that war was in progress, the supply of slaves would have been unending, but after 50 BC the potential of Gaul as a ready source for slaves diminished rapidly. It was now to the barbarian territories beyond, Britain and Germany, that the entrepreneurs began to look, and slave raiding in these lands would suddenly have increased (see pp.147 and 177–82).

Nor should the employment of mobile free labour be overlooked. Throughout the war, and the decades to follow, Gallic mercenaries, particularly the famous Gallic cavalry, were much in evidence in the ranks of the Roman auxiliaries. The Roman army provided a career structure which exactly suited the Gallic temperament. Each year hordes of young men, who would otherwise have been a disruptive influence, were siphoned off, those who survived returning after a period of 25 years or so fashioned into new men by their experience. This was a potent force for change. However, with the establishment of widespread peace throughout much of the Roman world after 30 BC, the need for large standing armies declined and the outlets for young adventurers became correspondingly fewer. The problem is impossible to quantify and difficult to assess, but the decrease in size of the standing army in Gaul, and the consequent fall in demand for recruits, may have been one factor in Augustus' desire to reorganize the tax base of the country, which began with the census of 27 BC.[16]

The change from the *ad hoc* organization of the immediate post-Caesar decade to the carefully administered provinces of the three Gauls, was probably initiated in 39 BC with the appointment of M. Vipsanius Agrippa as governor. According to Strabo it was Agrippa who was responsible for creating a series of new roads fanning out across Gaul to the Atlantic, the Channel and the Rhine (pp.138–9).[17] This major feat of planning and investment can only have meant the beginnings of a new era, looking forward to the time when the provinces would be closely administered and taxed. The context for this may well have been the plan to move troops gradually to the Rhine frontier. This process would have taken with it the need to transform the taxation system from a tax in kind, to feed the dispersed army, to a tax in cash to allow for the purchase and transport of military supplies to the army now concentrated in a military zone along the Rhine and soon to be campaigning deep in Germania. If this scenario is correct, there would have been a major change in the production systems at work in Gaul, the emphasis now being on the creation of a range of marketable commodities, and a corresponding upsurge in the development of a full market economy. In archaeological terms, one might expect to find the emergence of permanent market centres, a rapid increase in commodity production leading to a degree of industrialization and the appearance of low denomination coinage throughout the country.[18]

The Gaulish economy, which had already undergone rapid change in the first half of the first century BC, in response to the demands of the Roman entrepreneurs, was severely dislocated by the Caesarian campaigns. But after the war it picked up again and continued on its trajectory for another generation. This continuity can be seen in a variety of persistent customs, not least in the maintenance of native systems of coinage, which continued to be issued under the authority of chieftains. The coinage of the Arvernian ruler Epasnactus, mentioned in the *Gallic Wars*, is informative.[19] His issues are inscribed with his name, EPAD, but those post-dating the war copy the Roman denarius in style and weight, no doubt to facilitate exchange in the new Roman monetary system. One issue, even more revealing of the times, was minted by Q. Julius Togirix in Sequanian territory. His name betrays the fact that he had received Roman citizenship, possibly at the hands of Caesar, while the style in which he is sometimes depicted, wearing a Roman helmet, suggests that he may, at one stage in his career, have been the commander of a native auxiliary unit.[20]

Post-war coinage shares two characteristics: it is invariably low denomination, minted in bronze, or less often in silver, and its issues exhibit a bewildering variety which is best explained by suggesting that the minting authority was no longer the chieftain or the magistrate of the tribe, but the leader of each of the various *pagi* into which every tribe was divided. Recent work at Titelberg, an *oppidum* in the territory of the Treveri, has allowed the definition of seven different series of coins, all probably minted on the site in the period 50–30 BC. At Villeneuve-Saint-Germain, an *oppidum* in the Aisne valley belonging to the Suessiones, two series of cast coins were issued in the post-war period, in styles totally dissimilar to classic Suessiones coinage found in the nearby *oppidum* at Pommiers (probably the Noviodunum of the Gallic war). Here a change in location of the market centre is accompanied by a complete break in coinage tradition.[21]

On the one hand, then, coinage in Celtic style continued to be issued after 50 BC, while on the other it was evidently designed to serve a very different purpose to the pre-war or wartime issues. What we are now seeing is the small change of a market economy operating on an essentially local level. The gold and much of the silver was being removed from the system in the form of tribute, later systematized as taxes, and passed into the coffers of the Roman administration. It would, of course, have been recycled back into Gaul through army pay, but precious metal coinage was now essentially part of the international Roman system, while the low denomination issues remained exclusive to the local Gaulish system.

After the war, local craft production picked up and intensified. The organization of pottery manufacture and marketing is accessible through archaeological evidence, and a few examples will suffice. In central Gaul the fashion for wheel-made pottery painted in red, ochre and white, already well-established in the early part of the first century BC, continued, and from the distribution patterns of the various wares it is possible to distinguish between long-distance trade in selected vessels and local distribution based on the market areas of specialized producers. One such production area in operation by the Augustan period was based in the valley of the Allier, in the vicinity of Ledosus. The potters here produced a distinctive array of bowls, known now as Roanne ware, decorated with intricate, if rather formalized, painted motifs.[22] The skills of the potters of central Gaul were soon to form the basis of a very extensive pottery industry, making the glossy, red, slipped *terra sigillata* and a number of other specialist products, inspired initially by the demands of the permanent military market established along the Rhine frontier.

In the immediate post-war period many parts of Gaul were producing their own distinctive pottery, usually wheel-turned and displaying a high degree of technical competence. Regional styles abounded: grey and black rouletted wares from the region of Gergovia; fine black-cordoned wares, sometimes graphite-coated, from north-eastern Armorica; and an elegant array of tall pedestal-based jars and associated bowls from Belgica — all representing indigenous traditions which developed and flourished in the post-conquest era as local market economies picked up, before they were swamped by the phase of industrialization which was to get underway by the end of the century.[23]

Other craft skills made a similar revival. The Gauls were well known to be skilled metalworkers, and this is borne out by a number of outstanding bronzes which survive: the Celtic god from Bouray (Seine-et-Oise) and the remarkable collection of figures from Neuvy-en-Sullias (Loiret) are masterpieces of Gallo-Roman art. In these, the Celtic spirit is still clearly evident before the heavy hand of Roman classicism had settled too firmly upon the Celtic workshops.[24] Production of this kind, and of the more mundane items of everyday use, would, for the most part, have been based on the *oppida*. At Bibracte a group of small workshops, dating to the post-conquest period, have been found in a zone set aside for artisans flanking the main road just inside the gate. Here, small bronze items were made and decorated with enamel. Zoned development of this kind was probably widespread among the European *oppida* in the pre-conquest period, but the unusually dense development which seems to be implied by the plan of Bibracte must reflect the intensification of production experienced in the post-conquest decades.[25]

Economic intensification

The build-up and concentration of troops in the Rhine frontier zone, given fresh impetus by Augustus's visit to Gaul in 16 BC, was the prelude to the invasion of Germany which began four years later. By this time the military zone along the river was firmly established, with permanent bases supplied with food and raw materials produced largely in Gaul. Troop numbers are difficult to estimate precisely, but five or six legions were probably in position, together with a number of supporting auxiliary detachments. The overall size of the army must have exceeded 45,000.[26] The supply needs of such a force, now permanently stationed along the Rhine frontier and thrusting deep into Germany during the summer campaigning season, introduced a new factor into the economic system of Gaul — a factor which manifests itself most clearly in an intensification of production. At the same time, the development of long-distance trade and the attraction to entrepreneurs of the country, now firmly integrated into the administrative system of the empire, gave an added impetus to economic growth. The result of this complex interaction of forces was the emergence of a new urban aristocracy, and with it the rapid development of urban centres. Thus the decade 20–10 BC saw a further change in the economic trajectory, evidence for which can be found in the archaeological record.

The demand for high-quality ceramics by the army and also by the rapidly growing, Romanized, urban aristocracy created entrepreneurial opportunities for craftsmen to develop new industrialized centres of production, turning out a range of quality mass-produced wares designed to satisfy Roman tastes. Many such centres are known in Gaul. At Lombez (Gers), near the Pyrenees, a range of fine, thin-walled, orange-coloured pottery was in production by the beginning of the first century AD, and was distributed widely to a civilian market. White wares coated with green lead-glaze, made at Saint-Remy-en-Rolat in the valley of the Allier, were rather more popular from the end of the first century BC, and by the middle of the next century they were being exported as far afield as Britain. In neither case, however, did the producers supply the military market in bulk.[27]

The most popular Gallic wares in the frontier zone were *terra sigillata* and a range of fine-ware plates and cups known as Gallo-Belgic wares. These were either red (*terra rubra*) or grey/black (*terra nigra*) and were made at several centres in Belgica, and also in the territory of the Lingones. Production seems to have begun about 10 BC, presumably in direct response to the military demand for fine tableware. Another area producing a similar product to the northern *terra nigra* lay on the west coast of Gaul, near Saintes, in the territory of the Santones. The kilns are close to Agrippa's road west from Lugdunum, providing a reminder of the importance of the Atlantic-Channel route for the supply of the western end of the Rhine frontier.[28]

Terra sigillata became immensely popular. One of the earliest production centres was at Lezoux in the Allier valley, where *sigillata* was produced as early as AD 10. Further south, at two locations, in the vicinity of Montans and La Graufesenque, extensive workshops were in production a few years later. The products are so similar in style to the wares and forms produced at Arezzo in northern Italy that there can be little doubt that the earliest Gaulish *sigillata* manufacturers were craftsmen who had migrated from Italy to set up new workshops, more conveniently sited to supply the vast consumer market which Gaul and the Rhine frontier zone offered.[29]

The post-war revival encouraged the development of urban agglomerations which, for the most part, evolved from already existing *oppida*. The best known example is provided by Bibracte, the capital of the Aedui, set on a mountain top 800m up in the Morvan (fig 50). Sufficient is known, both from Caesar's accounts and from the excavations undertaken almost continuously from 1867–1907, to appreciate its pre-eminent position by and during the Gallic war. The defensive wall, of *murus gallicus* type, was a massive construction 5km in overall length. One of the early excavators suggested that it originally stood 5m high, and on this assumption estimated that nearly 40,000 cubic metres of wood would have been needed in its erection. The scale alone is an indication of the coercive power of the tribal authorities who oversaw its construction.

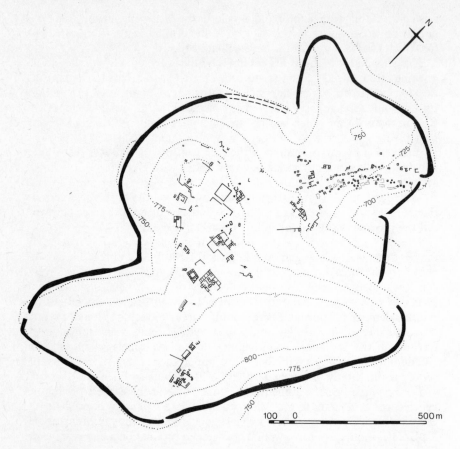

50 Mont Beuvray — the native oppidum *of Bibracte. The defences are pre-Roman but most of the buildings shown are of the early Augustan period. (After Déchelette 1904, opp. p. 8)*

After Caesar had left Gaul, the inhabitants continued to live within the defences and it is to this phase that most of the known buildings belong. The road leading into the *oppidum* was lined with small buildings, mostly of drystone and timber construction, some of them with rock-cut cellars. It was in this region that the metalworkers and enamellers lived. Further towards the centre, close to the crest, were larger courtyard houses, suitable for the aristocracy. Apart from this broad zoning, the plan shows little signs of ordered layout or planning, but this impression may be misleading, due to the ill-recorded and incomplete nature of the excavation.[30]

About 12 BC a new town, Augustodunum (Autun) was founded some 20km away in a more congenial valleyside location, convenient for the rapidly developing road system (fig 51). Augustodunum soon found favour, and in a comparatively short time the native population had abandoned the old tribal

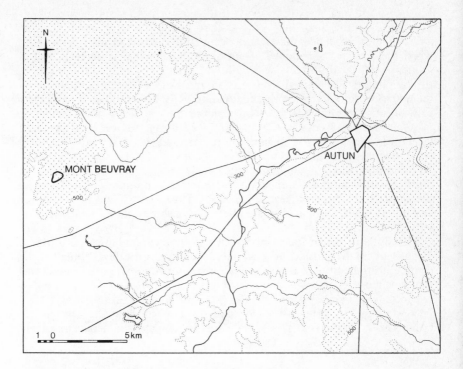

MONT BEUVRAY

AUTUN

51 The location of the Augustan town of Autun and its predecessor, the native site of Mont Beuvray

oppidum for the new Roman urban centre. There was no compulsion — it was simply that the road communications made Augustodunum a route node and this drew in the commercial and administrative systems: the population followed.[31]

The story so vividly exemplified by Bibracte/Augustodunum can be repeated, with variations, elsewhere in Gaul. Sometimes, as with Bibracte, the new road system demanded a shift of focus to a more convenient location; elsewhere, when the terrain allowed, the roads linked existing *oppida*, as for example Vesontio (Besançon), Cenabum (Orléans) and Caesarodunum (Chartres). It has been suggested, however, that this continuity of location is restricted to central Gaul, which is the area where development towards a state system of government and a fully urbanized economy was already underway before the war, the implication being that the Roman administration was at pains to accept the existing social and economic structure of this region with as little change as possible.

A rather different situation seems to have developed in the extreme west, in Armorica, in the territory of the Coriosolites (Côte du Nord). Here, the pre-conquest settlement was located on the promontory of St Servan (Roman Alet) which commands several good harbours in the estuary of the River

Rance, and it was here that a port, trading with central southern Britain, flourished in the first half of the first century BC (pp.98–101). The archaeological evidence shows that occupation continued until AD 15–20, when the site was abandoned — an abandonment which may have been influenced by the disorders in the west in the reign of Tiberius. By this time, the thoroughly Romanized town of Fanum Martius (Corseul), some 20km inland, had begun to take over the function of a *civitas* capital. Whether the shift of focus was a deliberate political act or the result of gradual economic factors is unclear. It may be that the longevity of Alet was due to its favoured location in relation to the western sea routes, and that when cross-Channel trade declined in the second half of the first century AD so did Alet. Significantly, Alet rose to importance again in the late third and fourth centuries AD when the Channel once more became an important sea-way. At the same time, there is clear evidence of a marked decline in activity at Corseul, emphasizing the intricate inter-relationship of the two sites and the importance of the sea-ways.[32]

The shifts of urban focus in the case of Bibracte and Alet were over a distance of 20km or so and were caused, primarily, by the development of the communications system. But there are cases where the change in location was slight, indicating perhaps political or symbolic dislocations. The case of Noviodunum in the Aisne valley provides a good example (fig 52). Noviodunum, the principal *oppidum* of the Suessiones at the time of the Gallic war, has been identified with the fortification of Pommiers, a massively

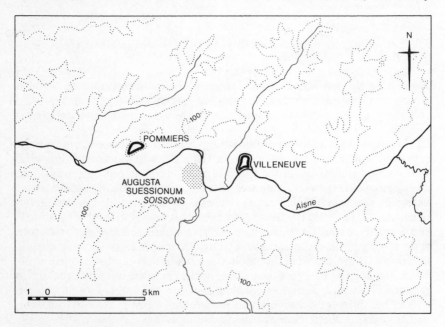

52 *The relationship of the native fortification of Pommiers to Villeneuve, founded soon after the conquest, and the Augustan town of Augusta Suessionum (Soissons)*

defended promontory fort of 40ha extent, occupying a commanding position overlooking the Aisne. Desultory excavation in the nineteenth century unearthed about 2600 coins, the study of which showed the site to have been intensively occupied in the period *c.* 70–51 BC with some form of occupation continuing after that into Augustan times. Barely 6km to the east of Pommiers, at Villeneuve-Saint-Germain, a new urban agglomeration developed within a deep meander of the Aisne. The river formed the defensive boundary on three sides, the fourth being defended by a rampart and ditch. Area excavation within has produced abundant evidence of a dense and organized layout of buildings, sometimes set in palisaded enclosures, arranged along straight streets (fig 53). The overriding impression is of planning and order, and yet the style of timber building, the defences, the location, and the general layout are typical of a Celtic *oppidum*.

In advance of detailed publication it is difficult to discuss the chronology in any detail, but the numismatic evidence strongly suggests that the floruit of Villeneuve followed that of Pommiers. In other words, it looks as though Villeneuve, still essentially a native *oppidum* in style, was created in the immediate post-conquest period to replace Pommiers.[33]

Between the two sites, the Roman settlement of *Augusta Suessionum* (Soissons) developed. As its name implies, it was probably a creation of the Augustan reorganization in the last decade or two of the first century BC, and is most likely to represent the official resettlement of the area. The reasons for the two shifts in location of the urban nucleus are elusive. At best they illustrate the fluidity of the situation following the Gallic war, and the extent to which Gaul was left very much to its own devices for 30 or 40 years after Caesar's conquest. That the three nuclei should cluster so close together is an indication that political change respected the economic reality of existing route nodes, while more subtle constraints — political or social — were also at work.

Long-distance trade

As Gaul came increasingly under Roman domination in the latter half of the first century BC, so the nature of its trading networks evolved. In the period of Gallic independence, goods had moved, essentially, within a system of gift-exchange governed by a framework of social obligation. External Roman pressure, and indeed the influence of Roman traders, now established in the native *oppida*, gave an added impetus to the volume and selection of the goods transported, but the actual mechanisms of exchange still lay largely within the native social system. With the conquest and the development of the German military zone all this changed, gradually at first, but with increasing pace in the last two decades of the first century. The productive capacity of Gaul could now be exploited within the Roman administrative framework, but Gaul also provided a convenient stepping-stone to the potential riches of Britain and Germany.

It is debatable how much the impetus for the upsurge of long-distance trade came from the need to supply the army, and how much from the sheer

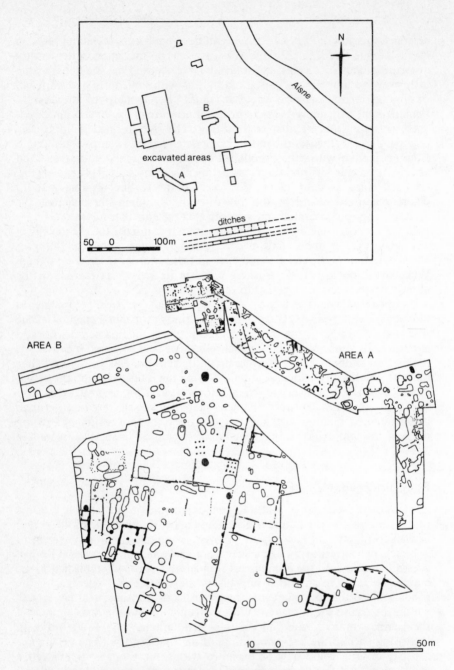

*53 The native-style settlement at Villeneuve-Saint-Germain
(see fig 52 for location) showing excavated areas and details of the native urban layout
exposed in the excavations. (Based on Debord 1982, 214–7 and Demoule & Ilett 1985,
fig 10.18)*

entrepreneurial flair of civilian traders and the demands of the civilian population, but there can be little doubt that the roads established by Agrippa, essentially to facilitate supplies to the frontier, provided a great incentive to the development of trade.

Ease of communication was paramount. Writing during the Augustan period, Strabo gives a precise assessment of the importance of river transport. The greatest of the Gaulish rivers was the Rhône, 'the voyage which [it] affords inland is a considerable one, even for vessels of great burden, and reaches numerous parts of the country on account of the fact that the rivers which fall into it are navigable, and in their turns receive most of the traffic.' By means of tributaries, and a short overland haul, traffic could reach the Seine; 'thence it begins its voyage down to the ocean and to the Lexovii and Caleti and from these peoples it is less than three days' run to Britain'.[34] However, since the Rhone was swift, and difficult to sail up, some of the traffic preferred to go by land, westwards, to join the upper reaches of the Loire and thence to the Atlantic. The third route was the long-established haul from Narbo across to Tolosa to join the River Garonne. There can be little doubt that these ancient river routes saw a greatly increased volume of traffic in the post-conquest era (fig 49).

Agrippa's road system added considerably to the ease and rapidity with which the far-flung parts of Gaul could be reached (fig 49). Using the pre-existing network of Transalpina and the new roads through the Alps, he created a major route node at Lugdunum (Lyon). From here, three new routes fanned out west and north.[35] One road ran due west to *Mediolanum* (Saintes), providing a new outlet on the Atlantic coast between the mouths of the Garonne and Loire. Another took a northern route across the watersheds of northern Gaul. At *Andemantunnum* (Langres) it divided, one branch passing well north of the Seine, through the territory of the Remi, the Suessiones and the Ambiani to the Channel port of *Gesoriacum* (Bologne), while the other ran along the Moselle valley to *Augusta Treverorum* (Trier) and thence north to *Colonia Agrippina* (Cologne) on the Rhine, which was itself a navigable river, providing another outlet to the North Sea. Thus by river and road, Gaul and the Mediterranean were linked to a western and northern seaboard at six principal outlets, seldom more than 200km apart.

The long-established route linking the Atlantic seaboard to Britain, which had been dramatically invigorated in the first half of the first century BC, remained in operation after the Gallic war, but the archaeological evidence so far available from central southern Britain suggests that the volume of shipping had drastically decreased. The two principal indicators of the trade route are amphorae and fine ware ceramics. Three types of amphorae were used in the bulk transport of wine in the post-Caesarian period: Dressel 1B and 2–4, and Pascual 1 types. A quantitative assessment of the central Italian Dressel 1B amphoras found in the west shows that they are significantly less numerous than the earlier 1A types. In Brittany, for example, where detailed statistics are available, 70% of the identifiable Dressel 1 types were 1A and only 30% were 1B. The figures from the port of Hengistbury are even more extreme (90.4% 1A and 9.6% 1B).[36] The implication is that in the post-war period there was a notable decrease in the volume of Italian wine reaching the west. This does not, however, necessarily mean that the wine trade had slumped, for the low volume of Italian wine being shipped was now augmented by products from the newly-developing wine-growing areas in north-eastern Spain and eastern Provence. This is shown by the appearance, along the Atlantic route, of Pascual 1 and Dressel 2–4 amphorae made in distinctive fabrics characteristic of the province of Tarraconensis (near modern Barcelona). The Spanish vineyards were widely known at the time to be a source of cheap wine. Similar amphora forms were also made in eastern Provence near Aspiran. The inescapable implication of this evidence is that the monopoly which the Italian producers had established over the Atlantic route in the pre-Caesarian period had now been broken and the Spanish and Gaulish shippers were fast moving in.

The distribution of Dressel 2–4 and Pascual 1 amphorae in the west shows that the traditional routes and ports were still in operation. In Armorica, there were concentrations about Vannes and Quimper, and both types have been found at the southern British ports of Hengistbury Head and Cleavel Point (in Poole Harbour). More direct evidence of trans-shipment is provided by the wreck discovered off Belle-Ile, containing Dressel 2–4 amphorae, and a further wreck, implied by the discovery of a Pascual 1 amphora, in the English Channel off Newhaven.[37]

The only other traded products which can so far be identified along the Atlantic route are fine ware ceramics: mica-gilt decorated vessels from central Gaul and a range of *terra nigra* bowls and plates, made around Saintes. Few have yet been formally identified in Armorica but the western *terra nigra* is known from several sites in Guernsey and occurs at Hengistbury and Cleavel Point.[38]

The recent excavations at Hengistbury show that the activities already established on the site in the first half of the first century BC — bronze-working, iron extraction, salt-working, and the concentration of cereal stocks from inland locations, were maintained in the post-Caesarian era, suggesting that much the same range of commodities continued to be exported from Britain. The port was now fully established as a production centre: a new range of wheel-made pottery was manufactured close by and exported into the hinterland, and early in the first century AD there is evidence to suggest that low denomination coinage was being minted there.[39] Thus it would seem that the conquest of Gaul had little immediate effect upon Atlantic trade. However, the new axes of contact which developed between Gaul and eastern Britain seem, eventually, to have eclipsed the long-established Atlantic system.

The situation in northern Gaul at this time is particularly interesting, but is still rather difficult to untangle because of the lack of a precise chronological control for the mass of disparate data that has accumulated over the years. Even so, general patterns can begin to be recognized which are likely to reflect social and economic changes throughout the second half of the first century BC.[40]

Crucial to the development of the area were the military dispositions in the late first century BC. Scattered finds and an assessment of the road network allow at least a skeleton of the system to be suggested (fig 54c). In the immediate post-Caesarian period troops were based near, or billeted at, native settlements, but as the roads were laid down by Agrippa and successive governors, there seems to have been a movement to new establishments along the roads, most of which subsequently developed into towns.[41]

Against this may be compared the distribution of rich burials and luxury goods. A recent survey of the Dressel 1 amphorae from Belgica has shown there to be two notable concentrations, one in the Aisne valley in the tribal area of the Suessiones and Remi, the other in the Moselle valley, in the territory of the Treveri.[42] A comparison of the two maps (fig 54b and c) shows that the two concentrations lie astride two of the northern roads built by Agrippa. While this could be a coincidence (or future work could show the apparent concentrations to be spurious), taken at its face value the evidence strongly suggests that the native communities of these two regions were able to acquire wine in quantity, while those further to the north were in some way excluded. One possible explanation is that the early roads passing through the two tribal territories provided the opportunity for the exploitation of the trading system. It may even be that the local communities were favoured with some kind of monopoly agreement, but this must remain speculative.

Additional evidence for wealth accumulation in these two regions is provided by the distribution of richly furnished burials (fig 54a) several of which were equipped with a full range of wine-drinking gear imported from northern Italy. One of the most impressive of these élite burials was found at Goeblingen-Nospelt in Luxembourg. The burial (grave B) was provided with a bronze patella and jug of north Italian manufacture, accompanied by an Aco beaker and samian ware.[43] Together, the finds suggest a date in the last quarter of the first century BC.

The overall impression given by this evidence is that we are seeing what is essentially a native system, the wealth which had accumulated in the hands of an aristocracy being conspicuously consumed in the ritual associated with burial. Whether or not the socio-economic system which this reflects was akin to the prestige goods economy of the Hallstatt period it is impossible to say. What is interesting is that the system was working *within* the Roman provincial structure rather than beyond it. That this could be so is a further indication of the lightness of the Roman hold over the Belgic region in the three or four decades following the conquest.

If we are correct in seeing these concentrations of wealth as reflections of the command of long-distance trade routes, it is necessary to consider what evidence there is for the direction of the trade. One area with a productive potential was the northern part of Belgica — the territory of the Menapii, Nervii and Tungri and the tribes beyond. The region produced grain, cattle, salt and iron and it may well have been from the Ardennes that some of the smoked hams, which Strabo singles out for mention as one of the choice products of Gaul, were exported. In this scenario the élite of the Remi, Suessiones and Treveri would serve as the middle-men in an essentially

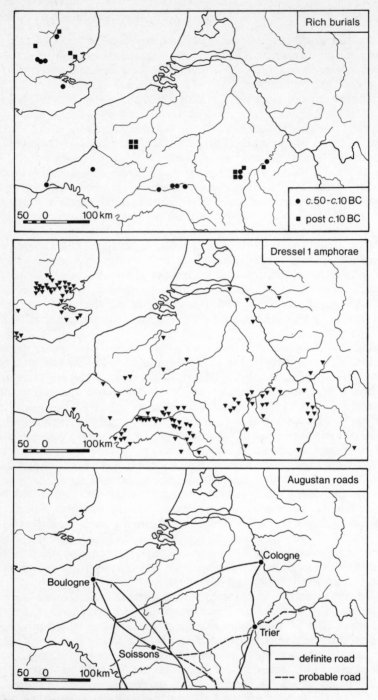

54 *Northern Gaul in the first century* BC: *aspects of social hierarchy in relation to communication.*
(After Haselgrove 1984, fig 1 [rich burials]; Fitzpatrick 1985, fig 5 [amphorae]; and Wightman 1977, fig 2 [roads])

native system of exchange, concentrating goods generated by the northern tribes and transferring them into the Roman economic system, relying on the road communications to transport supplies north to the military zone and south to the civilian markets of urbanized Gaul. If this view is broadly true, then it implies that the social and economic systems at work in Belgica in the forty or fifty years after Caesar remained essentially unromanized. The divide between Belgica and Lugdunensis would, then, reflect closely the different stages of political and urban development that the two regions had reached in the pre-Caesarian period.

Another area linked closely to the Belgic trading system was Britain. Indeed it may well have been for commercial as well as military reasons that one branch of the Augustan road system made for the Channel port of Gesoriacum (Boulogne). The effects of trade on the communities of Britain is vividly demonstrated by the distribution of Dressel 1B amphorae and richly furnished burials concentrating in the eastern part of the country around the estuary of the Thames, and the rivers flowing into the North Sea to the north of it.[44] The distribution underlines the importance of the Gesoriacum-Thames axis as the main cross-Channel route. A route via the Seine would have meant an unnecessarily long sea-journey, while the Rhine route was probably not yet sufficiently established to have become a major trading passage. It is particularly interesting to note that the area of eastern Britain most affected by the post-Caesarian trading contacts adopted many of the traits of Belgic Gaul, most noticeably the rite of cremation and a similar style and range of pottery. Some of the richer of the British burials were furnished in the Belgic manner, with buckets and sets of north Italian wine-drinking equipment. The details of this British development will be considered more fully in the next chapter. Here the point to be emphasized is that the two areas — southern Belgica and central eastern Britain — shared a broadly similar set of cultural traits in the post-Caesarian decades, sufficient to suggest that the communities on the two sides of the Channel were in intimate contact for some while. In Britain, the zone of rich burials denoted the emergence of the same kind of native economy that we have seen developing in two concentrations in southern Belgica.

When the British evidence is reviewed against indigenous developments, the phenomenon becomes even more remarkable in that it marks a total break with what has gone before. It may be significant that the area of 'Belgicization' in Britain is exactly coincident with that across which Caesar campaigned in 55 and 54 BC. He received the submission of a number of tribes, took hostages and established the level of tribute to be paid to Rome, thus creating a formal bond of relationships and obligations between central eastern Britain and the Roman world, where previously there had been only transient native alliances. What we are seeing in the acculturation of this area is rapid social and economic change brought about by regular long-distance trading contacts, operating within what was still a largely native system. It would not be unreasonable to consider southern Belgica and central eastern Britain as a single zone of conquered territory, responding in similar ways to the economic pressures generated by Rome.[45] From what little historical information survives from this period, it is clear that Augustus considered Britain to have been partially conquered, though unstable. In 34, 28 and again in 27 BC some thought was given to sending in expeditionary forces to maintain order, but nothing came of it. After the last occasion, the historian Cassius Dio recorded that Britain would not come to terms. This event, and not the departure of Caesar in 54 BC, signifies the split. After this, southern Belgica became increasingly Romanized, while the British communities continued in freedom.[46] It was in the early part of the first century AD that a fully developed prestige goods economy emerged (pp.149–153).

If the western branch of Agrippa's northern road system facilitated trade with Britain, the eastern branch, through Trier to Cologne, was the principal route, not only to the centre of the military zone, but also to free Germany beyond. Until 12 BC the Rhine had formed the boundary, and for forty years or so conditions had been stable enough to allow regular patterns of exchange to develop. After 12 BC, when the military advance into Germany began, and for nearly thirty years until the final withdrawal in AD 16, the need to supply the campaigning army was paramount. The Rhine itself became a major zone of communication while the territory behind it — Belgica — now underwent a period of Romanization that was to integrate it totally into the Roman world.

8 Progress through Britain

Throughout the later prehistoric period, well-established sea routes linked the British Isles to Continental Europe. Sometimes trade was brisk; on other occasions there were long periods when the island communities developed in isolation. The reasons for this ebb and flow were complex and are now largely inaccessible, but the approach of Rome in the late second or early first century BC introduced a new dynamic which, because of a scattering of relevant literary sources, can be more readily understood. But to put the Roman advance through Britain into its proper perspective it is necessary to begin in the first half of the first millennium BC, reviewing some of the points raised in previous chapters.

Prehistoric trade patterns

Throughout the Bronze Age, with increasing momentum, the redistribution of metals, copper, tin, their alloy bronze, and to a lesser extent gold, was carried out within a complex exchange system which involved the shipping of considerable quantities of metal, in the form of ingots, finished items or scrap, from the metal-producing areas of the west — Brittany, Cornwall, Wales and Ireland — to those parts of Britain and the Continent unable to supply their own needs from local sources. In the highly imperfect archaeological record, this 'trade' is manifest in the distribution of scrap hoards containing broken weapons and tool types manufactured sometimes many hundreds of kilometres away.[1] A particularly vivid example is provided by the distribution of Armorican axes, manufactured in Brittany in the middle of the first millennium BC. They were hoarded in vast numbers in Brittany, and seldom show any evidence of finishing or use, suggesting that, though a recognized axe form, they probably functioned as ingots. The type is found in Britain, concentrating on the south coast, where they must have been brought, as one item in mixed cargoes, by ships plying between Brittany and the British south-coast ports (fig 55). The distribution of many other bronze types tells much the same story of cross-Channel exchange.[2]

Within such a system, certain easily accessible south-coast sites would have become favoured ports-of-call. Three can be readily identified: Mount Batten, near Plymouth, the Portland–Weymouth Bay region and Hengistbury. All three lie in the centres of dense distributions of bronze artefacts, and each has produced some additional evidence of occupation in the early first millennium BC. At Mount Batten, for example, quantities of bronze scrap, ingots and evidence of bronze-working suggest a range of industrial

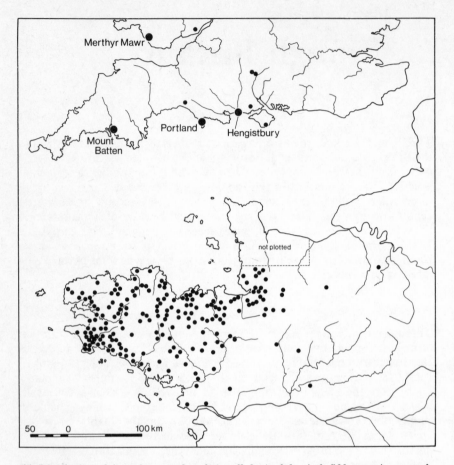

55 *Distribution of Armorican axe hoards (small dots) of the sixth-fifth centuries* BC *and major British ports (large dots) of the sixth-second centuries* BC.
(After Cunliffe 1982, fig 4 with additions)

activities, and proximity to the tin and copper sources of Dartmoor and the south-west would have made direct access to newly-won raw materials comparatively easy.[3] There must have been many other ports of this kind around the British coasts, serving both as contact points for Continental shippers and trans-shipment centres for short-haul coastal traffic. The discovery of two potential wreck sites, producing a range of bronzes, at Moor Sand, Salcombe, Devon, and Langdon Bay, Dover in Kent provides an added insight into the difficulties of maritime transport at this time.[4]

After the middle of the first millennium BC iron came increasingly into use and since the metal was more widely available the long-established trade in bronze dwindled, though not to extinction. Over much of Britain, evidence for long-distance trade becomes increasingly slight and the archaeological record suggests a developing inward-looking regionalism. Ports like Hengist-bury and probably Portland seem to have been abandoned. But the decline in overseas trade was not universal: Mount Batten certainly continued to be active and, as we have suggested above (p.28), it may well have been one of the principal ports involved in the tin trade. There are suggestions too that other ports may have developed to facilitate the exploitation of western metals. At Merthyr Mawr Warren in south Wales, near Bridgend, suggestive evidence pointing to a late first millennium BC industrial site on the river Ogmore has been amassed over the years.[5]

The re-invigoration of long-distance trade

The continuation of the old metal-trading routes of the south- west into the third and second centuries BC can best be seen as the maintenance of traditional systems, intensified perhaps by the increasing demand for tin by the Greek colonists of the western Mediterranean. But in about 100 BC, as we have seen (pp.98–104), a great transformation took place, when the Roman entrepreneurs, established in southern Gaul, began to manipulate and extend the Atlantic routes, drawing from Britain the products now so much in demand: metals, corn, hides and slaves.

The initial thrust of this new enterprise focused on the coast of central southern Britain, the port of Hengistbury serving as a collecting base for commodities from central southern and south-western Britain. Imported Roman luxury goods such as wine, figs and exotic glass items were probably widely distributed to the inland communities, but the principal components of the trading system were accompanied by a number of more locally-generated exchanges, manifest in the importation of quantities of north-western French pottery and the manufacture and distribution of local wheel-turned pottery and shale armlets.[6]

The effects of all this on the local community must have been considerable. The long-established socio-economic system, comprising a series of territorial chiefdoms based on centrally placed and strongly defended hillforts, appears to have come to an abrupt end at about this time, with the forts and many of the farming settlements being abandoned. The social reformation which followed is at present difficult to disentangle, but it seems to have involved the emergence of large and sometimes undefended settlements located at route nodes, particularly at river crossings, implying that control of the movement of commodities was now a paramount consideration.[7]

The situation was further confused by folk movement. Caesar, referring to the Belgic tribes of northern Gaul, explicitly states that sometime in the recent past (*c.* 100–80 BC?), raiding parties, having attacked the shores of Britain, decided to settle. He gives no further details. The geography, chronology and indeed the reality of this Belgic incursion has been hotly debated in the past. The traditional belief was that they penetrated Kent and the Thames estuary and caused widespread cultural upheaval, but several scholars have recently argued that all these changes, in ceramic styles, burial rite, coinage, etc. were in fact post-Caesarian. The simplest approach to the question would be to ask: where did the later Roman settlers believe the Belgae to have settled? The answer is central southern Britain, focused on the Solent and the Test and Itchen valleys, with Winchester (*Venta Belgarum*) later becoming the Roman administrative centre (fig 56). This makes good sense of a slightly later event in the 40s BC when Commius, a chieftain of the Atrebates, fled to Britain 'to join his people already here' and carved out a kingdom for himself with its capital at Silchester (*Calleva Atrebatum*), inland from the Belgic enclave.[8] If this interpretation is correct, then the collapse of the old socio-economic system in central southern Britain in the early first century BC may have been caused by a coincidence of events, including the rapid development of Roman-inspired overseas trade *and* the incursion of

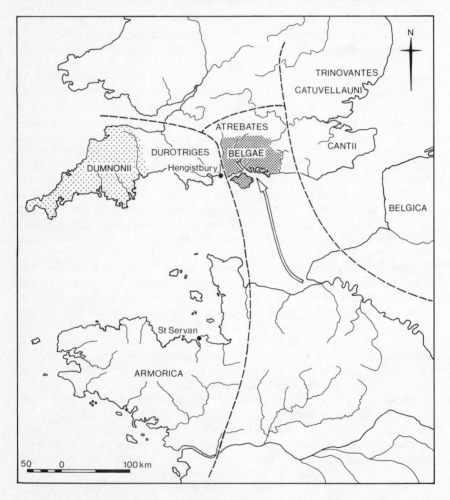

56 *Zones of cross-channel contact in the first century BC showing possible movement of the Belgae to Britain*

Belgic settlers. It is difficult, on present evidence, to distinguish the relative importance of these factors and to assess to what extent they were geographically and chronologically distinct.

A separate issue which deserves consideration is the increasingly close relationship between the tribes of northern France and eastern Britain. Probably as early as 125 BC, Gallo-Belgic coins minted by the principal Belgic tribes began to reach Britain.[9] Gallo–Belgic A and B probably arrived during the same period, and their joint distribution focuses on the lower Thames Valley, covering Kent and Essex, with some slight penetration inland and occasional appearances on the south coast. The slightly later Gallo–Belgic C, which develops imperceptibly from A, occupies much the same area. All three are gold coinages of the kind that would have featured in gift exchange. It is tempting to see these distributions as a reflection of social interchange between the communities of the lower Thames zone and the adjacent coasts of Belgic Gaul. That such relationships existed is made clear by Caesar who, referring to Diviacus (high king of the Suessiones), says that he held sway over large areas of Britain. These traditional social allegiances were later put to good use by the Romans, as we shall see below.

The acceptance in eastern Britain of gold coinage as a suitable item for gift exchange led to the minting of a range of local gold coinages in the peripheral areas stretching from Dorset to Lincolnshire. The exact chronology of these British developments is still in some doubt, but it has recently been argued that all the early British types developed roughly together in the period 80–60 BC.[10] It is highly unlikely that the gold issues would have been used in any form of market exchange, since their value would always have been far too high, but in Kent and the lower Thames valley there developed a low denomination coinage made in high tin-bronze. These issues, sometimes called '*potin*' after similar French types, were probably made initially in imitation of coins issued by Massalia, and the series is now thought to have begun before the Caesarian conquest. If this dating is correct then these Kentish cast bronze issues may well represent the local production of low denomination coins designed to facilitate exchange at the market level. In other words they may reflect a development from the traditional embedded economy to more organized trade of a market kind.[11] The extreme paucity of Roman goods in the lower Thames zone in the pre-Caesarian period strongly suggests that whatever cross-Channel trade took place at this time between the Belgae of northern Gaul and their British neighbours in eastern Britain it suffered no Roman interference and was articulated solely by the exchange of goods and services produced and distributed within the two neighbouring zones. It was therefore in stark contrast to the Atlantic route, which brought a range of Mediterranean luxuries to central southern Britain.

Britain after Caesar

Caesar's conquest of Gaul in the 50s BC introduced a totally new situation. Gaul to the Channel coast was now Roman territory. However, as we have seen, Romanization was delayed for several decades, especially in the north, and for a while there seems to have been little dramatic change. In the west the Atlantic sea-ways continued to be used, but if quantities of imported wine amphorae are a fair reflection of its intensity, the actual bulk of trade greatly declined and the wine supplied tended now to come from eastern Spanish and southern French vineyards rather than from Italy. In parallel with this, the eastern contacts between Belgic Gaul and the lower Thames zone now intensified. In the archaeological record this manifests itself in the way in which the British communities began to adopt many aspects of Belgic culture.

Distinctive ceramic forms, the rite of cremation in small cemeteries and the fitting out of the richer burials with wine-drinking equipment are all characteristics which can be found on both sides of the Channel, but were unknown in eastern Britain in the earlier decades. The explanation must be that the social and economic contacts between the two regions intensified in the post-Caesarian period, the aristocracy of the British communities adopting attributes of status from their neighbours. The early sets of wine-drinking equipment were of north Italian manufacture and were most likely to have been imported as high status goods which could be passed into the essentially native social system as diplomatic gifts. That the Aylesford-Swarling culture of the lower Thames zone became virtually indistinguishable from that of Belgic Gaul is a measure of the intensity of the contact between the two regions in the period *c.* 50–10 BC.[12]

The rich burials of this period are not numerous, but together they fairly reflect the range of imports available. At Aylesford, the richest burial of the cemetery (burial Y) consisted of a large circular chalk-lined pit furnished with a bronze-plated wooden bucket, containing the cremation and a brooch, together with a number of pots, a bronze *oenochoe* (jug) and a bronze *patella* (pan), both manufactured in northern Italy in the second half of the first century BC. It is the only rich burial of this date found in Kent. The others come from the vicinity of Welwyn in Hertfordshire, commanding the point where the valley of the river Lea emerges from the Chiltern ridge (fig 57). Three graves, Welwyn A and B and Welwyn Garden City produced imported bronze vessels; two, Welwyn B and Welwyn Garden City, also contained Roman silver cups of Augustan date, while all three, together with Hertford Heath, were furnished with Dressel 1B amphorae. Hertford Heath also yielded an imported glass bowl.

This tight cluster of richly furnished burials, no more than 15km apart, must represent the emergence of an aristocracy able to control the movement of luxury goods and to capture select status-related items for conspicuous consumption in the burials of the leading nobles. The parallel with the Hallstatt D chieftain burials of western central Europe is striking, and may well reflect the emergence of a similar prestige goods economy.

Once established in the east of Britain, the fashion for rich burial continues up to the time of the Roman conquest of AD 43. Graves at Mount Bures, Stanfordbury (A and B), Lexden and Snailwell maintain the tradition, each containing one or more amphorae, and a range of imported pottery — both Gallo-Belgic and *terra sigillata*. Imported bronze and glass vessels occur, but

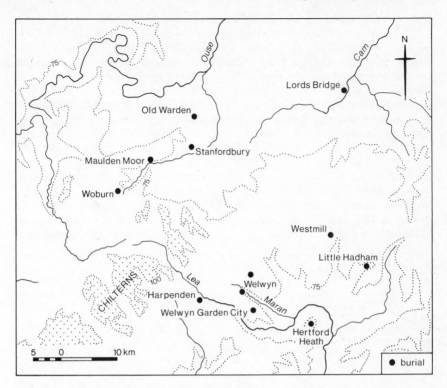

57 Elite burials of the period 50 BC–AD 50 in relation to routes through the Chilterns between the Thames valley and the valleys of the Ouse and Cam

less regularly, and hearth furniture in the form of iron spits and fire-dogs is a frequent accompaniment. It is the presence of imported fine tablewares that enable the later group to be distinguished from the earlier, and dated to after *c.* 10 BC. For convenience, the early rich burials are referred to as belonging to the Welwyn phase (50–10 BC); the later to the Lexden phase (10 BC–AD 50).

With so few burials to consider, it is difficult to make reliable generalizations about shifts in centres of power, but two points stand out: first, there is a marked shift away from Kent during the second half of the first century BC, and second, after an initial early focus on the upper reaches of the river Lea in the period 50–10 BC, the later centres of power appear to be more dispersed. There is a distinct concentration on the Essex coast and another west of the Chilterns, close to the Great Ouse-Ivel confluence (fig 57). An isolated example at Snailwell, in the Little Ouse valley, may be the sole recorded survival of another group to the north. If each concentration reflects a centre of aristocratic power controlling trade then the conclusion would seem to be that there was a movement away from the Thames estuary to more peripheral regions during the hundred years or so before the conquest. It would be wise, however, to remind ourselves that rich burial is only one of the ways in which status and wealth may be demonstrated, and it is quite possible that in some regions wholly different methods of display were in operation. The surprising scatter of gold torcs of first-century BC date found in East Anglia is an indication that other systems of wealth concentration, whether comparable or not to the burials, were practised nearby.

The rich burials, with their wide range of imported Roman luxury goods, show that a lively trade was maintained with the Roman world, initially through the middle-men of Belgic Gaul, and later, as the road system and ports developed, more directly by Roman entrepreneurs. The concentration of luxury goods, and in particular Dressel 1B amphorae, demonstrates beyond doubt that the thrust of the trading expeditions was towards eastern Britain, north of the Thames (fig 58). This area was controlled by a tribal complex which comes down to us, through the coin evidence, under the names of the Trinovantes and Catuvellauni.[13] In this area Caesar concentrated his two short campaigns of 55 and 54 BC, claiming, when he returned

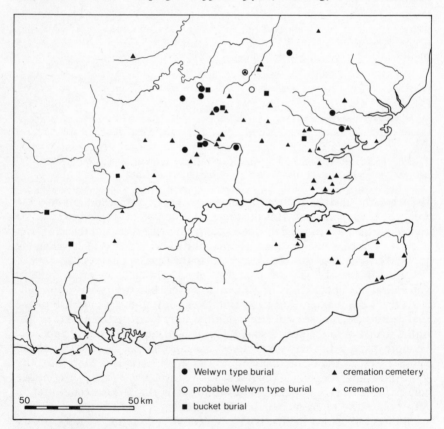

58 *Elite burials of the period 50 BC–AD 50 in eastern Britain.*
(After Cunliffe 1978, fig 6.4)

to Gaul, that he had established diplomatic relations with the principal tribes. It was no doubt the effects of these campaigns, and the political and social obligations established at the time, that made the eastern zone the focus of Roman interest after the conquest of Gaul. There is, however, little direct evidence to suggest what form the contact took. On the one hand, the imports in the graves could be little more than diplomatic gifts, supplied by the Roman administration to maintain established links of clientage and patronage; on the other, they could represent one manifestation of a flood of imports introduced during commercial transactions. In all probability both systems were in operation at the same time.

That some form of regular commercial activity developed in southern Britain is suggested by the numismatic and settlement evidence. After the Gallic war, marked by the minting of Gallo–Belgic E coinage in Belgic Gaul and its spread to the south-east of Britain, a number of local coinages developed, many including both gold staters and coins of lesser denomination. The distribution patterns of the various issues are complex and overlapping, but it is possible to discern sixteen or so recurring zones in the south-east, each of which probably represented a discrete socio-economic region (fig 59). The finds cluster into two broad groupings: the central southern zone, where issues of Commius and his successors were dominant, and an eastern zone, north of the Thames, where Trinovantian/Catuvellaunian coins concentrated. Along the interface, particularly in east Kent and the middle Thames, there is a high degree of overlapping. It is tempting to see, in this two-fold division, a reflection of an earlier political divide — between the intrusive Belgic element in the centre south and the indigenous tribes of eastern Britain — emphasized by the political allegiances of the Caesarian period, which seem to have left the Belgic zone of the centre south in economic isolation.[14]

In most of the smaller socio-economic regions it is possible to recognize one or more urban settlement, usually sited to command important route nodes (fig 60). In east Kent, for example, the earliest settlement at Bigbury seems to have been abandoned some time during this period in favour of a site closer to the river, now beneath the Roman (and later) town of Canterbury. In west Kent, however, the *oppidum* of Oldbury occupied a hilltop location. The focus in the St Albans region of Hertfordshire seems to have shifted from the riverside site of Wheathampstead to a similar location on the river Ver, where later the Roman town of Verulamium was to develop. Similar continuity from the Late Iron Age to the Roman period can be detected at Winchester (*Venta Belgarum*), Silchester (*Calleva Atrebatum*) and Colchester (*Camulodunum*). Dorchester-on-Thames, in Oxfordshire, provides an interesting example of an even longer implied continuity, from the Early-Middle Iron Age hillfort of Wittenham Clumps to the Thames-side siting of Dyke Hills (for which a Late Iron Age date is suggested but not proved) and then to the Roman fort and later town of Dorchester.

Far too little of any of these Late Iron Age *oppida* has been excavated to throw light on layout or overall planning, but it is possible to suggest that there may have been a change over time from the enclosed form of *oppidum*,

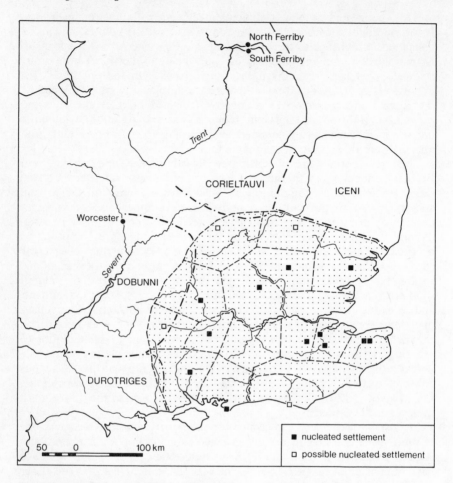

59 *The dynastic coinages of south-eastern Britain (stippled) and the tribal coinages of the surrounding area, showing nucleated settlements and their theoretical territories in the dynastic zone. (After Cunliffe 1981, figs. 15 and 20)*

like Dyke Hills, Dorchester, defended by ramparts and ditches, to a more open form in which a large territory, delineated by earthworks, was utilized for a variety of functions focusing at different locations within. Camulodunum is the best known example of one of these. Not all of the potential urban sites conform to these characteristics and many may have remained quite small throughout.[15]

Central southern and eastern Britain constituted a core zone, characterized by a well-developed system of coinage, by urban settlement and by the consumption of quantities of imported Roman luxury goods. Around that core were four peripheral tribal groups, each of which developed its own coinage — the Iceni, the Corieltauvi, the Dobunni and the Durotriges (fig 59). The

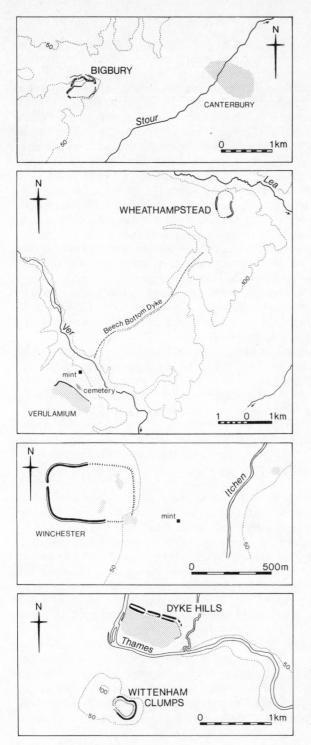

60 Selected oppida *in south-eastern Britain. (After Cunliffe 1976, fig 5 and 1978, fig 6.6)*

distribution of each tribe's coins was largely restricted to the area within the tribal borders, implying that it was minted for purposes of internal exchange, whereas the coinage of the core area extended rather more freely into the zones of the peripheral tribes. This numismatic evidence is suggestive of a classic core-periphery relationship, the peripheral tribes acting as both producers and middle-men for commodities passing to the core. Thus, slaves won in Wales might be moved through Dobunnic territory, changing hands several times in a pattern of gift exchanges, involving the use of local coins, before reaching the core area at an *oppidum* like Dorchester-on-Thames. Once in the core zone, more regular forms of market exchange would have taken over, hastening the movement of the commodity to one of the east coast ports for trans-shipment to the Roman world. Roman luxury goods were drawn into the core zone, but little that is recognizable in the archaeological record found its way into the hands of the peripheral tribes. The medium of exchange in this direction may well have been bullion in the form of coins, which could be melted down and restruck to tribal models for internal transactions. To give some idea of the intensity of minting of coinage it may be pointed out that one of the eastern leaders, Cunobelin, who was in power for about 30 years, is estimated to have issued a million coins. How much of this coinage was circulated within the core region, and how much passed into the periphery, is impossible to know.

Each of the tribal regions is likely to have developed centres providing facilities for exchange, but few have yet been recognized with any degree of certainty. The Dobunni, we know, had three major *foci*: an enclosed *oppidum* at Salmonsbury, on the River Windrush; a larger *oppidum* of territorial type at Bagendon, north of Cirencester, on the River Churn; and a site of unknown type at Camerton, on a tributary of the Somerset Avon. Salmonsbury and Camerton were both occupied in the Middle Iron Age and continued to be so into the Roman period; the origins of Bagendon are obscure but nothing that need pre-date the first century AD has yet been found.[16]

The Durotriges seem to have relied on some of their long-established hillforts to provide centres for exchange in the Late Iron Age, but the evidence which is now beginning to accumulate suggests that the focus of activity may well now have been outside the ramparts, in large sprawling settlements which began to develop at the time. The old port-of-trade at Hengistbury continued in use and was the centre of production of wheel-made pottery and iron; it also probably housed a mint. The only site in the territory of the Durotriges which has the appearance of an enclosed *oppidum* has recently been identified near Ilchester, in the valley of the River Yeo.[17]

Of the centres of the Iceni in the pre-conquest period practically nothing is known, except by way of an unusual concentration of coins and other artefacts in the vicinity of Saham Toney which may prove to have had an early market function. The Corieltauvi were better served. Two major undefined settlements have been located at Old Sleaford and Dragonby, while there is some possibility that Leicester (*Ratae*) may have had a pre-Roman origin. Old Sleaford is known to have been a site where coin flans were made and probably struck.[18]

The relationship between the peripheral tribes and the communities beyond, living in the south-west, Wales and the north is difficult to define. These areas were the source of most of the non-ferrous metals produced in Britain and probably provided the majority of the slaves exported from the country. They could also have supplied hides and furs. Some form of exchange mechanism must have been maintained to ensure the regular flow of goods but how the exchange was articulated it is beyond the limit of the evidence to say. It is quite possible that regular meeting-places were in existence, on or close to tribal boundaries, perhaps associated with shrines. One possibility is the site of Worcester, on the River Severn close to the western boundary of the Dobunni, where a number of coins have come to light and an earthwork enclosure has been identified. Another is on either side of the Humber crossing, at South and North Ferriby, the border between the Corieltauvi and Parisi. The South Ferriby site has produced a range of coins and brooches, while North Ferriby has yielded an impressive variety of Gallo–Roman fine wares. This assemblage, however, is more likely to be of the conquest period and is therefore relevant to a later part of this chapter.[19]

Standing back from the range of evidence briefly reviewed here for the pre-conquest period in Britain, a clear picture begins to emerge. The country can be divided into three broad zones — core, periphery and beyond. In the core zone, occupying much of the south-east, a complex pattern of socio-economic zones can be defined, each with one or more 'urban' centre. A well- developed system of coinage provided the means by which a range of commodities could be drawn through the system and concentrated for export to the Roman consumer market in Gaul and beyond. Reciprocal systems allowed luxury imports to disseminate within the core zone. Around the core, the peripheral tribes were organized into four broad groupings, each with its own coinage and with some specialist settlements, of urban or proto-urban character, where commodities could be exchanged. Some of these locations lay close to the borders of the tribe, on the inner interface with the core and the outer interface with the less developed tribes beyond. The coinage systems and the settlement evidence suggests a considerable variation in the level of socio-economic organization reached by the four peripheral tribes. The situation in each was fluid, and developing. Beyond, to the north and west of the Exe-Severn-Trent line, the tribes show little sign of having developed significantly from the simple economic systems already in force in the Early and Middle Iron Age. Slave-raiding as a means of producing a marketable surplus was a new disruptive factor in traditional endemic warfare and cattle-raiding, ensuring that the communities remained alienated and fragmented. Thus, at the time of the Roman invasion in AD 43, Britain could be divided into three parts. It is against this division that the progress of the Roman conquest can best be understood.

The Roman conquest

The conquest initiated by Claudius in AD 43 had been in the minds of the Roman leadership since the time of Caesar's daring sorties in 55 and 54 BC. The ninety years which separated the two events saw a growing relationship between the leaders of the British tribes and Rome. On several occasions, British aristocrats fled to Rome for protection when ousted by rivals, and by AD 43 there must have been a considerable expatriate British community living under Roman protection. Clearly, several of the leading families of Britain were bound in a system of clientage and obligation to the head of the Roman state, who, in return, provided patronage in the form of protection, gifts and probably trading monopolies going back to the treaties negotiated by Caesar. The system would have suited Rome for as long as equilibrium was maintained.[20]

The invasion of AD 43 was preceded by the flight of one of the Atrebatic chieftains to Rome, implying a degree of enhanced unrest in the south, but this can hardly have been a reason for conquest, even though it might have been presented as such. The real reason lay in the aspirations of the Emperor Claudius, and the need he felt to establish his position in Rome by a military triumph; to qualify he had to conquer a new territory with minimal loss of Roman life.[21]

The invasion had been carefully planned, in full knowledge of the geography and tribal politics of the country. The initial landing took place in Kent and, after overcoming concerted opposition at the Medway, the troops moved onwards to the Thames, which they crossed with ease. A short pause allowed the emperor to travel from Rome to join his men at the assault of Camulodunum, one of the principal *oppida*, after which he was able to leave the rest of the mopping-up to the troops and return to Rome to enjoy his triumph. What followed was the systematic advance across the south-east to the Exe-Severn-Trent line, where, by AD 47, a frontier had been established — supported in the rear by a military road known now as the Fosseway. In other words, it seems to have been the intention at the outset to take over the territory of the core and peripheral zone, up to the interface between the peripheral tribes and the underdeveloped tribes beyond. This would have brought the settled and semi-urbanized part of Britain under direct Roman control, leaving the less civilized part of the island to its own devices. The clear-sighted logic of this decision had been born in the disastrous German campaigns of thirty to forty years before, when the Roman leadership learnt that while conquest of urbanized barbarians was comparatively simple, control of a non-centralized and fragmented enemy with space to manoeuvre was virtually impossible.

The initial conquest was accomplished without significant difficulty. After the capitulation of Camulodunum, the *Legio XX* remained in reserve, while *Legio IX* and *Legio XIV* fanned out across the Midlands. The *Legio II* may already have been in Atrebatic territory by this time, ready to take the Durotriges and Dobunni. It was only here that serious resistance was recorded. Two tribes had to be subdued and more than twenty fortified native capitals taken by force. From this it seems reasonable to suppose that the legions, led by Vespasian, came up against the hillforts of the Durotriges, which were refortified in opposition to the Roman advance. The task of subduing the south-west was quickly accomplished, but Vespasian clearly thought it expedient to disperse part of his military force throughout Durotrigan territory — in permanent forts — to maintain surveillance. The behaviour of the Durotriges might, at first sight, seem to suggest that they were far less centralized than the other tribes, resorting to hillforts for their opposition, but this need not have been so. There is no evidence to suggest that the hillforts had been *continuously* occupied. It could well be that the tribe was unified in its opposition to Rome and took to the old hillforts merely as a convenient means of organizing its resistance. At any event, confrontation with Rome failed, although opposition and hostility remained for at least two decades.[22]

The initial advance had been fast and its momentum had carried it forward without significant hindrance, but opposition was soon to come, in the winter of AD 47–8, when the Silures of south Wales, led by Caractacus, a renegade warlord from the south-east, initiated a series of fierce attacks against a tribe allied to Rome. This would seem to suggest that the Dobunni may originally have extended to the west side of the Severn, and that this part of the tribe, though beyond the newly-imposed frontier, maintained friendly relations with Rome. By this stage, the potential instability of the frontier must have begun to be realized and, with a growing awareness of the geography of free Britain, the next commander, Ostorius Scapula, embarked upon a limited advance, south-west into Cornwall and west into the Midlands to the Welsh Marches. The occupation of Cornwall was a sensible move, not only in shortening the land frontier, but in providing more easy control of the Severn estuary, while the advance into the Midlands had the effect of isolating the native opposition in the mountainous areas of Wales, separating them from easy combination with the potential opposition in the north. The advance was virtually complete by AD 51, but much of the following decade had to be spent campaigning in Wales and monitoring events in the north.

The early Romanization of the south-east (fig 61)

The territory south and east of the Fosse frontier was immediately developed as a Roman province, but in an *ad hoc* manner reflecting the variety of its socio-political tradition.[23] Two semi-independent client kingdoms were set up or, more probably, were allowed to continue in existence. The Regni in the south occupied part of the original Belgic area, which had more recently come under the control of the Atrebatic ruling house. Their king, Cogidubnus, was well-favoured by the Roman administration and was given additional territories to rule. He maintained his nominal autonomy until his death in the mid-seventies AD. The Iceni of eastern England were also allowed to retain their independence, even after a brief uprising in AD 47 following which King Prasutagus was confirmed in power. It was his death in

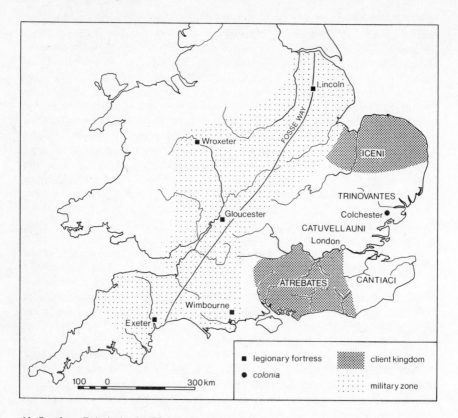

61 Southern Britain in the Claudio-Neronian period

AD 60 which precipitated the rebellion led by his wife Boudica. Elsewhere, the Roman administrative structure was erected largely on the basis of the original tribal system, and many of the pre-Roman urban centres were developed to become the urban administrative centres of the tribal territories. At Verulamium, for example, a street grid was created, and in one area a row of timber-built shops was erected. It is quite possible that military engineers were employed to design and lay out these early settlements.

Not all early towns were built on previously occupied sites. London, for example, appears to have been a completely new foundation. By AD 60 Tacitus tells us that it was 'teeming with traders and settlers', many of whom were no doubt foreigners attracted to the new province by the prospect of growing rich on the economic possibilities which its exploitation offered.

The heavy hand of the Roman administrator was all too apparent, and many of the acts of official consolidation must have been seen by the native communities as deliberate provocation. Within the old tribal capital of Camulodunum a large legionary fortress was built for the *Legio XX*, held in reserve in the rear of the advance, and after the legion had moved forward to

Gloucester in AD 48–9 the site was developed as a *colonia* for veterans. This meant that large tracts of tribal land were confiscated from the native population and reallocated to retired soldiers — an act which cannot have failed to arouse deep resentment. To add to the injury, a huge temple was erected in the new *colonia*, dedicated to the deified emperor. It was an arrogant statement that Rome was here to stay.

What happened at Camulodunum was an outstanding example of the effects of Roman imperialism, but everywhere in the conquered territories there would have been many lesser acts of heavy-handed arrogance. At Bath, for example, a road, possibly the Fosseway, sliced through the centre of what would have been the *temenos* sacred to the native goddess Sulis, dividing one of the thermal springs from another. Such sacrilege must have infuriated the local population.

The invasion of AD 43 and the subsequent advance into the Midlands and Wales would have seen the slaughter of a substantial portion of the young male population. Others would have been captured and sold into slavery and many would have thrown in their lot with Rome and joined the army as auxiliaries, to serve abroad. In this way, the potential for native resistance was greatly weakened for a generation, while the province was being reorganized, but in AD 60 a rebellion broke out among the Iceni and spread rapidly to much of the rest of the country. The immediate cause was the Roman administration's mismanagement of the events following the death of the client king, Prasutagus. It seems that the Roman intention was to absorb the kingdom into the province. This was opposed by Prasutagus's wife Boudica, and the military detachment sent in to deal with the situation made matters worse by flogging the queen and raping her daughters. Then, as Tacitus tells us, 'the Icenian nobles were deprived of their ancestral estates'.[24]

The rebellion which followed was a severe set-back for Rome. It was soon put down, but the cost was considerable. The three major towns, London, Verulamium and Camulodunum, had been burnt down, the countryside was ravaged and one estimate put the British dead as high as 80,000. The entire economic system must have been destroyed. It is no wonder that the emperor Nero seriously considered abandoning the province. In the event, no withdrawal took place, but it was a decade before the damage could be made good.

Northern Britain

Throughout this time, AD 60–70, Wales and the north remained comparatively calm. Beyond the northern frontier lay the Brigantes, a loose confederacy of communities occupying a territory stretching, as Tacitus tells us, from sea to sea. These people were allied to Rome and therefore formed a buffer state protecting Roman-occupied territory from the tribes beyond. The rebel Caractacus, who had led resistance to Rome in Wales, fled to the Brigantian royal household for protection in AD 51, but was turned over to the Roman authorities by Queen Cartimandua — who was no doubt acting within the strict limits of her agreement with Rome. The confederacy was, however, unstable, not least because of the antagonism which soon developed between Cartimandua and her husband Venutius. In AD 57–8 a legion had to be sent in to protect the queen's interests. The situation deteriorated still further when open revolt against the pro-Roman group, stirred up by Venutius, forced the army to intervene once more, this time to snatch Cartimandua to safety. Thus, by about AD 70, as Tacitus so effectively puts it, 'the throne was left to Venutius, the war to us'.[25]

For nearly thirty years, therefore, the north of Britain beyond the military zone had been in direct and often friendly contact with Rome. Before the invasion, the tribes had been far from the influence of Rome, beyond the periphery of coin-issuing tribes, but in the years immediately following AD 43 they suddenly found themselves in immediate physical proximity to the Romans.

It was inevitable that complex trading relations would spring up. One site which deserves consideration in this regard is North Ferriby, on the north shore of the Humber estuary. Quantities of imported pottery — Gallo–Belgic and *terra sigillata* — found here suggest an unusual degree of activity in the Claudian period.[26] It is tempting to see North Ferriby as a trading base in free Britain, so sited that it would be in easy communication with the Roman bridgehead on the opposite side of the river, a few kilometres upstream at Winteringham, where a road led south to the legionary base at Lincoln. From North Ferriby, long-established routeways led north to the Yorkshire Wolds and the valley of the Swale, and beyond to the densely settled landscape of Durham and Northumberland. There is now ample evidence to show that these areas of north-eastern Britain practised a mixed farming régime and could, no doubt, have managed to produce a surplus of grain and cattle to satisfy part of the demands of the Roman quartermasters serving the frontier troops south of the Humber-Mersey axis.

The establishment of regular trade with the Romans must have brought about changes in the social and economic systems of these northern barbarian tribes. Most dramatic was the development of a massive *oppidum* at Stanwick, strategically sited between the rivers Swale and Tees, at the point where the Stainmoor Pass leads westwards across the Pennines.[27] Stanwick thus commanded a major route node. Its importance is reflected in its size — three hundred hectares enclosed within massive defences. Recent archaeological work has shown that occupation began soon after the invasion, and already, in the 40s, imported Roman fine wares including *terra sigillata* were reaching the site. If the great earthworks began to be erected as early as this, which now seems highly likely, then Stanwick is best seen as a direct reflection of the remarkable socio-economic change gripping the northern barbarians in the three decades or so following the invasion. From being an economically underdeveloped area in AD 40, without coinage and well beyond the immediate influence of Rome, by AD 70 it had developed many of the attributes of the urbanized pre-conquest south-east.

Political unrest and the constant conflict between the pro-and anti-Roman factions among the Brigantes culminated in the expulsion of Cartimandua.

The Roman authorities could no longer tolerate a potentially dangerous situation on their northern flank and consequently, in AD 71, the governor Petillius Cerialis began the systematic conquest of the region. Within three years, if Tacitus is to be believed, he had triumphed over a major part of Brigantian territory. After an interlude of five years or so, while the Welsh tribes were being subdued, the northern advance was again driven forward, this time by Julius Agricola, and by AD 84 most of the north up to the foothills of the Grampian Mountains had been brought under Roman military control, while the army had campaigned far beyond.

Into Scotland (figs 62 and 63)

The mid-eighties were a time of consolidation. A line of forts was established, blocking the mouths of the glens leading deep into the Grampians, quite possibly in preparation for a final thrust into the mountains, but a crisis on the Rhine and Danube frontiers in AD 85–6 brought to an end any idea of the total conquest of Britain. In AD 86 the *Legio II Adiutrix* was recalled from Britain and the retreat from the north began, culminating, in the early years of the second century, during the reign of Trajan, with the creation of a frontier line across the Tyne-Solway isthmus, between the military bases at Carlisle and Corbridge. This Stanegate 'frontier' was soon to be consolidated, under the aegis of Hadrian, into the permanent complex of frontier defences known as Hadrian's Wall.

For about twenty years (*c.* 122–142) Hadrian's front line was maintained, though throughout its short life it was constantly being modified. The essential element was the complex of continuous barriers stretching across Britain, manned with permanent garrisons stationed in forts spaced at roughly regular intervals. To the north, in barbarian territory, outpost forts were maintained, linked to the frontier defences by roads.

In *c.* AD 142 the decision was taken to advance northwards through southern Scotland and to create a new frontier — the Antonine Wall — between the Clyde and the Firth of Forth. With one temporary break in the late 150s, the Antonine Wall was the frontier of Britain until about AD 163, when once more the old Hadrianic line was brought back into commission. Apart from the maintenance of outposts, and one brief period of campaigning into the far north under the Emperor Severus in the early third century, the Tyne-Solway line formed the effective boundary of Roman-administered territory until the collapse of Roman rule in the early years of the fifth century AD.[28]

This brief summary highlights the complexity of military activities in the north. Clearly, with frequently changing policies creating periodic advances and withdrawals, the relationship between the Roman administrative system and the native communities must have been in a state of constant flux. There was hardly time for a system to stabilize before it was upset by another military decision. This being said, Scotland can be divided into two regions: the south, from the Tyne northwards to the foothills of the Grampians; and the north, comprising the Grampians and beyond, and including the Western

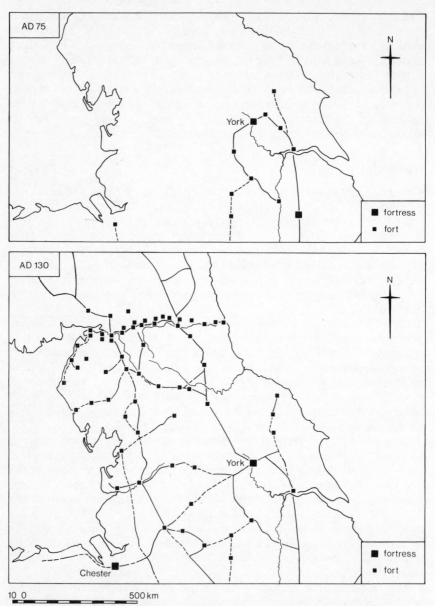

62 The military dispositions in northern Britain in AD 75 and AD 130. (After Breeze &
Dobson 1985, figs 1 and 5)

and Northern Isles. The southern region, thus defined, was the zone of
maximum Roman contact, sometimes wholly or partially occupied,
sometimes campaigned through and always within close reach of the Roman

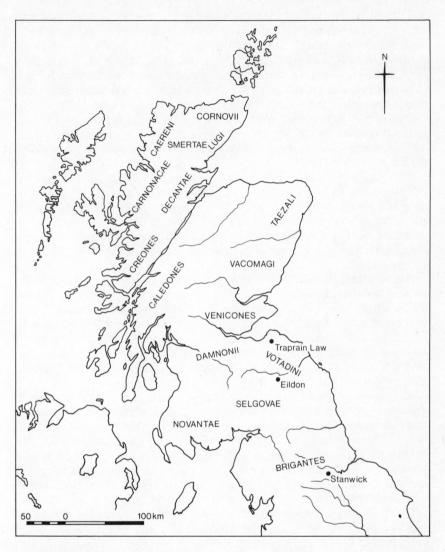

63 The tribes of northern Britain. (After Cunliffe 1978, fig 8.3)

military presence. The northern zone, apart from the brief campaigns of Agricola in the late first century AD and Severus in the early third, can be regarded as free Britain, safely beyond the direct influence of Rome.

The southern region was occupied by six tribes: the Novantae and Damnonii in the west, the Selgovae and Votadini in the east between the Tyne and Forth, with the Venicones and Vacomagi to the north of the Forth, separated from each other by the Tay. The eastern side of southern Scotland was far more densely occupied than the west. The land was more congenial and through the Cheviots led the main routes north. The midland axis between the Forth and the Clyde provided the main access from east to west. It is hardly surprising, therefore, that it is in these zones that the main distribution of Roman artefacts is to be found. Opinions vary as to how these items made their way into native hands. One interpretation favours the view that most material was pilfered from abandoned Roman sites or stolen during raids, the other that the items were transferred through processes of legitimate gift exchange or marketing. In reality, both processes are likely to have been in operation, but the balance is in favour of the majority of the Roman goods passing legally and regularly into native hands through exchange mechanisms.[29]

The range of Roman material found on native sites is interesting: fine bronze vessels including paterae, jugs and strainers, high quality brooches, glass and *terra sigillata* vessels and gold and silver coinage. A detailed study of the coinage shows a close correspondence between the range of those found on native sites and the currency in use in neighbouring forts — a further factor in favour of the theory of legitimate transfer of goods to the native communities.

In southern Scotland much of this material may have changed hands in the vicinity of the forts themselves, the natives bringing for exchange the commodities which the troops needed. Celtic wheeled vehicles, horse harness, swords, tools, glass armlets, quernstones and oysters have all been found on fort sites, indicating the range of native products on offer. Occasionally there may have been substantial diplomatic gifts, as is implied by Dio Cassius' statement that the Emperor Severus 'bought peace from the Maeatae' in the early third century AD.

The general scatter of material and the apparent lack of concentration in graves or settlements would seem to suggest that society was not structured in such a way that a native aristocracy could control the flow of goods and grow rich on the proceeds, but there may be another explanation. Perhaps the volume of goods exchanged was too low to permit the development of a prestige goods economy. The productive capacity of Scotland was not great, nor did it have rare resources in any measure. The bulk of the material consumed by the army was transported from the south and it is even doubtful whether the native economy could have produced sufficient corn to feed the resident garrison. Another point which should not be overlooked is the considerable depth of the military zone — from York to the Tay is over 300km. Civilian traders would not have found the transport of bulk goods across such distances a particularly attractive prospect. Taken together then, a series of factors seem to have combined to ensure that the volume of goods exchanged between Roman and native (whether the native was beyond the military zone or temporarily engulfed by it) was never very great: it was probably little more than small-scale trading carried out on a one-to-one basis in the vicinity of the garrisons.

Beyond southern Scotland, very little Roman material penetrated, though a few items passed up the eastern coastal zone and by the second century AD Roman objects had reached Orkney, Shetland and the Western Isles. This trickle continued into the fourth century AD. While regular trading missions cannot be ruled out, the volume of material is so small that simple down-the-line exchange is a more likely mechanism.

The settlement archaeology of northern Britain is now sufficiently well known for the effects of the Roman presence or proximity to be recognized. The general pattern in southern Scotland and northern England was for the hillforts to be abandoned in favour of farmsteads or larger agglomerations, a number of which are found to overlie the earlier, now-defunct, fortifications. Another tendency was for drystone to replace earth and timber as a building material. But more impressive than these changes is the complete lack of any form of aggrandizement or Romanization: the native social structure seems to have remained largely unchanged.

One site which deserves particular note is the massive hillfort of Traprain Law dominating the plain of East Lothian looking across to the Firth of Forth (fig 64).[30] The earliest fortifications are prehistoric and enclose some 4ha. The area was later doubled, and in the late first or early second century AD it increased again to about 16ha, making it by far the largest and most impressive settlement north of Stanwick. Excavation in the interior has been somewhat limited but sufficient has been uncovered to show that by late Roman times settlement, at least in some parts, was dense. Drystone-walled houses of sub- rectangular shape clustered together along roads and around open 'squares'. The finds made during the excavations included much imported Roman material. *Terra sigillata* found its way to the site in quantity, beginning in the late first century AD, and Roman coins span the period up to the early fifth century.

The community was engaged in a wide range of activities in addition to farming. It is possible that distinctive, and widely distributed, glass bracelets were manufactured on the site, though no direct evidence of this has been found — only many broken examples. More certainty attaches to bronze-working. Crucibles and moulds have been discovered, together with an impressive array of small bronze artefacts including dress fasteners, dragonesque *fibulae*, penannular brooches, pins and horse-gear.

The overall impression given by Traprain is that it served as a major manufacturing and distribution centre throughout much of the period of Roman occupation, and it is tempting to see it as the principal *oppidum* of the Votadini — a seat of legitimate native power, allowed to remain in existence during the Roman interlude as the focus of the tribe. That in the early first millennium AD it maintained manufacturing and redistribution functions similar to those of the Middle Iron Age hillforts of central southern Britain is an indication of the comparatively low level of economic development experienced by the northern tribes, in spite of centuries of Roman contact.

The last stage of redefence at Traprain involved a reduction in size of the enclosed area to about 12ha by the construction of a massive stone-faced wall. The exact time of building is unknown, but a late fourth century date seems likely. By this stage, Britain north of the Tyne-Solway line was fast reverting to sub-Roman tribalism. A tantalizing glimpse of the situation is given by the *Ravenna Cosmography*, a list of place-names in the Roman world, compiled in

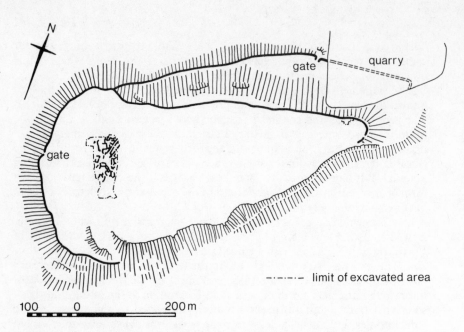

quarry

gate

gate

—·—·—·— limit of excavated area

100   0   200 m

64 The hillfort of Traprain Law showing in detail the buildings of the excavated area. After Hogg 1951, figs 53 and 54)

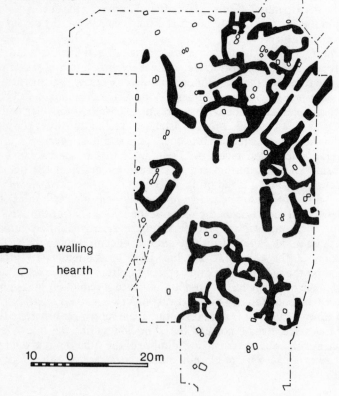

walling

hearth

10   0   20m

the seventh century AD. In one section, mention is made of a number of *loca*, or meeting places, several of which are evidently in Scotland. That they are listed implies official recognition.[31] Here, presumably, we are seeing the re-emergence of the native system of tribal meeting-places where, at fixed times during the year, justice could be dispensed, social contracts agreed, exchanges take place and the gods be worshipped. Significantly, at least four of the names begin with 'Maponi', referring to the Celtic god, Maponus. This is a further reminder of how thin the veneer of Romanization was in these northern regions.

Across the Celtic Sea

Finally, it remains to consider Ireland.[32] In AD 82 the Roman general, Agricola, stood on the west coast of Scotland and looked across to Ireland. His biographer, Tacitus, writes:

> I have often heard Agricola say that Ireland could be invaded and conquered with one legion and a few auxiliaries. It would be an advantage, especially with the pacification of Britain, if Roman arms were everywhere to be seen and independence swept from the map.

He goes on to say that the interior of Ireland is little known, but 'through commercial intercourse and the merchants there is better knowledge of harbours and approaches'.[33]

In the event, the conquest of Ireland was not attempted, wisely if later history is any guide, but the concentration of Roman objects on Irish sites in the hinterland of the harbours of Dublin and Cork is an indication that trading missions were not infrequent in the late first and second centuries AD. The merchants brought with them a range of trinkets, brooches and toilet sets, together with some *terra sigillata* and bronze vessels, mainly paterae. A few coins also found their way in. In return, the merchants acquired the much-famed Irish wolfhounds, hides and cattle. Significantly, hunting dogs, hides and cattle are among the commodities listed by Strabo as the principal exports of Britain in the late first century BC.

The context of Roman goods in Ireland is not well-known, but some have been found on the Crannog sites of Ballinderry and Lagore and there is a concentration of finds at the Rath of the Synods — a high-status site in the complex at Tara, one of the seats of legitimization of the Irish kings. Distributions of this kind are only to be expected, but there is nothing in the Irish archaeological record to suggest that trade with Britannia, and the manipulation of Roman goods, in any way influenced the Irish socio-economic system. That traditional systems of exchange were maintained over long periods is vividly demonstrated in the *Confessio* of St Patrick, written in the mid-fifth century AD. Captured in an Irish raid on a villa estate in Britain, Patrick spent six years as a slave on an Irish farm before he joined a merchant ship bound for Gaul with a cargo of dogs.

The wheel had come full circle. In the first century BC Mediterranean luxury goods were reaching the south-east of Britain in exchange for raw materials and slaves, binding the Mediterranean and barbarian systems together in a web of mutual dependence. Half a millennium later, similar processes were in operation. The communities of the Irish Sea were still exporting their dogs and slaves south along the Atlantic sea-ways, and in return Mediterranean wine amphorae and pottery made in western France were returning northwards, to appear on many sites in the Celtic west.[34]

9 Beyond the Rhine

To Julius Caesar the Rhine formed the logical boundary of the Roman world. Twice, in 55 and 53 BC, he had crossed the river to campaign among the Germans beyond, but this was an act of bravura irresistible to a man of Caesar's drive, rather than an attempt at conquest. At best it demonstrated to those beyond the river Rome's ability to instigate rapid, highly organized movements of troops: it also showed them the force of Roman arms. A few years later, in 38 BC, Agrippa mounted a punitive campaign, but again there was little thought of conquest.[1] In the decades following Caesar's Gaulish campaigns, the winter quarters of the legions were probably placed well back in Gaulish territory, though there must have been temporary works in the vicinity of the Rhine, with an adequate system of communications linking them. Little is yet known of these arrangements.

The military situation and the German campaigns

The period of apparent military inactivity in northern Gaul, *c.* 50–12 BC, was a time of consolidation elsewhere in the empire. After the Civil War, Augustus began a long process of limited expansion and reorganization. Campaigns in Illyricum and in Spain, followed by activity in Africa, Egypt and Arabia gradually brought the frontiers of the Roman world to their sensible geographical limits, in the case of Spain, freeing large numbers of Roman troops for activities elsewhere. In 20 BC Parthia was brought to heel with the return of Roman standards, lost years before, and the client kingdom of Armenia was created. By 19 BC a degree of stability had been established in the west, south and east and Augustus could now begin to look to the northern frontiers.

The advance began in 15 BC with the conquest of the Raeti and Vindelici in the Central Alps and Voralpenland and the annexation of the kingdom of Noricum, bringing under direct Roman control all the peoples south of the Danube.[2] It was probably during this period, *c.* 15–12 BC, that legions were established in permanent bases along the Rhine at Xanten, Vetera and probably also at Mainz and Neuss, in preparation for the greatest, and in many ways most audacious, of Augustus' military enterprises — the conquest of Germany. The preparations had been careful and systematic. The occupation of the Voralpenland had consolidated the eastern flank; the final conquest of Iberia had freed a considerable military force not only in Spain but also Aquitania; and the systematic consolidation of Gaul, culminating in the inauguration of the altar to Rome and Augustus at Lyon in 12 BC, had brought Caesar's conquered territories firmly within the Roman administrative system.

In 12 BC Drusus, the stepson of Augustus, crossed the Rhine to inflict defeat on the Sagambri, whose attempt to cross into Roman territory provided the immediate excuse for the advance. In 11 BC Drusus crossed the Rhine again, using the valley of the River Lippe for his main advance and establishing forts there (fig 65). In 10 and 9 BC he was again campaigning in Germany, thrusting first north, most probably from Mainz, and eventually reaching the River Elbe, which was probably considered to be the maximum extent of Germany it was necessary to conquer in order to create a stable and efficient frontier. Drusus died in 9 BC and was replaced by his brother

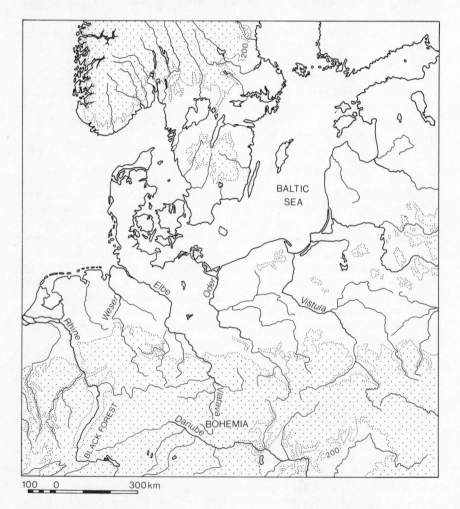

65 *Germania: high land and principal rivers*

Tiberius, who led further campaigns throughout Germany in 8–7 BC and in AD 4–5, at the end of which Germany seemed to be secure.[3]

It was now that attention turned to the Bohemian plateau — a fertile area held by a German tribe, the Marcomanni, who had recently ousted the Celtic Boii. The geographical position of Bohemia dissected by the River Vlatava, a tributary of the Elbe, made it of considerable importance to Rome, since it lay between the Elbe frontier and the Upper Danube. Control of Bohemia would have allowed the creation of a single frontier running from the Black Sea to the North Sea following major rivers in an almost straight line. In addition, Bohemia lay astride the ancient trade route linking the head of the Adriatic and the north European plain whence came a variety of desirable products including amber and furs. For the Roman merchants, control of the Vlatava valley would have ensured ease of access to commodities all too rare in the Mediterranean world.

Plans for the conquest of Bohemia were well underway in AD 6 when a revolt broke out in Illyricum.[4] Tiberius was sent in to pacify the region, but so serious was the uprising and so difficult the terrain that it took three years to restore order, and then only at considerable cost. At one time a colossal force of 15 legions and supporting auxiliaries was deployed, and it was necessary to raise a special war tax to pay for the exceptional costs.

Hardly had the rebellion been put down than news reached Rome of an uprising in Germany. Three legions under the command of Varus had been annihilated in the Teutenburg forest and virtually all the Roman garrisons north of the Rhine had been wiped out by the German war leader, Arminius.[5] Arminius, like so many able young warriors, Gallic or German, had spent some years as a cavalry officer in the service of the Romans. He was now turning his knowledge and experience of the Roman army to good use. His onslaught was so sudden and unexpected that the surviving Roman forces in Germany only just managed to hold the Rhine. Two decades of conquest and consolidation in Germany had been totally destroyed in a matter of weeks.

In the next year, AD 10, Tiberius was present in the military zone along the south bank of the Rhine, presumably consolidating his forces to prevent further incursions: in the following season he was confident enough to cross the river in a limited show of strength. The events of the next few years are obscure, but some limited advances were evidently being undertaken. However, it was not until after Augustus' death in AD 14 that the reconquest of Germany began in earnest, now under the command of Germanicus.[6] In AD 15 and 16 his campaigns began with land and sea forces converging on the River Ems, and in 16 he had crossed the River Weser. According to Tacitus, Germanicus believed that had he been allowed to continue in the field he would have reached the Elbe in another year and would thus have restored Germany to Rome, but this was not to be. After the campaigning season of AD 16 was over, Germanicus was recalled to enjoy his triumph in Rome before being sent on a new command to the east. Tiberius, who had succeeded Augustus as emperor, had decided that the German wars had gone on long enough.

In the aftermath, the troops were withdrawn to the south bank while the north bank was treated in a variety of ways. In the middle section the land was cleared of hostile communities and a number of bridgehead garrisons established. Along the Lower Rhine, the Frisii and Batavi were accepted as faithful allies, paying dues to Rome, while on the Middle Danube a client kingdom was set up. Apart from minor readjustment, little more was done until the accession of Vespasian in AD 69. Then began a systematic reorganization, accompanied by a limited advance across the difficult re-entrant between the upper reaches of the Rhine and Danube. It was Vespasian's successor, Domitian, who, in AD 83–5, completed the new linear barrier from north of Coblenz on the Rhine to the vicinity of Regensburg on the Danube, creating a frontier which was to last for more than three centuries.[7]

The intention of Augustus had been to conquer Germany, and for nearly thirty years that dream had held good, even after the Varus disaster, but in the cold light of experience — much of it gained first-hand — Tiberius had decided that conquest was impossible and that the Rhine and not the Elbe was the natural limit of the empire. That this policy was maintained, even by the Flavian emperors, whose limited advance was simply designed to iron out a small irregularity, shows that Rome fully accepted the logic of Tiberius's policies.

The reasons for the Roman failure to conquer Germany were many, but of prime importance was the nature of the socio-economic and political systems prevalent among the German people. Although, as we have seen (p.116–17), there had been a wide band of Celtic-style settlement, based on an *oppidum* economy, extending in a zone 150km or so deep, north of the Danube-Rhine axis, considerable population pressures had been building up among the less developed tribes to the north-east, and even as early as Caesar's time bands of these 'primitive Germans' were thrusting into the *oppidum* zone and even crossing the Rhine. Around the middle of the first century BC this process intensified. The result was that the Roman armies had to face, not a stable semi-urban-based population who would succumb once their *oppida* had been taken, but a far more mobile foe who would melt away into the forest in the face of Roman pressure. More to the point, the subsistence economies of these groups were such that large areas of arable land were not maintained. This posed very serious problems of supply for the Roman armies, especially during the winter, and it is not surprising therefore that successive commanders were forced to withdraw troops to winter camps on the Rhine, in easier reach of the corn supplies of northern Gaul. A further point that should not be overlooked is that this was a period of population increase among the Germans: as one army was defeated another would amass to take its place. A shrewd observer like Tiberius, with years of experience in the field in Germany, would readily have appreciated the problem and realized that the conquest of Germany was a lost cause.

Germanic society

Two principal sources provide an insight into the nature of early German society: Julius Caesar's *Commentaries* of the Gallic wars, completed in 51 BC, and a descriptive account — *Germania* — written by the historian Tacitus in AD 98. The former described the Germans at the moment of their first contact with Rome; the latter was composed 150 years later, 85 years after the abortive occupation of Germania, by which time the close proximity of Roman systems had had time to affect the very roots of German society.[8]

Caesar's description is superficial, generalized, probably inaccurate and certainly incomplete, but it is nonetheless useful in offering a picture reflecting the very simple structure of German society. Above all he emphasizes the lack of concern for agriculture and the importance of pastoral activities. Land was not held as private property, but each year the magistrates and leading men of the tribe allotted territory to the clans; the following year, 'they compel them to move to another piece of land'.[9] In this way their society maintained a degree of equality, preventing wealth from building up in the hands of any one group and preserving a mobility, considered to be beneficial. However, by acquiring, through raid or other methods, large flocks and herds, an individual could rise to a pre-eminent position.

Warfare and raiding were endemic:

> The Germans claim that it is good training for the young men and stops them becoming lazy. When one of the chiefs announces at an assembly that he is going to lead a raid and calls for volunteers to go with him, those who agree with the raid and approve of the man proposing it stand up, and, applauded by the whole gathering, promise him their help. If any of these men then fail to go with him they are regarded as deserters and traitors and no one ever trusts them again in anything.[10]

The procedure closely echoes that of archaic Celtic society. Prowess was measured by the ability of the would-be leader to attract followers. They, in return, would expect to share the spoils — goods, cattle and females — thus increasing their own wealth, and their ability to bestow patronage.

The mid-first-century social system, then, was based on clans which were grouped together in larger units called tribes. Tribal leaders might constitute a council for allocating land but they had no powers of coercion beyond this except in times of warfare, when elected chieftains might lead confederate armies.

Very significant changes had taken place by the end of the first century AD when Tacitus was writing. Arable land was now distributed according to social standing, suggesting that their society had evolved from one based on the equality of kinship groups to one in which class and status were enshrined within the social structure.[11] The council of the leading men was now held regularly, not only in times of war. Those eligible to attend were either of noble birth or could claim that their fathers had provided outstanding services. When an external danger threatened the tribe, a war leader, or *dux*, would be elected to conduct the war. In Caesar's time it was usual for a number of individuals to be appointed; now one or two were the norm, reflecting once again the centralization of power. Another type of leader was the king, 'rex', who was elected, probably for life, from among the members of the royal clan. He performed religious duties and led the council.

In addition to the council there was the general assembly of warriors, open to all who had not disgraced themselves in battle. They met at regular intervals to debate matters of general interest, but it seems that the assembly could not initiate action — they could only adopt or reject proposals put before them by the *dux* or one of the leading men. Tacitus gives a vivid account of such a meeting:

> They assemble on certain particular days, either shortly after the new moon or shortly before the full moon. . . . When the assembled crowd thinks fit, they take their seats fully armed. Silence is then commanded by the priests who on such occasions have power to enforce obedience. Then such hearing is given to the king or chief as his age, rank, military distinction, or eloquence can secure. . . . If a proposal displeases them, the people shout their dissent; if they approve, they clash their spears. To express approbation with their weapons is their most complementary way of showing agreement.[12]

The leaders and the general assembly constituted the principal mechanisms for controlling and motivating the tribe, and together they provided a degree of stability, but the third element — the retinue — cut across tribal boundaries and created a potential for instability. The focus of the retinue was a charismatic leader — a nobleman of prowess who could attract young nobles to his following, irrespective of their tribal origins. As Tacitus so succinctly puts it:

> The chiefs fight for victory, the followers for their chief. Many noble youths, if the land of their birth is stagnating in a long period of peace or inactivity, deliberately seek out other tribes which have some war in hand. For the Germans have no taste for peace; renown is more easily won among perils, and a large body of retainers cannot be kept together except by means of violence and war.[13]

The implications of this are clear; there must have existed extra-tribal retinues feeding upon and fuelling the system of endemic warfare, and these retinues were composed of warriors alienated from the land, whose livelihood was based entirely upon obtaining spoils. Tacitus again:

> A German is not so easily prevailed upon to plough the land and wait patiently for harvest as to challenge a foe and earn wounds for his reward. He thinks it tame and spiritless to accumulate slowly by the sweat of his brow what can be got quickly by the loss of a little blood. . . . The boldest and most warlike men have no regular employment, the care of house, home, and fields being left to the women, old men, and weaklings of the family.[14]

The emergence of retinues, owing personal allegiance to their leader and alienated from productive agrarian labour, was a step towards the establishment of tyrannies. Two examples show this process in action.

At the end of the first century BC the Marcomanni, living in the valley of the Main, came under increasing pressure from the Romans, with the result that they decided to migrate to a new and safer territory, now Bohemia. In the course of this migration their chieftain, Maroboduus, seized power, setting himself up as a leader for life, ruling in an autocratic manner with no regard for the will of the assembly. From his new base in Bohemia he extended his personal authority over a number of neighbouring tribes.[15] The parallels with the situation among the Helvetii, sixty years earlier, are fascinating. In both, a mass migration is planned and in both, a leader with a powerful retinue attempts to use the situation to seize absolute power. In the case of the Helvetii, the ambitions of Orgetorix were exposed and he was removed; Maroboduus was more successful and lived to enjoy the fruits of his tyranny for some years.

The second example is provided by the career of Arminius.[16] As a young man he had served as a mercenary commander in the Roman army, his noble status entitling him to the rank of knight. On returning to his tribe, the Cherusci, he was elected as a war leader and proceeded to organize the military revolt against Rome, which met with its first startling success in AD 9 with the annihilation of Varus and his three legions. But Arminius was not without opponents among his kin. His father-in-law, Segestes, pursued a consistently pro-Roman policy in the early years of the revolt, and later, after Arminius had turned against Maroboduus, his uncle, Inguiomerus, changed sides and fought against him. In both cases, Segestes and Inguiomerus were leading their personal retinues in opposition to the chosen war leader of their own tribe and against their own kinsman, thus demonstrating that the power of the retinue leader now transcended traditional loyalties to tribe and kin.

But there is more to learn from the story of Arminius. In AD 19, having fought successfully for his tribe for twelve years, it seems that he took the final step towards tyranny. Our only source is a terse reference by Tacitus: 'The Roman evacuation of Germany and the fall of Maroboduus had induced Arminius to aim at kingship. But his freedom-loving compatriots forcibly resisted. The fortunes of the fight fluctuated but finally Arminius succumbed to treachery from his relations.'[17] The implication seems clear enough — his prowess as a war leader was great, but when the moment came and he made a bid for autocratic power, the will of the people was stronger than the might of his retinue. Once more there are clear echoes of the situation in Gaul seventy years earlier.

If Tacitus, in *Germania* and the *Annals*, provides a very detailed picture of German society in the first century AD, it must be stressed that Caesar's picture of the mid-first-century BC situation is far more summary and there are, therefore, considerable dangers inherent in contrasting the two and assuming that the differences reflect social change. Nonetheless, at a general level, the differences are striking. In Caesar's time the kinship group and the clan were socially dominant and society was so structured that wealth could not accumulate in the hands of a few, but by the first century AD the nobility were acquiring great wealth, to such an extent that they, and their retinues, could ride roughshod over the desires of the tribe in their bids for absolute power. It is inconceivable that the proximity of Rome had not been instrumental in effecting these changes.

Roman interaction with free Germany (figs 66–8)

The presence of Rome as a near neighbour introduced two new dislocating factors into German society — trade and patronage — and it is to the evidence for both that we must now turn.

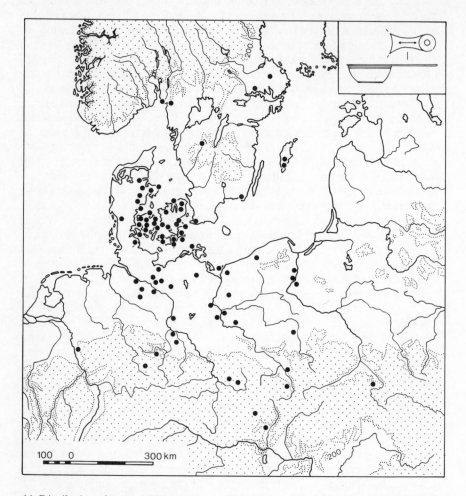

66 *Distribution of a type of Roman* patera *(Eggers type 139–144) in barbarian Europe beyond the frontier.*
(After Eggers 1951, Karte 41)

Germany, viewed from the south through the eyes of the Roman entrepreneurs, was a vast, almost limitless market, traditionally providing a variety of rare goods for the southern consumers. Its exploitation was rapid. Even in Caesar's time the Suebi, described as by far the largest and most warlike of all the German tribes, 'admitted traders to their country so that they will have purchasers for their booty rather than because they want to import anything'. Caesar goes on to say that 'the importation of wine into their country is absolutely forbidden: they think that it makes men soft and effeminate and incapable of enduring hardship'.[18] This is confirmed

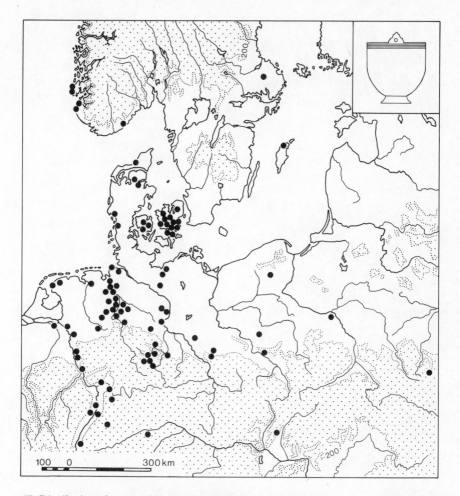

67 *Distribution of a type of Roman bronze bucket*
(Eggers type 55–66) in barbarian Europe beyond the frontier.
(After Eggers 1951, Karte 23)

archaeologically by the absence of Roman wine amphorae from Germany and indeed from much of northern Belgica.

The Suebian booty to which Caesar refers will almost certainly have included slaves and cattle, together perhaps with commodities such as amber from the Baltic coasts and furs from the north. In return, the Roman traders provided gold and silver, in the form of coin, and a range of bronze table ware.

Coins are found widely distributed throughout Germany, but the dangers inherent in basing too complex an argument on the distribution of the

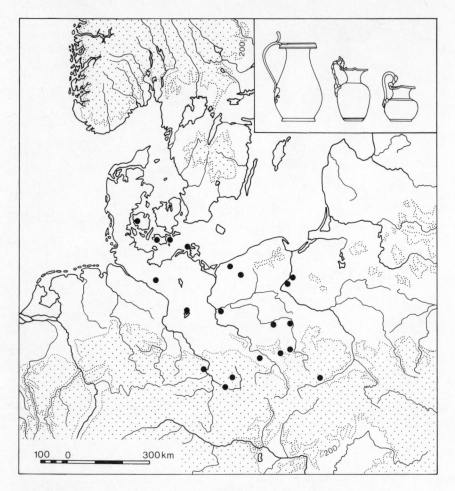

68 *Distribution of Roman bronze flagons (Eggers types 122–6) in barbarian Europe*
beyond the frontier.
(After Eggers 1951, Karte 37 and 38)

different types are nicely underlined by the comments of Tacitus, writing at
the end of the first century AD, when he says,

> The Germans nearest us value gold and silver for their use in trade and
> recognize and prefer certain types of Roman coins . . . they like coins that are
> old and familiar, *denarii* with the notched edge and the type of two-horse
> chariot . . . they try to get silver in preference to gold . . . they find plenty of
> silver change more serviceable in buying cheap and common goods.[19]

This is indeed borne out by the archaeological evidence. Gold is rare and
Republican *denarii*, with their higher silver content, were favoured. Even in

hoards deposited in the early second century AD there is a marked preference for *denarii* issued before Nero's coinage reforms of AD 64. It is also interesting to note that the great majority of the first-century AD coin hoards from Germany lie within a zone some 200km wide immediately adjacent to the frontier, supporting Tacitus's statement that it was the Germans 'nearest to us' who used Roman coins.

A restricted range of Roman table ware was also reaching deep into barbarian territory — dolphin-handled *situlae*, *paterae* with swan-headed or ring-ended handles together with plain bronze buckets (figs 66–8). Differential distributions reflect changes with time as well as local political factors, but some of the material was reaching as far north as Sweden and Norway by the end of the first century AD.[20]

Two concentrations of imports deserve special mention: one in Bohemia, the other on the Danish Islands. The Bohemian distribution is focused on the upper reaches of the Vlatava, the area which, as we have seen, was occupied by the Germanic Marcomanni, led by Maroboduus who had ousted the Celtic Boii. Maroboduus had probably spent his early life as a cavalry officer in the Roman army and for this reason retained some philo-Roman feelings. When, in AD 18, he was forced to flee, following a revolution led by Catualda, in his palace and the adjacent fort were found 'businessmen and camp followers from the Roman province. They had been induced first by a trade agreement and then by hopes of making more money, to migrate from their various homes to enemy territory. Finally they had forgotten their own country'.[21] The attraction of the Marcomannic kingdom to entrepreneurs is not difficult to understand. Maroboduus, by virtue of his position in the Vlatava valley, controlled a major trade route from the north European plain leading down to the Danube in the vicinity of the Roman frontier settlement at Carnuntum (fig 69), but more important was the fact that in his accession to kingship he must have acquired obligations to nobles that were best exercised by the distribution of high-quality luxury goods. By inviting the traders into his court he ensured total control over the inflow of these commodities.[22]

The concentration of luxury goods on the Danish Islands cannot be explained in terms of any historical reference, but as the maps will show, the islands occupy a vital position in relation to north-south and east-west trade routes, and the simplest suggestion is that the unnamed leaders of this region were able to maintain control over the flow of goods (below, pp.189–90). The importance of these northern regions is brought out in a story told by Pliny of a Roman knight who, in the reign of Nero, made an expedition across Germany to the Baltic coast in search of beasts for gladiatorial shows. Whilst there, he visited *commercia*, or trading centres, and acquired considerable quantities of amber, which he brought back to Rome.[23] Whether this was a pioneering venture, or simply one of many such trips made by entrepreneurs along well-trodden routes, it is impossible to say.

Nor was the movement of traders always from the Roman world into barbarian lands. Tacitus tells of the Hermunduri, 'our faithful allies', who, because of their proven loyalty 'are the only Germans who trade with us not merely on the river bank but far within our borders, and indeed in the

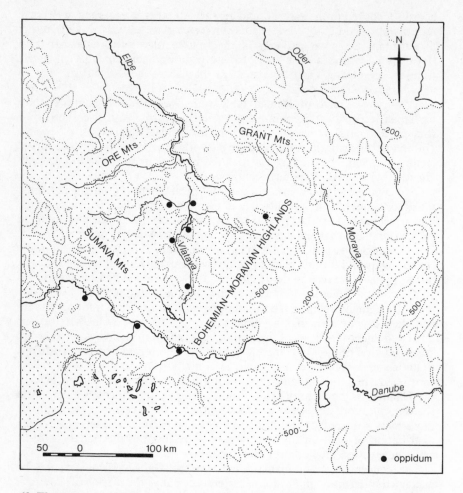

69 *The geography of Bohemia, centred on the valley of the Vlatava, with its enclosing ring of mountains*

splendid colony that is the capital of Raetia. They come over where they will, and without a guard set over them'.[24]

Trade then was well established. The north had much to offer: amber, wild animals for the beast shows, furs, cattle and hides, and slaves. It is impossible to quantify the flow of goods or to offer any estimate of relative proportions, but of the items listed we can be tolerably certain that the two most sought-after were hides, to make the tents and other equipment of the army, and slaves, to be employed widely throughout the Roman provinces.

Direct trade was one form of intercourse between the Romans and Germans; the other was diplomacy. This took many forms, but the principle upon which the Roman state usually worked was one of subversion, manipulating chieftains and their retinues in such a way that they adopted a pro-Roman attitude. Writing of the Marcomanni and Quadi, Tacitus is explicit: 'The power of the kings depends entirely on the authority of Rome. They occasionally receive armed assistance from us, more often financial aid, which proves equally effective.'[25]

The strengths and weaknesses of the policy are well illustrated by the careers of Segestes and Maroboduus. Segestes was the father-in-law of the war leader, Arminius. Both were noblemen of the Cherusci and both commanded large retinues. The attitudes of Segestes were pro-Roman throughout even though, in AD 9, he was compelled through weight of public opinion to take part in the revolt against Rome. In the following year he and his followers maintained their pro-Roman attitudes amid increasing hostilities, until, in AD 15, they had to be rescued by Germanicus and settled on the Roman south bank. Had the Romans pursued their attempts to reconquer Germania there can be little doubt that they would have restored Segestes to some position of power. In the event he and his people remained within the Roman province.

The case of Maroboduus was in many ways similar. Although troublesome to Rome, Maroboduus owed much of his power to tacit, and sometimes direct, Roman support. Arminius could say of him 'he is a traitor, an Imperial agent'. Even so, by *c*. AD 18 he had served his usefulness and was driven out by Catualda, whose task was aided by a gift of Roman gold. In spite of Rome's involvement in his downfall, Maroboduus was eventually settled in Ravenna and allowed to live out the rest of his life in comfort. Later, Catualda was also ousted by internal intrigue and made his home at Fréjus.[26]

The stories of Segestes, Maroboduus and Catualda show one aspect of Roman opportunist diplomacy — the selection of nobles as agents and the acceptance of the transience of the native situation. A more positive case is that of Italicus. Italicus was the nephew of Arminius. His father, Flavius, had fought consistently for Rome, thus engendering the hatred of the majority of his own tribe. By AD 47, internal dissension among the Cherusci had wiped out the entire 'royal family' with the exception of Italicus, who had been born in Rome and was now living there. The policy of Claudius was simple: conquest of Germany was out of the question, but control of the German tribes through Roman surrogates was distinctly desirable. In this context, Italicus was 'restored' to his people. With a grant of money and an escort, Claudius 'encouraged him to enter upon his heritage', adding that Italicus was the first man born at Rome as a citizen, not a hostage, to proceed to a foreign throne. The venture was not an unqualified success and at one stage he was ejected only to be returned to power by the Lombardi, the northern neighbours of the Cherusci.[27]

In all these examples, Rome manipulated the German tribes through legitimate leaders embedded within the traditional social system, but occasionally their interference was more direct — as in the case of the Frisians, who lived in the coastal regions of what is now Holland. They had been subdued by Drusus and had agreed to pay tribute to Rome in the form of leather hides for use by the army. The arrangement continued amicably for forty years, but in AD 28 they rebelled after heavy-handed treatment by the centurions sent to oversee the collection of the tribute. The revolt was successful and for a further twenty years they maintained their freedom, until AD 47 when the legate of Lower Germany, Domitius Corbulo, moved against them. The result was complete capitulation. Corbulo resettled the people and 'allocated to them a senate, officials and laws — and constructed a fort to ensure obedience'.[28] The clear implication of this is that the tribe submitted to a total restructuring of its socio-political system, accompanied by a redistribution of land.

The example of the Frisians is an extreme case — generally Rome was content to sit back and manipulate from a distance, bolstering up the coercive power of the pro-Roman chieftains with gifts of cash. These subsidies would have been redistributed to the retinues to ensure their loyalty. The system which developed had, then, many characteristics of the prestige goods economy discussed earlier (Chapter 2). So long as the subsidies continued on a regular basis, the stability of the retinue could be maintained, but if for some reason subsidy ceased then the chieftain's power would collapse. It is possible that Rome used this ploy to destabilize Maroboduus before he was toppled.

Socio-economic zones in Germany

We have already seen that the Roman government used coin, both gold and silver, as payment to their German supporters, and that the distribution of first-century AD hoards concentrates in a 200km zone along the frontier. This presumably indicates the region dominated by the pro-Roman chieftains, forming a buffer zone, in advance of the frontier, within which a Roman-manipulated form of a prestige goods economy was practised — the input being coins, the output loyalty. In the proximal zone of free Germany we must distinguish therefore between two distinct socio-economic systems, one official with a direct political motive, the other entrepreneurial with the aim of acquiring raw materials and manpower. In some cases, as in the example of the Marcomanni, the two systems were intertwined on a single territory and within a single court; elsewhere they may have been discrete.[29]

Beyond the 200km zone the distribution of Roman items is altogether different since it is here that the bulk of the luxury goods — the *situlae*, *paterae*, buckets, glassware and weapons — concentrates and it is within this region that rich burials begin to appear in the first century AD.

The beginnings of social differentiation among the burials of free Germany can be traced back to the first century BC, with the appearance of occasional high-status burials in the cemeteries of the western Baltic region, but it was not until the first and early second centuries AD that the very rich burials (*Fürstengräber*) of the north European Plain appear. These are named after the Pomeranian cemetery of Lübsow where five rich burials have been found in close proximity.[30] As the map (fig 70) will show, the Lübsow burials are not very numerous, but they extend over a vast region stretching from Bohemia to Norway.

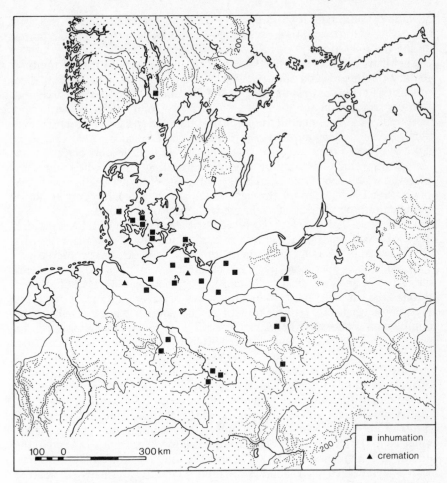

70 *Rich burials of the Lübsow group. (After Eggers 1951, Textkarte C)*

The group share a number of linking characteristics. Most were inhumations (the normal indigenous rite was cremation) and many were buried in coffins or specially constructed chambers under cairns or barrows. All contained a wide range of imported Roman grave goods usually including sets of wine-drinking and banqueting equipment in bronze, silver and glass. One example, from Hoby, on the Danish island of Lolland, will suffice to indicate the variety of luxury objects accessible.[31] The burial was that of a man who had probably been laid in a wooden coffin. He was accompanied by joints of pork and the equipment of the feast, two silver cups on a bronze tray, a silver ladle, a bronze *situla*, a *patera*, a jug and two bronze mounted drinking horns. In addition to this there were brooches of bronze, silver and gold, gold rings, bronze belt-fittings and knife, and three pottery vessels, all of local manufacture. The assemblage dates to the beginning of the first century AD and represents one of the most elaborate to be found in Germania during the Roman era.

The distribution of Lübsow burials is complementary to that of the first century coin hoards and must reflect a different socio-economic system. The similarities of the burials to those of the Hallstatt D period of west central Europe, half a millennium earlier, are striking: inhumation in contrast to local traditions of cremation; the emphasis on impressive grave structure; and the conspicuous consumption of rare luxury goods of alien production. It is difficult to resist the conclusion that, like the Hallstatt leaders before them, the Lübsow chieftains were an élite demonstrating their exalted status by adopting what they conceived to be the burial rite of higher civilization to the south, and by consuming, through burial, goods accessible only to those commanding the systems of exchange with the Roman world.

Thus, in the first and early second centuries the German world was divided into two broad zones — a southern zone in which power was maintained by the exchange of coin, and a northern zone in which a classic prestige goods economy was in operation (fig 71). One must assume that the two systems interacted in such a way that Roman luxury goods could pass unhindered through the southern zone. The simplest way of envisaging such a process is to suppose that the retinue leaders of the southern zone acted as the middle-men conducting the exchanges with their northern neighbours in the wilds of free Germany, and with the Roman entrepreneurs on their own territory or at the frontier posts. The wealth derived from such transactions was used to acquire Roman pottery and personal trinkets from the Roman markets, or more coin with which to maintain and extend their retinues. All the time that the frontier remained static, as it did for more than 150 years, the system could continue in operation little changed, but a new forward thrust from Rome would totally upset the equilibrium. This is neatly reflected in the fact that rich burials of the Lübsow type came to an end in the middle of the second century AD, at just the time that the emperor Marcus Aurelius embarked upon another attempt to conquer Germany. It was not that the war halted the supply of Roman luxury goods, but that it totally disrupted the socio-economic systems by which the goods had previously been distributed.

The late second century (fig 72)

The Marcomannic War (AD 166–80) was not the result of Roman Imperialist aggression, but was caused by population pressures, generated in the northern Germanic zone, forcing the tribes of the southern zone to migrate south through the frontier into the Roman provinces. The prelude was a raid made by the Chatti in AD 162, which was successfully repulsed by the Roman governor. A few years later, the northern pressures had grown to such an extent that vast hoards of Langobardi and Marcomanni crossed to Pannonia to demand land and were driven back. Then, in AD 167, another massive folk movement, this time of Marcomanni, Quadi and Sarmatian Iazyges, thrust

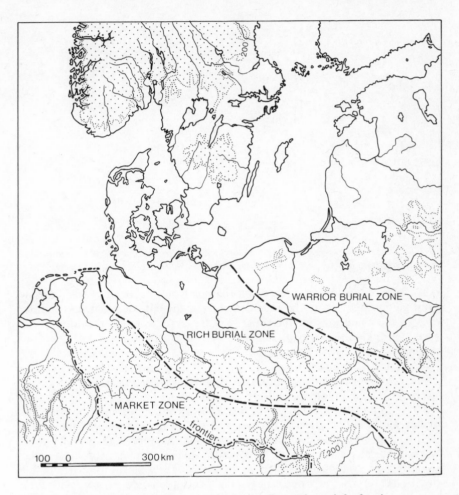

71 The principal socio-economic zones of barbarian Europe beyond the frontier

south, reaching the head of the Adriatic and besieging the town of Aquileia. Once more the invaders were driven back, and in AD 172 and 173 Marcus Aurelius moved first against the Quadi and then the Marcomanni in their homelands. It was only the pressure of events in the east that prevented Rome from annexing the entire territory.

The causes of the southward migration are of considerable potential interest, but are not well-known. Increase in population in the eastern German regions and beyond may well have been the prime cause, but once more there are echoes of what had happened in western central Europe more than half a millennium before, when pressure from the Celtic tribes beyond the Hallstatt D chieftain zone had caused the collapse of the prestige goods economy and the mass migration of warrior bands south and east. Could it be

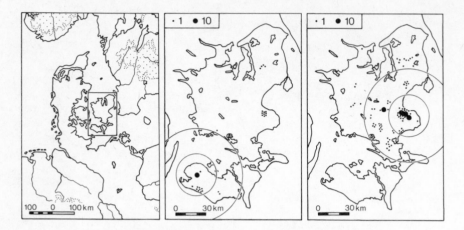

72 *The island of Bornholm showing the change in focus of the élite burial concentration between the early and late Roman periods. (After Hedeager 1978b, figs 6 and 8)*

that the social instability caused, on the north-eastern flank of the Lübsow prestige goods zone, by the very demands of the élite-dominated economy, created the conditions for the collapse of the systems there, resulting in the social turmoil which eventually forced the Marcomanni and the Quadi to attempt their southern migration?

In eastern Germania at this time, two distinct cultural groupings can be recognized — the Oksywie culture of the lower Vistula region and the Bay of Danzig, and the Przeworsk culture centred on the basins of the Vistula and Oder.[32] The Przeworsk culture is best known, but almost entirely from the evidence of its cemeteries. Cremation was the norm, and what is significant, from the point of view of our discussion, is the very high percentage of warrior burials, accompanied by swords, shields (represented by circular shield-bosses and hand-grips) and, in many cases, spurs. A considerable degree of uniformity existed, suggesting a society of free warriors with little significant social differentiation, though a few 'chieftain' graves have been distinguished by their silver and gold *fibulae*.

The Oksywie culture presents a similar range of warrior burials, with occasional richer interments like that at Szwajcaria — a mounted warrior provided with a long sword, a lance decorated with silver inlay, a hemispherical shield-boss and spurs, together with personal ornaments decorated with silver and gold foil. Though status was differentiated, the disparity between a 'warrior' and a 'chieftain' was not great.

In terms of the known tribes, the Przworsk and Oksywie cultures covered the territory within which the Burgundians and Vandals are thought to have emerged as historically attested tribes. The archaeological evidence suggests a noticeable change in burial pattern, apparently accompanied by a thinning out of settlement density in the late second or early third century AD. It is tempting to see this as evidence of the movement of these north-eastern

Germanic warrior bands away from their traditional homes, drawn to the west and the south by the lure of the prestige goods economies.

Late Roman economic reformations

At any event, the Marcomannic wars marked the end of the old systems of exchange. Thereafter, the north was in a state of instability, caused by constant and increasing folk movements, and it was out of this that new economic systems emerged — some of them linked in networks of exchange to the Roman frontier zone. Some areas, for example eastern Jutland, the Elbe–Saale basin and Silesia/Slovakia, developed social systems in which *Fürstengräber* reappeared.

The Elbe–Saale group has been extensively studied.[33] The rite was inhumation in wooden coffins or chambers, usually accompanied by luxury goods of Roman origin such as bronze and glass tableware. In addition, there can be found locally-made textiles and jewellery, and frequent sets of three bronze or silver arrowheads, which must have been emblems denoting status. The Slovakian burials form another distinct and restricted group, the interred often accompanied by silver vessels and plate of very considerable value.[34] Both groups are sufficiently close to the frontier for the luxury goods to represent diplomatic gifts handed out by Roman military commanders in return for allegiance, but it could equally well be that we are seeing the emergence, for comparatively short periods, of local élites controlling trade routes.

The situation in eastern Denmark presents an interesting contrast because here luxury goods tend to accumulate throughout the early (first and second centuries AD) and late (third and fourth centuries) Roman period.[35] There are, however, two significant differences between these periods. First, in terms of distribution, there is a shift of emphasis from Lolland in the early period, where the graves with Roman imports cluster around the grave of Hoby, to the Stevns region of east Zealand in the late period. And secondly, whereas in the early period luxury goods were found in only a small percentage of the total number of graves, in the later period, not only is there a much greater quantity of luxury material available, but it is more widely distributed among a larger number of graves. The inescapable conclusions are: that there had been a minor shift in focus of the contact-point with the Roman world; that the volume of trade had greatly increased; and that Roman grave-sets no longer served to distinguish a small élite. It may be that we are seeing here the emergence of 'administered trade', in which the processes of exchange were based on an agreed set of value systems, beneficial to all parties, rather than on gift exchange wholly embedded within the social system. Eastern Denmark, then, provides a rare example of a system of exchange in a state of transformation, and one which survived the upheavals of the late second century AD.

The location of the centres of élite burial on the Danish Islands shows the importance of the sea in facilitating trade. The intensification of that trade, reflected in the greatly increased volume of imports after the late second century AD, could be the direct result of the dislocations caused to the old land-based systems of exchange by the upheavals which led to the Marcomannic wars. Zealand and Lolland were well placed to serve as exchange centres for hides and other northern commodities, bought from the Baltic islands of Öland and Gotland *en route* for the Roman bases at the Rhine mouth.[36]

A further indication of coastal trade is given by the very considerable quantities of samian pottery found on coastal sites in Holland, much of it second to early third century AD in date. It is tempting to see this as the result of low-level exchange systems operating between the local villagers and those who manned the craft plying along the North Sea coasts to the Baltic ports.

The settlements of Holland north of the Rhine and the German coastal zone exhibit significant changes, beginning in the third century AD and extending into the fourth. Flögeln, Feddersen Wierde, and Wijster all show an intensification of local manufacturing activities such as metal-working and weaving, coupled with the emergence of one of the farmstead units as the principal homestead.[37] At Flögeln, near Cuxhaven in Lower Saxony, for example, extensive excavation of a village, occupied during the first half of the first millennium AD, showed how the number of sunken huts, used as workshops, had significantly increased from the third century AD. Hearths in the huts may have been for metal-working. Other buildings were found associated with shallow ditches or basins, possibly used as tanning-pits or for treating flax. At Feddersen Wierde, north of Bremerhaven, eight successive villages spanning the period from the first to fourth centuries AD have been totally uncovered. From the second century onwards differences in the size of the individual farms become apparent and one farm in particular begins to take on the appearance of being of special importance. It was here that imported Roman items — *terra sigillata*, beads and bronze vessels — were concentrated.

Much the same patterns appear to be true for Jutland.[38] At Drengsted in south-west Jutland, evidence of extensive iron production, far in excess of the needs of the villages, has been found, while at the nearby settlement of Dankirke quantities of luxury goods have been discovered, including a stock of glass found in one house, together with lead scale-weights. The quantities were such that surplus trading stock is the implied explanation. This intensification of secondary (i.e. non-subsistence) activity is a characteristic of most of the settlements examined on Jutland. Another noticeable characteristic is the general increase in the size of the individual holdings. At Vorbasse, in southern Jutland, the farmyard enclosures of the fourth century AD were four times bigger than their first-century equivalents, and the individual houses more than twice as long. In the last phase each house had its own workshop and the village had grown to comprise 20 individual farmsteads.

The overall increase in settlement size and complexity over the first half of the first millennium AD must have been accompanied by a growth in the subsistence economy. Sufficient is now known of agricultural activity in the region to suggest that a technological level had been reached such that there was little room for significant change in crop-growing regimes. Expansion must therefore have been made in the sphere of animal husbandry, principally cattle-rearing.

It is tempting to suggest that there may be a close link between the economic changes so clearly documented in the settlements of the North Sea zone and the increase in luxury commodities reaching the contact-zone of the Danish Islands in the third and fourth centuries AD. Could it be that regular 'administered trade' with the Roman world, developing after the Marcomannic wars, created the stability and the demand for hides and other commodities that enabled the economic expansion of the communities of the North Sea zone to get underway? If so, it is quite possible that the eventual breakdown of the Roman frontier system was one of the more significant factors contributing to the collapse of the native settlement systems in the early fifth century AD.

The late third century and after

The stability of the coastal region is in marked contrast to much of the rest of Germany, which, from the early third century, was in a turmoil of folk movement caused by the increasingly mobile confederacies of warriors. Many of the old tribal names are no longer heard of and new ones appear, suggesting widespread regrouping. One of the more troublesome of these confederacies was the Alemanni (literally 'all people'). In AD 215 they broke through the *limes* of Upper Germany, only to be driven back. Thereafter, the raids continued with increasing intensity until, in AD 259–60, they and their confederate allies overran the Roman land frontier that protected the *agri decumantes* — the re-entrant of land between the Upper Rhine and the Upper Danube — and occupied the entire territory, forcing the Roman armies to retreat behind the two rivers which now became the effective frontier.[39]

Meanwhile, in the Lower and Middle Rhine, another confederacy, the Franks, was amassing, and in the 270's they too crossed the Rhine, thrusting deep into the Roman empire, ravaging much of Gaul. Other tribes were also on the move: the Goths (traditionally from southern Sweden) had appeared in Poland in the second century AD and had begun their push towards the Black Sea, one group replacing the Romans in Dacia in 270; meanwhile, the Vandals, occupying the lower reaches of the Oder basin at the end of the first century AD, had expanded and split, one group — the Siling Vandals — settling in Silesia, while the others — the Asding Vandals — moved to the Danube frontier. Another eastern German tribe, the Burgundians, moved up to the Rhine frontier to occupy land between the Franks and the Alemanni. If the detail is confused, the overall pattern is clear enough: the peoples of eastern Germania were inexorably moving south and west towards the frontier, creating pressures in the old buffer zone and, in their newly-formed confederacies, occasionally spilling over into the empire.

The events of the 270s brought home to the Roman administration, probably for the first time, the seriousness of the situation — a situation which had been gradually worsening since the beginning of the Marcomannic wars. In the face of the barbarian threat, a complete change of frontier policy took place. No longer was the intention to maintain a narrow heavily fortified forward defence, but instead to create a defence in depth. This was accomplished by settling a new frontier force (*limitanei*) in forward positions, backed by an internal buffer zone of fortlets and fortified roads, where a highly mobile field army (*comitatenses*) was stationed. In addition, peasant militias (*laeti*), composed largely of German families, were settled in the large tracts of depopulated land which had by now appeared in northern Gaul.[40]

The new arrangements were successful for a while, but in the early years of the fifth century AD they finally broke down, allowing the pent-up hordes of northern barbarians to flood into the Roman world. In many ways the situation in the early fourth century AD was not unlike that in the late fifth century BC. Then, a mobile force of Celts had thrust south into the Roman and Hellenistic world, attracted by the plunder which was to be had. The main difference was that they had met the nascent Roman Republic with all its youthful energy and had been driven back and conquered. Their Germanic successors 800 years later found only the decaying carcass of the empire, and stayed to create the foundations of modern Europe.

10 Retrospect

In the previous chapters sufficient has been said of the complexity of the interactions between the classical and barbarian worlds in the period from 600 BC to AD 400 to justify the assertion that the two were inextricably bound together in a network of economic interdependence. On some occasions the links were direct, on others more distant, but at no time during this period could it be said that barbarian Europe and the Mediterranean states were not in some way influencing each other.

In Chapter I we briefly explored something of the theoretical background to core-periphery relationships and the processes of trade and exchange operating in systems of this kind. An awareness of these models has necessarily influenced the selection and presentation of the evidence considered in succeeding chapters, but as far as possible the evidence has been allowed to stand in its own right with the minimum of theoretical structuring. It remains now to stand back from the mass of data to see if broad generalizations and recurring patterns can be detected in the fast-moving situation which began with early Greek colonization and ended with the collapse of the Roman West. The comparatively high quality of the archaeological data, and the range of controls offered by the contemporary documentary accounts, make western Europe in the millennium under discussion a region of high potential in the study of the many subtleties of core-periphery relationships. To begin with we will offer a simple summary of the changing situation, before going on to consider the validity of current theoretical frameworks.

At the risk of over-simplifying it is possible to define four major periods of comparative stability, each followed by a time of disruption caused by folk movement or conquest. In the periods of stability networks of exchange sprang up, each one differing in subtle and informative ways from the other.

In the first period, roughly 530–480 BC, a classic core-periphery situation obtained (fig 73). Along the Mediterranean coast of Gaul a series of Greek colonies, with Massalia predominant, served the function of gateway communities, existing essentially on the interface between the two worlds and articulating exchange between them. Inland, in west central Europe, there emerged a zone of rich chiefdoms whose power and prestige were founded upon the ability of the paramount chiefs to control the incoming and internal redistribution of rare and valuable Mediterranean goods. This conforms to the general model of the prestige goods economy. Beyond the zone of chiefdoms lay the procurement zone, through which the commodities for export to the south were obtained.

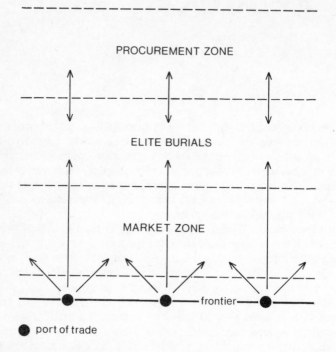

PROCUREMENT ZONE

ELITE BURIALS

MARKET ZONE

frontier

● port of trade

73 Model for trade in Gaul c.500 BC

The chiefdom zone was characterized by the rich burials of the aristocracy, reflecting, in the rites performed, the perceived manners of Mediterranean society, together with dominant fortified residences wherein a range of manufacturing activities generated the commodities needed for distribution down the chain of social hierarchy. The procurement zone to the north was entirely differently structured around a warrior society with two foci, one on the Marne and the other on the Moselle. The warlike aspect of the burials suggests a society in which raiding and looting may well have formed an essential economic sub-system, the products of these activities being exchanged with the communities to the south, in the chiefdom zone, whence they were trans-shipped south again to the Mediterranean. It could be argued that the existence of the Mediterranean littoral market was the prime cause for the emergence of the chiefdom zone (developing from a warrior aristocracy) and that the demands of this economy in turn created the situation in which the warrior aristocracy of the Marne-Moselle region could develop.

It is comparatively easy to visualize how these two peripheral socio-economic systems could interdigitate, but the mechanisms by which the Mediterranean littoral interacted with the chiefdom zone are more obscure. The two are more than 350km apart and virtually nothing is known, in useful detail, of the situation between, except for some rich burials in the vicinity of the Italian lakes commanding the southern ends of the central Alpine passes. The simplest way to model the situation is in terms of corridors of trans-shipment through this intermediate zone, along which the prestige goods could flow without being diverted. How the goods were carried and by what means the flow was effected through the tribal controls of the intermediate zone are questions to which no clear answers can yet be given. It is a problem which will recur later.

It would be wrong to give the impression that the system was static; indeed, a clear development through time can be detected. Before *c.* 530 BC there was extensive trade between Italy and southern Gaul, but only very few of the imported products found their way far inland. Even so, some costly bronzes of Greek manufacture were reaching west central Europe. After *c.* 530 BC, for about half a century, the volume of imports increased dramatically, first along the Rhône route, via Massalia, and later through the Alpine passes from Etruria and from the Adriatic via Spina and Adria. The change in the route of supplies was probably the cause of shifts in the centres of power detectable in the chiefdom zone. Those no longer able to command a consistent volume of southern luxuries fell from power, while those able to control the newly developing routes acquired new status and prestige. These readjustments in trading routes were driven by political changes in the Mediterranean.

The collapse of the system, in the middle of the fifth century BC, is best explained, on present evidence, by growing instability in the periphery. The most likely scenario is that instability originated in the warrior aristocracy of the Marne-Moselle region, and manifested itself as the beginnings of a folk movement which grew to become the Celtic migrations of the early and middle La Tène period. This would require us to accept that the social system of the region, which involved endemic raiding, escalated, possibly under pressures created by population growth, until the point was reached when the raiders no longer returned to their home territories.

The Celtic folk movements, passing through the old chiefdom zone, brought about the collapse of the prestige goods economy, and the continued migration to the south and east even threatened the stability of the Greco-Roman world. The turbulence caused by the mobile Celtic bands was soon overtaken by almost continuous warfare among the west Mediterranean states — most notably the Punic Wars, which eventually led to the competing armies of Carthage and Rome crossing and re-crossing the southern Gaulish littoral zone.

Thus from the mid-fifth to mid-second centuries BC, unstable conditions militated against the creation of well-established systems of exchange (of a kind that can be clearly distinguished in the archaeological record). But that long-distance trade persisted is not in doubt. Quantities of imported Greek and Italian pottery are found in the coastal regions of southern Gaul, and imports found their way north along the Rhône route to Vienne and west towards Tolosa. Moreover, the documentary sources imply that the tin trade with Brittany and Britain was also in operation, middle-men bringing the metal by ship to the Gironde estuary, from where it was trans-shipped by river and land to Massalia. These activities have left little recognizable impression on the adjacent barbarian communities.

By 120 BC a new situation had emerged: Rome had been drawn into southern Gaul, nominally by military considerations, but no doubt with her eyes firmly fixed on the attractive economic possibilities which now presented themselves. In the sixty years which followed, a totally new set of core-periphery relationships had developed, instigated by Roman entrepreneurs who had been gradually exploiting the area long before the military takeover occurred.

In the new system which emerged in the period 120–60 BC, it is possible to distinguish several levels of economic contact (fig 74). The first is represented by the two very remarkable sites of Tolosa and Chalon, where enormous quantities of wine amphorae have been found, most probably discarded after the wine had been decanted into barrels or skins for trans-shipment to native

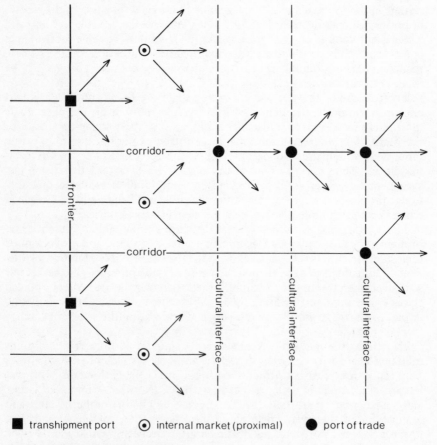

■ transhipment port   ⊙ internal market (proximal)   ● port of trade

74 *Model for trade in Gaul c.100 BC*

communities beyond Roman-held territory. A second group of sites comprised a series of large native *oppida*, 50km or so away from the frontier, in barbarian territory. The many amphorae recovered suggest that these *oppida* might have been 'internal markets', in Polanyi's sense, to which wine was shipped for redistribution within the native socio-economic system.

In addition to these two modes of distribution there is a third which implies the existence of corridors of trans-shipment — the wine and other commodities being carried through the barbarian hinterland beyond the frontier to a second range of internal markets, deep in barbarian territory. The examples here are provided by Quiberon and Quimper in Armorica, and Hengistbury on the coast of southern Britain. These are strictly ports-of-trade, on the interfaces of barbarian territory at the end of a corridor, partly riverine and partly maritime. Each of these ports had hinterlands of their own within which the imported products were redistributed.

The recognition of these three distinct methods of trans-shipment and exchange is a reminder of the complexity of the system. But this, in itself, is a simplification; no doubt the true situation was far more involved than we can begin to comprehend.

The mechanisms by which the goods were actually moved through the social system are beyond recovery; we can only guess. At the trans-shipment ports like Toulouse and Chalon it is quite possible that small-scale exchanges took place with barbarian Gaulish middle-men travelling to the centres under Roman jurisdiction. The 'internal markets' are quite different. To these, we must suppose that the Roman products were transported in bulk (the wine in its original containers) to be exchanged with the native élite, who would then redistribute the luxury goods down the hierarchy. Trans-shipment through the corridors is altogether more difficult to model. Cargoes leaving Toulouse by boat would have to be offloaded on to sea-going vessels, probably in the vicinity of Bordeaux, for their trip across the Bay of Biscay to the southern ports of Armorica. There is no reason why the whole of this process should not have been in the hands of Roman entrepreneurs, but whether they were involved in the last leg of the voyage between Armorica and central southern Britain is less certain. The wide range of products reaching Britain, including Armorican pottery, might suggest that the Armorican communities acted as the middle-men, but it is equally possible that the British ports received both Roman and Breton merchant ships.

This second phase of stability was short-lived, for in 58 BC Julius Caesar began his conquest of Gaul, which was to last for the rest of the decade.

From 50 to roughly 10 BC a new and most interesting equilibrium emerged. Gaul was now conquered up to the Rhine, and in all probability the south-eastern corner of Britain, where Caesar had campaigned, was also regarded as part of the Roman domain, though the unwillingness of the British tribes to come to heel soon made it clear to Augustus that he had no real power over the Islands.

For much of the period, Roman influence over the newly-won territory was slight and in northern Gaul native socio-economic systems seem to have been left largely untouched (fig 75). In two areas, roughly centred on the

Aisne valley and the Moselle valley, groups of rich burials containing Roman wine-drinking equipment begin to appear. It is also in these areas that Dressel I wine amphorae are seen to concentrate. On the other side of the Channel a similar phenomenon can be found in eastern Britain, north of the Thames. The implication would seem to be that a distinct zone — the North Gaulish-East British zone — had developed an economy in which the élite could in some way command the inflow of Roman luxury goods, presumably by articulating the movement of goods and commodities between the north and the now-Romanized south. In many ways this is not dissimilar to the prestige goods economy of west central Europe in the Late Hallstatt period, but with two important differences: the entire zone lay within the empire; and to the north, between the North Gaulish-East British zone and the unconquered barbarians, lay the Roman military frontier. Thus an essentially native socio-economic system seems to have been functioning *within* a loosely administered part of the empire. Where the procurement zone lay is a matter of debate. Britain certainly formed part of it, and it is reasonable to suppose that the northern part of Belgica should also be included. In all probability, Germania, beyond the frontier, was not involved at this stage. The simplest explanation would be to see a direct relationship between the Roman entrepreneurs (and administrators) and the native élite of the North Gaulish-East British zone, the procured commodities flowing through to the south in exchange for Roman luxury goods. But if so, how did the military frontier zone relate to this? It is inconceivable that there was not some flow of goods from the collection zone northwards, to supply the frontier forces, and the roads which Agrippa constructed would have facilitated such a movement.

Sufficient will have been said to indicate the potential complexities of the situation, and to this must be added the thought that there must also have

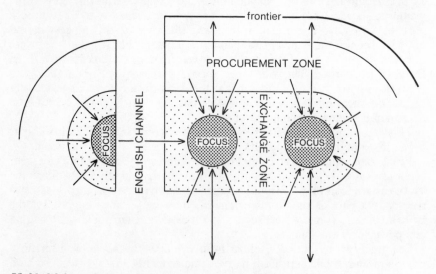

75 *Model for trade in northern Gaul and Britain c.10* BC

been change with time as a formalized administrative structure took shape. By about 10 BC, when the military advance into Germania had begun, it is highly likely that Roman systems had largely replaced the native, except in Britain where a classic core-periphery situation survived until the conquest of AD 43.

The interlude of disturbance caused by the advance into Germania was over by AD 20. Thereafter, a new interface was created along the Rhine, and for the next century and a half, until the Marcomannic Wars, a new equilibrium was created (fig 76). The archaeological evidence strongly suggests that Free Germania can be divided into three separate zones. From the frontier, to a depth of about 200km, lay a 'market zone' which seems to have had direct and easy access to Roman goods. Then came a zone of rich burials (the Lübsow burials), suggesting an élite controlling the through-flow of commodities, and beyond lay a zone dominated by warrior graves, which we might regard as a procurement zone. Once again, the general model seems

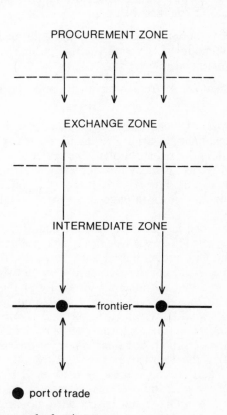

76 Model for trade between the frontier zone and free Germany c. AD 100

to conform very closely to that of the west central European chiefdoms of the Late Hallstatt period, even more so when the collapse of the two systems is considered. In both cases it was pressure and eventually the migration of warriors from the procurement zone that destroyed the equilibrium and led to widespread folk movement.

What has been said so far in this chapter is a brief summary of a vastly complex and constantly changing situation, only dimly visible to us through very fragmentary archaeological and historical evidence. Simplifications of this kind can be misleading and the desire to recognize patterns in historical data is fraught with difficulty. Yet it does seem that we can recognize the main elements of a generalized *developed core-periphery system* which recurs on various scales throughout the period we are considering, when the interface between the Greco-Roman and barbarian worlds had remained stable for a sufficient period of time. The recurring elements are:

(a) Ports-of-trade (or gateway communities) at or close to the interface.

(b) An intermediate zone within which a market economy develops, the individual internal markets being linked directly to the ports-of-trade.

(c) An élite redistribution zone in which the élite maintains control over incoming commodities, retaining prestige goods for their own use and organizing commodity flow.

(d) A procurement zone from which the bulk of raw materials and manpower are derived.

Luxury goods pass through the intermediate zone, which allows, and possibly facilitates, their passage, receiving in return low-value goods. They are retained in the élite redistribution zone where they generate, through processes of reciprocity, commodities for exchange with the procurement zone. The bulk of the raw materials and manpower produced in the procurement zone flow down through the system, largely unaltered, to the ports-of-trade.

The system was one in a state of unstable equilibrium. If the supply of luxury goods fluctuated there was a danger of collapse. It is also probable that the failure of the élite redistribution zone to satisfy the demands of the procurement zone would have caused destructive forces to emerge, and it may be in this area that the inherent instability of the system really lay. Perhaps the escalating expectations of the raiding communities of the procurement zone would always end in the raiders turning upon the élite redistribution zone. It may be significant that in the mid-fifth century BC and mid-second century AD, both occasions when the system was not suffering upset from without, the destructive drive came from the procurement zone.

These two systems we can regard as mature. Between them we have defined two slightly different systems developing in c. 120–60 BC and c. 50–10 BC, both of which could be regarded as immature, having been overtaken by events from without — in these cases Roman military advances. But both display other peculiarities. Some Gaulish tribes in the period

120–60 BC were in the throes of developing state systems, and this prevented élites from emerging as they might have done in less structured political systems. But one could argue that the internal markets we are able to define at native *oppida* were characteristic of the intermediate zone, and it may be that elements of an evolving élite redistribution remain to be discovered. Indeed, a group of chariot burials in the Seine valley, concentrating around Paris, may be one such group. Others might be expected in the mid-Loire and perhaps even the Garonne, but there are no convincing traces of such activity in the archaeological record. The system was further complicated by long-distance sea routes to Brittany and to Britain, which created discrete sub-systems.

The second immature system, northern Gaul in the period 50–10 BC, is also an anomaly because it occurred within the empire, but if we were to leave aside the question of the frontier zone, then many of the attributes of a classic system are present, especially in eastern Britain where the frontier anomaly does not exist anyway. One way to approach the problem would be to regard the frontier zone as part of a totally different system superimposed across the other, but not directly related to it. These matters will necessarily remain unresolved until the archaeological record is better understood.

Sufficient has by now been said to justify the assertion, implicit in the opening chapter, that barbarian Europe and the Mediterranean world must be studied together, since for much of the time their development was interdependent. For a clearer understanding there is much to be said for standing back and taking a broader chronological perspective. Only in this way will the recurring patterns reflecting like human responses to like situations come into focus. The approach is invigorating, but it is also humbling, showing how little we yet know of even the fundamental issues of early European history.

Notes

1 Themes and approaches (pp.1–11)

1. Jacobstahl, 1944, remains the standard work on Celtic art. Wheeler's little book *Rome Beyond the Imperial Frontiers* (1954) deals extensively with barbarian Europe and is still a very useful account.
2. For an entertaining and perceptive review of the question, see Snodgrass 1986.
3. The approach was pioneered by Moses Finley (1973). Other highly significant contributions include Duncan-Jones 1974, Hopkins 1978a, 1978b and 1980, Whittaker 1978 and 1980, and Garnsey, Hopkins & Whittaker 1983. The literature is now growing rapidly.
4. These issues are carefully explored by Hopkins (1980).
5. Polanyi 1957.
6. Polanyi 1975.
7. Polanyi 1963. The two basic works on the subject of ancient trade are Sabloff & Lamberg-Karlovsky 1975 and Earle & Ericson 1977. Both contain papers of considerable significance which are widely read and even more widely quoted.
8. Hirth 1978, 37.

2 The Greek adventure (pp.12–37)

1. For brief assessments of Phocaea and Phocaean activities in the west Mediterranean, see Boardman 1980 and Cook 1962. For the town of Phocaea, see Akurgal 1956, 3–14, and for Phocaean influence in the west Mediterranean, Langlotz 1966 and Morel 1975.
2. For short, recent, discussions of Greek colonization see Boardman 1980 and Murray 1980. For more detailed accounts, see Dunbabin 1948 and Graham 1964.
3. Snodgrass 1977.
4. Herodotus 4, 149–58.
5. Kimmig (1983a) gives a detailed consideration of the effects of Greek colonization on developments in barbarian Europe. For a general review of the Greek colonies themselves, see Woodhead 1962.
6. Ridgeway 1973; Boardman 1980, 165–8 with detailed references.
7. Buchner 1966, 12 and 1970, 97. Though could it be that imported blooms were being refined?
8. Boardman 1980, 168–9 with detailed references.
9. Thucydides 6.3.
10. For a full general account of the Phoenicians, fully referenced, see Harden 1972 (revision of 1962).
11. Herodotus 1.163.
12. Tartessus: Arribas 1962 for general account of Iberian development, also Schulten 1945.

13. Herodotus 1.163.
14. Rolland 1951; Villard 1960, 75.
15. I have here accepted the date of 600, widely adopted by archaeologists. The material remains have been considered at length by Villard 1960 and Gallet de Santerre 1962. Recent work by Michael Vickers has cast doubt on the early foundation preferring instead to accept the date of 540 given by Thucydides (Vickers 1984), but there are problems and until the arguments have been presented and debated in full there is no strong reason to reject the usually held foundation date of 600.
16. Emporion (García y Bellido 1948); Tauroention (Duprat 1935); Antipolis (Schoder 1974); Nikaia (Benoît 1968b); Olbia (Coupry 1964); Alalia (Jehasse 1963 and Jehasse & Jehasse 1973).
17. The standard work on Marseille is Clerc 1927-9. For more recent work, see Benoit 1966 and 1972, and Euzennat & Salviat 1968 and 1976 (with very extensive bibliographies of recent discoveries). Clavel-Leveque 1977 discusses aspects of trade.
18. Villard 1960; Benoît 1965. A recent survey of the evidence from Marseilles and Saint Blaise, by Bouloumie (1982), emphasizes the significance of Etruscan trade in the period 625-575 and charts the rise of Marseilles at the expense of Saint Blaise after the mid-sixth century.
19. Fully discussed in Benoît 1965.
20. For up-to-date distribution maps showing the find-spots of Greek and Massaliot material along the Mediterranean littoral in western central Europe, see Kimmig 1983a, Abb. 25, 27, 28, 29. The analytical work on the Massaliot amphorae is published by Echallier 1982.
21. A simplified outline of the trading potential of Massalia is given by Wells (1980, 61-76) together with the relevant classical references.
22. See note 18.
23. See Kimmig 1983a, Abb. 6 for a general distribution map, and Arnal et al. 1974 for details of the port of Latara, giving changing quantities of imports (see p.46-7 above).
24. These processes are usefully discussed by Nash (1985, 55-9). For a summary of relations between the Greeks and Etruscans in Italy, see Boardman 1980, 198-210.
25. Brief summaries of Spina and Adria are to be found in Boardman 1980, 227-9, with recent references. For the Po plains in the sixth and fifth centuries, Wells (1980, 130-4) provides the major references.
26. The archaeological literature dealing with the Hallstatt C period is extensive. Most useful are Kossack's two detailed studies of southern Bavaria (Kossack 1959; 1972). To these can be added Kimmig & Hell 1958 and Neuffer 1974 for Württemberg, Freidin 1982 for the Paris Basin and Härke 1979 for a discussion of West Hallstatt settlement types. All have extensive bibliographies.
27. Much has been written on the subject. The settlement sites are all considered with full references in Härke 1979. A useful summary of the major burials (again with full references) is to be found in Wells 1980, but the most significant recent overview is Spindler 1983.
28. See, for example, Shefton 1979, on *oinochoai* and Frey 1955 on Etruscan beaked flagons. For a general discussion of Mediterranean imported bronzes in barbarian Europe, see Dehn & Frey 1962.
29. Recent excavations, 1983-5, to be published in Cunliffe forthcoming. Meanwhile for a summary of site, see Cunliffe 1983.

30. Enthusiastic support for the importance of the slave trade is to be found in Nash 1985; for the minimalist view see Wells 1980, 69. The most accessible discussion of Greek slavery is given by Finley (1959), but see also Peschel 1971.
31. Heuneburg. The literature is considerable but for an up-to-date summary with a full bibliography see Kimmig 1983b.
32. Vix (Joffroy 1954); Grafenbühl (Zürn 1970); Homichele (Riek 1962, Hundt 1969); La Garenne (Joffroy 1960); Grächwil (Jucker 1973).
33. The classic statement of the model with regard to south-west Germany is Frankenstein & Rowlands 1978 where references to the important *Fürstensitze* and *Fürstengräber* are conveniently collated. The following paragraphs paraphrase Frankenstein's and Rowlands's principal arguments.
34. Härke 1979 for spatial analysis of hillforts, etc.
35. For discussion of Hunsrück-Eifel, see Driehaus 1965 and Haffner 1976.
36. Driehaus 1965.
37. For the Late Hallstatt in the Paris Basin, see Freidin 1982. For the La Tène culture of the Marne region, Bretz-Mahler 1971.
38. The question has been considered recently by Pauli 1985, where the literature is briefly referred to and thoroughly referenced. Nash (1985) offers explanations for the social change in this period.
39. A much discussed subject. For recent views, see Nash 1985 and Pauli 1985. Only the beginnings concern us here.
40. Pliny, *Nat. Hist.*, 12.2.5.
41. Quoted in Justin, 20 and 24.
42. Clusium: Livy, 5.33.2–6. Bellovesus and Segovesus: Livy, 5.34.1–4.

3 The southern shores of Gaul (pp.38–58)

1. 'Stable' is used relatively. Most archaeologists writing on recent excavations stress the continuity of occupation while noting occasional phases of destruction, which they assign to 'historical' events such as the movement of the Volcae Tectosages into Languedoc or the passage of Hannibal through the region in 218 BC. Disruptive events such as these will undoubtedly have caused occasional discontinuities in the archaeological record, but it is dangerous to assign every settlement fire to a major historical event. For a general discussion of the peoples of southern Gaul, largely from an historical viewpoint, see Barruol 1969. A brief summary of recent work in the urban settlements is given by Fevrier 1973 with copious references, while Py (1982) surveys developing urbanism against the protohistoric background in Languedoc-Roussillon. Py (1968) discusses the effects of Greek influence on the development of native settlements in the Vaunage. A perceptive overview of the question of urbanization in the region is offered by Goudineau (1980).
2. The settlements of eastern Transalpina (Var and Alpes-Maritimes) have been well mapped (Goudineau 1980, 154). A detailed listing of fortifications in the Alpes-Maritimes is provided by Octobon 1962. Recent excavations of significance are Mont-Garou (Var), Arcelin, Arcelin-Pradelle & Gasco 1982, and Taradeau (Var), *Gallia* 27 (1969), 455; 29 (1971), 460–1; 31 (1973), 563; 33 (1975), 565; 35 (1977), 505.
3. There is extensive literature on St Blaise and Glanon, but for St Blaise, see Rolland 1951, 1956 and 1964 and for Glanon, see Rolland 1958 and 1960. For an interesting discussion of the relationship between these Hellenized towns and Marseilles, see Goudineau 1983 *passim*.

4. Echallier 1982, Reille 1985 and Ricq-de Bovard 1985.
5. Such a view would seem to be in conflict with that of Goudineau 1983 who sees the economic influence of Marseilles, in the third century and later, as strictly limited.
6. Gallet de Santerre 1980.
7. Cayla de Maillac: Louis & Taffanel 1955–60, Taffanel & Taffanel 1956 and 1960.
8. Enserune: Jannoray 1955, and Gallet de Santerre 1978 and 1980.
9. Nages: Py 1978. Thereafter, *Gallia* 36 (1978), 452–4; 37 (1979), 540–3; 39 (1981), 519–21; 41 (1983), 512–3.
10. Montlaurés: useful summary in Clemente 1974, 61–6 with full references. Thereafter, *Gallia* 37 (1979), 525 and 39 (1981), 504.
11. Diodorus 5.22.38.
12. Pech Maho: Campardou 1957, Solier 1961, 1976, 1979, 55–124. Peyriac-de-Mer: Solier & Fabre 1969.
13. Agde: the site is not well known archaeologically but aerial photography has indicated something of the land allotment pattern. Most finds come from dredging the Hérault and from the sea nearby. Brief notes in *Gallia* 6 (1948), 203; 7 (1950), 111; 20 (1962), 622; 22 (1964), 486–8; 24 (1966), 462–4. See also Clavel 1970.
14. Arnel, Majurel and Pradès 1974.
15. Entremont. The principal references are: Benoît 1947, 1954, 1957, 1968a. Thereafter, notes in *Gallia* 27 (1969), 419; 30 (1972), 511–14; 32 (1974), 501–5; 35 (1977), 511. There are problems with the date of destruction by the Romans, which is usually assigned to the campaigns of 125–3. Two phases of destruction have been recognized, with rebuilding and relaying of streets in between. Could they represent destruction in two successive campaigns (124 and 123) or destruction in 123 and again in 90 to 80? Both scenarios present problems. An alternative is that the first destruction was in 154, when a Roman force was sent at the request of Massalia, to relieve the besieged cities of Antipolis and Nikaia (see p.55). Strabo (4.6.3) specifically mentions the Salyans (Saluvii), along with the Ligurians, as causing trouble at about this time.
16. Diodorus 5.29.
17. Roquepertuse: Gérin-Ricard 1927. Thereafter, *Gallia* 18 (1960), 295; 20 (1962), 693; 27 (1969), 446.
18. Le Pègue: the principal references are Perraud 1955 and Hatt et al.* 1961. Thereafter, notes in *Gallia*.
19. Vienne: for the early levels, see Pelletier 1966 and notes in *Gallia* 22 (1964), 511–17; 24 (1966), 505–6; 26 (1968), 583–5.
20. Carcassonne: *Gallia* 31 (1973), 476–7 and Rancoule 1979. Toulouse: Labrousse 1968. For a recent discussion of the distribution of Attic red figured ware in the Mediterranean coastal area, see Gallet de Santerre 1977. This reflects something of the early trading patterns in the region.
21. *Monnaies-à-la-croix*: the literature is considerable but for useful summaries, Soutou 1969, Allen 1969, Colbert de Beaulieu 1971 and Richard 1972. The date of origin of the series is debated. Soutou and Allen prefer a late third- century date; Colbert de Beaulieu and Richard suggest a later origin.
22. Cunliffe 1983, and forthcoming.
23. And the modern scholarly literature is legion. It begins with Cary 1924. An excellent summary is to be found in Hencken 1932, 158–88. Thereafter, Maxwell 1972 and Hawkes 1977 and 1984, with copious references updating

Cary, and Penhallurick 1986, 115ff. The hard facts are few; for this reason interpretation and speculation are unbridled. For transport of tin across France, see Dion 1970.

24. Diodorus 5.38.

25. The three most useful general accounts of Roman influence in southern Gaul are Benedict 1942, Ebel 1976 and Goudineau 1983. Full references to the classical sources will be found in Ebel. A characteristically stimulating interpretation of the events of 125–118 is offered by Stevens (1980). For the question of acculturation see Clavel-Lévêque 1975.

26. It has been claimed that the events of 218 can be seen as destruction layers at a number of sites in the Languedoc, e.g. Enserune.

27. Livy 37.57.1. Orosius 4.20.24.

28. Livy 40.18.4–8.

29. Polybius 33.7–11. See note 16 for suggestion that Entremont may have suffered at this time.

30. For the campaigns of 125–1, with full references, see Benedict 1942 and Ebel 1976. Stevens (1980) presents the events against a background of native social development.

31. See Ebel 1976, 71–2 and notes for full references.

32. Ebel (1976, 76–88) discusses the achievements of Domitius, pointing out that the evidence which has been put forward in the past to suggest that Domitius was the great organizer of the province is by no means unequivocable.

33. See Benedict 1941. The date of foundation has been disputed. The traditional date of 118 given by Velleius (1.15.5) was said to be too early by Mattingly (1922 and 1958) and Sydenham (1952), interpreting the earliest coinage. But more recently Levick (1971) has convincingly argued against the Mattingly view. Most scholars now agree with a foundation date of 118.

34. Orosius 5.15.25; Strabo 4.1.3; Justin *Epit.* 32.3.9–11.

4 Roman estates and entrepreneurs (pp.59–79)

1. These figures are taken from Hopkins 1978, 16–17. Keith Hopkins' brilliant book *Conquerors and Slaves* has been the major inspiration for parts of this chapter. I found his main thesis entirely convincing and differ from it only in the emphasis which I put on the provinces ás consumers of Italy's surplus agricultural product. The other major sources upon which I have relied are Finley 1973 and the numerous writings of Peter Brunt, in particular Brunt 1962 and 1971 a and b. My debt to these authors runs throughout this chapter.

2. Hopkins 1978, 25–37 especially 28.

3. Hopkins 1978, 30.

4. Hopkins 1978, 36.

5. The literature on Gracchus and the social problems is immense. For a convenient and challenging summary, see Brunt 1971A, 74–111. For more detail, see Brunt 1971B (with full bibliography).

6. The most convenient discussion of the Republican colonization is Salmon 1969.

7. The commission went and began to lay out the land-grid, but the Roman opposition talked of the markers being mysteriously ripped up by the spirits. It was Julius Caesar who was to successfully establish the colony eighty years later.

8. Hopkins 1978, 66–7.

9. The question of senatorial involvement in trading ventures is considered by D'Arms 1980.

10. On the growth of large estates, see Hopkins 1978, 49–64.
11. Duncan-Jones 1974, 33.
12. The literature on ancient slavery is immense. Among the most useful recent sources in English are Harris 1980, Finley 1960, Westermann 1955 and, in particular, Hopkins 1978 — all with extensive bibliographies. A major collection of papers by many authors will be found in *Opus 1* (1982).
13. Columella 1.8.8.
14. Varro, *On Agriculture* 1.17.
15. Duncan-Jones 1974, 34–8.
16. Duncan-Jones 1974, 35, and Purcell 1985. The standard work on Roman wine production is Tchernia's masterly overview (1986).
17. Cicero *de repub.* 3.16. For a discussion of the significance of this passage, see Paterson 1978.
18. Suetonius, *Dom.* 7.2. It is unlikely that Domitian was trying to limit wine production solely in the interests of maintaining profits for the wine growers.
19. For a full discussion of Columella's statistics, exploring their difficulties and inconsistencies, see Duncan-Jones 1974, 39–54.
20. The literature on Cosa and the *Ager Cosanus* grows. For a brief summary, Salmon 1969, 29–39. For the town of Cosa, in the sad absence of a definitive excavation report, see Brown 1951 and 1980. For a settlement survey of the Ager Cosanus, see Dyson 1978. The port of Cosa and the fisheries are dealt with by McCann 1979 and 1985; the question of amphora production by Manacorda 1978 and Will 1979; and the villa at Settefinestre by Carandini and Tatton-Brown 1980 (interim report), and Carandini 1985 (definitive report). The social and economic problems posed by the archaeological evidence are critically discussed by Carandini and Settis (1979) and Rathbone (1981). There is much more besides, but these sources provide an introduction to the literature.
21. Carandini 1985.
22. Rathbone (1981) offers a closely argued assessment of the economy of the *Ager Cosanus*. His figures are adopted here.
23. McCann 1979 and 1985.
24. The Sestius amphorae are fast becoming a favourite topic. The most detailed study is that of Will (1979 and 1982), but see also Manacorda 1978.
25. The discussion in D'Arms 1980 is full and contains references to the original texts.
26. See Roman 1983, fig 54 and supporting text for the Narbonne region.
27. The definitive report on the Grand Congloue wreck was published by Benoit (1961), but for a frank discussion of the problems of dating (with full documentation) see Will 1979, 339–41.
28. The threads are brought together in a convincing manner in D'Arms 1980, 81–4.
29. Tchernia 1968–70.
30. Parker 1984.
31. Tchernia, Pomey and Hesnard 1978 and Tchernia 1978.
32. Py 1978, 247, 325.
33. Amphorae from Chalon: Bonnamour 1975. The evidence from Toulouse is summarized (with references) in Labrousse 1968, 143–60.
34. Tchernia 1983, 92. See also Roman 1985.
35. Carandini 1980.
36. Hopkins 1978, 73.

37. See note 12.
38. D'Arms 1980, 121.
39. Hopkins 1978, 102–3.
40. De Bello Gallico 2.33. Plutarch Caes. 15.
41. For a discussion of the question in relation to the possible sudden development of slave trade with Dacia (argued on the basis of the denarii hoards) see Crawford 1977.
42. Strabo on Aquileia, 5.1.8; on Tanais, 11.2.3; on Britain, 4.5.2. Tacitus on the adventure of the Usipi, Agricola 28.
43. These calculations are Tchernia's (1983, 98).

5 Gaul: continuity and change, 125–59 BC (pp.80–105)

1. These matters are discussed in detail by Badian 1966.
2. The main events of the Sertorian episode are most conveniently discussed in Schulten 1926.
3. The dates of Fonteius' commission are in dispute. Most recent writers, e.g. Broughton (1952, II, 109) and Badian (1966, 912) prefer 74–72, though Jullian (1908–26, III, 111) argues for 76–74.
4. The recent evidence has been presented in full by Vidal and Magnol 1983.
5. For the ports of Narbo, see Guy 1955.
6. A full discussion of the epigraphic evidence for trade and industry at Narbo is given in Benedict 1941, 67–78.
7. The Pro Fonteio text: the plausible reconstruction used here is given by Jullian (1908–26, III, 99). See also Labrousse 1968, 143 and Clemente 1974, 132 for its interpretation. Middleton (1983) argues that the movement of the wine was part of the military supply system.
8. The point is emphasized by Tchernia 1983, 93–4. For Aquileia see Strabo (5.1.8); for Gallic barrels used in siege warfare, Caesar (B.G. 8.42.1).
9. For a general statement, see Tchernia 1983, 95–6. More specifically for the metal sources and a full discussion of the documentary evidence, see Ramin 1974. Significant sites are discussed by Rancoule and Solier 1977 (Corbières); Rancoule and Rigaud 1978, and Rancoule and Guiraud 1979 (Lastours); and Dubois and Guilbaut 1980 (Pyrénées).
10. Montmerlhe has passed largely unnoticed in the literature. I am particularly grateful to Richard Boudet who told me about the site and about his current programme of work there; see Boudet 1985.
11. For the Rhône–Saône axis as a route by which Mediterranean commodities penetrated Gaul: Morel 1985, 198 (Campanian ware) and Roman 1985 (amphorae).
12. Bibracte, Essalois and Joeuvres. A convenient summary of all three with references to earlier work will be found in Cotton 1957. More recently, for Essalois, see Preynat 1962 and 1982, and Renaud 1962; and for Joeuvres, Pèrichon 1960, Besset and Pèrichon 1964, and Grosbelet and Pèrichon 1965.
13. Diodorus Siculus 5.26.3.
14. The question is explored by Daubigney (1981).
15. Tchernia 1983, 98–9.
16. For a general assessment of the classical sources see Tierney 1960, with critical comments and reservations by Nash 1976. The Irish literature as a source for archaic Celtic society is discussed by Jackson 1964. On the Irish literature see also Green 1954.

17. Strabo 5.29.
18. Caesar *B.G.* 6.13–14.
19. Caesar *B.G.* 1.1. The archaeological evidence for the division has not been considered fully but is summarized by Duval (1984), whence fig 37. The case of the distinct nature of the Aquitani is argued by Mohen 1980.
20. The Aedui: Caesar *B.G.* 1.11; 3.20. Strabo 4.3.3.
21. Caesar *B.G.* 1.4.
22. Caesar *B.G.* 7.4.
23. The case for early state development in central Gaul is championed by Nash (1978a), but Ralston (1984) argues that it is overstated.
24. The most convenient recent survey of the coinage of central Gaul is presented by Nash (1978b) who discusses its political and economic implications.
25. The literature on *oppida* in Gaul is diffuse and often excessively unhelpful. An extremely valuable survey of *oppida* enclosed with *muri gallici* (timber-laced walls) together with full references is to be found in Cotton 1957. A more up-to-date listing of Iron Age fortifications in non-Mediterranean France is given by Buchsenschultz (1984) with selected references.
26. For Cenabum: *B.G.* 7.3 and 11. For Avaricum: *B.G.* 7.13–15, 17 and 22–3.
27. For amphorae in Armorica, see Galliou 1982 for detailed listing and 1984 for a summary discussion.
28. Quimper: the various Late Iron Age discoveries are listed with references in Le Bihan 1984, 10–17 with a summary of current work at Le Braden.
29. Alet: for general survey of the evidence, see Langouet 1984 with full references.
30. The best survey of Armorican hillforts and *oppida* is Wheeler and Richardson 1957, where details of the excavations at Camp d'Artus and Le Petit Celland will be found.
31. Scipio's researches: Strabo 4.2.1; visit of Crassus: Strabo 3.5.11.
32. Caesar *B.G.* 3.7–11.
33. For general discussion of these questions, see Cunliffe 1982.
34. The results of the recent excavations at Hengistbury with an assessment of the earlier finds are given in Cunliffe 1987.
35. Details of the trade in Armorican pottery northwards to Britain are given in Cunliffe 1982, with full listings and references.
36. For general overview of the context, see Cunliffe 1984b. For the burials in particular, see Duval 1975a, 1975b, and Duval and Blanchet 1974.
37. For a recent distribution map (and listing) of Dressel 1 amphorae in northern Gaul, see Fitzpatrick 1985. (See pp.137–44 below for a more detailed consideration).
38. The anthropology of the north Belgic tribes is considered by Roymans 1983.

6 The Battle for Gaul: 58–50 BC (pp.106–124)

1. Works of the life of Julius Caesar are legion. Two readily accessible are Adcock 1956 and Geizer 1968. For a general background to Roman imperialism, see Badian 1968.
2. Still one of the best commentaries on the course of the war is Holmes 1899. Many of the locations attributed to battles are based on Napolean's *Histoire de Jules César* and are not as well founded as was once believed.
3. Quotations from the *Commentaries* are taken from A. and P. Wiseman's translation, published as *Julius Caesar. The Battle for Gaul* (London: 1980).

4. Crassus to Aquitania and Sabinus to Normandy, *B.G.* 3.11.
5. *B.G.* 6.1.
6. *B.G.* 6.2.
7. *B.G.* 7.1.
8. *B.G.* 1.2.
9. The question is neatly debated, with copious references, by Hachmann, Kossack and Kuhn 1962 and summarized by Wells (1972), 14–31.
10. Belgae of German origin, *B.G.* 2.4; Condrusi, etc., *B.G.* 2.4 and 6.32; Usipetes and Tencteri, *B.G.* 4.4; Menapii, *B.G.* 4.4.
11. For Suebi see *B.G.* 4.1–3.
12. Remi in *B.G.* Emissaries sent to Caesar, 2.3. Remi become dominant due to Caesar's protection, 6.12. Lingones as dependants, 7.63. Lingones and Remi provide cavalry, 8.11. Caesar protects them from Bellovaci, 7.90 and 8.76.
13. Aedui in *B.G.* Struggle against Arverni, 1.31, 33. Sequani return hostages, 7.12. Aeduian dependants, 7.75.
14. Aedui used against Bellovaci, *B.G.* 2.5, 10. Bellovaci clients of Aedui, *B.G.* 2.14.
15. Dumnorix of the Aedui, *B.G.* 1.3, 9, 18–20.
16. Dumnorix opposes Caesar, *B.G.* 5.5–7.
17. Caesar's uncertainty about the Aedui, *B.G.* 7.9. The subsequent revolt, *B.G.* 7.33–56.
18. Return of Aeduian captives, *B.G.* 7.89–90.
19. The rise of Vercingetorix, *B.G.* 7.4.
20. 'Scorched earth policy' in territory of Bituriges, *B.G.* 7.14. Nitiobriges join rebellion, *B.G.* 7.31. Council of war at Bibracte, *B.G.* 7.63.
21. *B.G.* 7.75–6.
22. *B.G.* 7.89–90.
23. Commius in *B.G.* Appointed king of Atrebates and in Britain, 4.21, 27. Commius in Britain in 54 BC, 5.22. Control of the Morini, 7.76. In command at Alesia, 7.76.
24. Commius after Alesia. In concert with Bellovaci, *B.G.* 8.6–7, 10. Attacked in Roman ambush, *B.G.* 8.21–3. Agreement with Mark Anthony, *B.G.* 8.47–8. Escape to Britain, Frontinus, *Strategemeta* 2.13, 11.
25. *B.G.* 2.28.
26. *B.G.* 3.16.
27. *B.G.* 2.33.
28. *B.G.* 7.11.
29. *B.G.* 7.28.
30. *B.G.* 8.44.

7 The creation of the three Gauls (pp.125–144)

1. For brief but balanced surveys of Caesar's settlement of Gaul, see Drinkwater 1983, Chapter 1 and Wightman 1985, 44–62.
2. Février 1973. For Arles and Narbonne, see also Suetonius, *Tiberius* 4.1.
3. Staehlin 1948, 91–6.
4. Gallic cavalry, Drinkwater 1978; also Julian 1921, 571–2. As an example of misfire: the rising of AD 21 led by Julius Florus and Julius Sacrovir, the former Treverian, the latter an Aeduian.
5. The revolt of the Bellovaci, Livy *Epitome* 114. The Raetian campaigns, Wells 1972, 36.

6. Visit in 39/8, Apian, 5.75. See also Drinkwater 1983, 121.
7. General summary of these events with references, Drinkwater 1983, 121.
8. Visit in 27, Dio, 53.22, 5. For organization, see Drinkwater 1983 *passim*.
9. Dio 54.4, 1.
10. Defeat of Salassi 25/4 and foundation of Augusta Praetoria (Aosta), Staehlin 1948, 163. For the Tropaeum, Pliny, *Nat. Hist.* 3.136 and Formigé 1949. The Alpine campaigns of Augustus are fully discussed by Wells (1972, Chapter 4).
11. For the choice of Lugdunum, Drinkwater 1975. For Lugdunum in general, Audin 1956.
12. Concilium Galliarum at Lugdunum, Seneca, *Epist.* 91.
13. We return to the German campaigns in more detail in Chapter 9. For a full and thoroughly referenced account see Wells 1972.
14. Drinkwater (1983, Chapter 6) argues convincingly that the development of Gaul in the late first century BC was closely linked to military policies and activity on the Rhine.
15. Caesar, *B.G.* 3.7 for the winter of 57/6 and 5.24 for the effects of the drought in 54/3.
16. This interesting point is made by Drinkwater (1983, 21 and 1978, 831).
17. Strabo, 4.6.11.
18. The question of the influence of the army on trade and supplies in Gaul is considered in two papers by Middleton (1979 and 1983).
19. Caesar *B.G.* 8.44.
20. Doyet 1962
21. For general listing of the post-Caesarian coinage, see Scheers 1977a. Sheers 1977b deals with the coinage of the Treveri while Sheers 1981, 20–22, looks at the coins found at Villeneuve and Pommiers. For a general discussion of post-Caesarian coinage with full references, see Wightman 1977, 117–23.
22. Cabotse and Pèrichon 1966
23. For pottery from the Gergovia region, see Ward-Perkins 1940 and Hatt 1945. For eastern Armorican graphite wares, see Cunliffe 1982, 59 with full bibliography. The best selection of Belgic pottery is illustrated by Hawkes and Dunning 1931, and Birchall 1965.
24. See Pliny, *Nat. Hist.* 34.162 for metal-working skills of the Gauls.
25. See Cotton 1957, 190–5 for summary with full bibliography to earlier work. A new programme of excavations has recently begun.
26. For discussion of the army size, see Wightman 1977, 107–8.
27. For wares from Lombez, see Mesplé 1951. For Saint-Rémy-en-Rollat, see Déchelette 1904, Vertet 1961.
28. Gallo–Belgic wares: see Green 1972 for succinct summary. Hatt 1949 gives a general account of wares produced in north-east Gaul. For the Santonge area TN: Santrot 1979 and 1984. Kilns producing a similar range of wares have recently been identified near Rennes (Menez 1985).
29. Early samian workshops by 10 BC at Lyon: see Picon and Garmier 1974, and Hartley 1977; at La Grafesenque, Hartley 1977. For a general consideration of the trading of samian in Gaul in the early Roman period, see Dannell 1979.
30. The early excavation reports are confusing and often uninformative. A useful summary with references is provided by Cotton 1957, 190–5.
31. Grenier 1931–60 iii, 234.
32. St Servan/Alet/Corseul: see Langouet 1977 and 1984; Corseul, Galliou 1983, 64–5 and *passim*; Guennon 1981, 159–75.
33. For Pommiers, see Wheeler and Richardson 1957, 129–30 with references. For

Villeneuve-Saint-Germain, see Scheers 1981, 21–2, and Debord and Scheers 1984 (coins); Debord 1982 (settlement and coins).

34. Strabo, 4.1.14.
35. Strabo, 4.6.11, 'Lugdunum is the centre of the country — an acropolis as it were; not only because the rivers meet there, but also because it is near all parts of the country. And it was on this account also, that Agrippa began at Lugdunum when he cut his roads'.
36. For Armorica, Galliliou 1982; for Hengistbury, see Cunliffe 1987, 309–10 with detailed report on the amphorae by Williams, 271–6.
37. The distribution of Pascual 1 amphorae, Williams 1981 and Fitzpatrick 1985, fig 8.
38. The western *terra nigra* production centres, Santrot 1979 and 1984. For the western Gaulish imports to Hengistbury, Rigby 1987. Those from Cleavel Point are not yet published. It is, however, possible that some of the finds in central southern Britain come from the kilns of the Rennes area (Menez 1985).
39. Cunliffe 1987 *passim*, but for summary see pp. 339–45.
40. For a general summary of social development in North Belgica, see Roymans 1983.
41. Wightman 1977 gives a comprehensive assessment of military dispositions in northern Gaul in the late first century BC
42. Fitzpatrick 1985, especially fig 5.
43. For a brief survey of north Gaulish burials, Collis 1977, 5–6 and appendix 1, p. 12. For Goeblingen-Nospelt, Thill 1966 and 1967.
44. For a brief review of the burial evidence from eastern Britain, Cunliffe 1978, 83–9.
45. For years archaeologists have argued that the 'Belgicization' of eastern Britain was the result of Belgic immigration. For the principal references, and a statement of the alternative view put forward here, see Cunliffe 1984b, 19–21.
46. For a stimulating review of the political aspirations of Rome and the attitude of Augustus to Britain, see Stevens 1951.

8 Progress through Britain (pp.145–170)

1. A recent review of Bronze Age trade between Britain and the Continent, giving copious detail of the exchange of metalwork, is to be found in O'Connor 1980. For a more theoretical approach, see Rowlands 1980.
2. Briard 1965.
3. The evidence from Mount Batten is briefly summarized in Pearce 1983. The results of the recent excavations by the present author are yet to be published.
4. The most convenient summary of these two sites, together with an assessment of cross-Channel trade and navigation in the Middle Bronze Age, is given in Muckelroy 1981.
5. Merthyr Mawr Warren is a site of considerable potential interest. Material collected over a period of time is listed and briefly discussed by Grimes (1951, especially 126–8) but deserves complete reassessment.
6. A full assessment of Hengistbury including material found in the earlier excavations as well as the most recent work will be found in Cunliffe 1987.
7. Cunliffe 1976 and 1984a for discussion of social and economic change in southern Britain in the Iron Age.
8. Cunliffe 1984b with bibliography for the earlier discussions. See also Hachmann 1976 for a general statement of the problem.

9. This was the traditional view originally puforward by Derek Allen. In recent years John Kent has preferred a later date for the introduction of the Gallo–Belgic issues (Kent 1981) but a reassessment by Robert Van Arsdell (soon to be published) supports the earlier dating.

10. The arguments are those of Robert Van Ardell to whom the author is indebted for the information soon to be published

11. For the potin series in general, see Van Ardell 1983 and 1986. For potin coinage as an indicator of early market economies in Britain, see Cunliffe 1981.

12. The literature is extensive. Central to the discussion is the work on burials and metalwork published by Stead (1967 and 1976). Tyres (1980) provides an interesting insight into the dating of ceramics.

13. Peacock 1984.

14. These points are enlarged upon, with maps, in Cunliffe 1981.

15. The problem of earlier *oppida* in Britain is summarized with an extensive bibliography in Cunliffe 1976 and 1978 *passim*. More recently for Camulodunum see Crummy 1980a and b; for Silchester, Fulford 1985; and for Verulamium Hunn 1980.

16. Salmonsbury, Dunning 1976; Bagendon, Clifford 1961; and Camerton, Wedlake 1958 and reassessment in progress by the present author. On the question of tribal boundaries defined numismatically see Sellwood 1984.

17. Leach and Thew 1985.

18. The site near Saham Toney: see Brown 1986. For a recent assessment of the major settlements of Lincolnshire with full bibliography see May 1984.

19. North Ferriby, Corder and Davies Pryce 1938; South Ferriby, Allen 1963 and Hawkes 1963. A new programme of excavation has begun at North Ferriby.

20. For a view of British politics between the invasions, see Frere 1974, chapter 4, written before the Iron Age background was extensively reinterpreted.

21. For the invasion and subsequent military history of Britain, see Frere 1974 and Salway 1981.

22. Conventional wisdom has it that the Durotrigan forts were continuously occupied from the Middle Iron Age. This view was based entirely upon Wheeler's interpretation of the sequence exposed in his excavations at Maiden Castle (Wheeler 1943). If so, then the Durotriges must have differed from neighbouring tribes to the north and east (a view accepted by Cunliffe 1971, 67–8). More recently Alcock (1980) has shown that South Cadbury was abandoned at the end of the Middle Iron Age and redefended at the time of the invasion in *c*. AD 43. Current excavation at Maiden Castle may yet modify Wheeler's interpretation.

23. A useful summary of the early stages of urban development in the province is to be found in Wacher 1975.

24. The causes and events of the Boudican rebellion have been frequently discussed, in summary by Frere (1974) and Salway (1981) and in more detail by Webster (1978).

25. Frere 1974, 92–103, 115–7, and for an extensive review of the evidence, Hanson and Campbell 1986.

26. See note 18 for references. Large numbers of Celtic coins have recently been recovered.

27. The classic description of the Stanwick earthworks and of the excavations of 1951 is given by Wheeler (1954). Since then, his interpretaions have been questioned (Dobson 1970). A new assessment incorporating the results of the most recent excavations is given by Turnbull (1984).

28. The literature on the Scottish campaigns and the northern frontiers is legion. The most convenient up-to-date summary, fully referenced, is offered by Breeze (1982). Maxwell (1980) summarizes views on the native situation.
29. Rivet (ed.) 1966 offers a collection of papers reflecting on the variety of Iron Age sites in northern Britain. The question of Roman imports in Scotland has been reviewed from time to time, most usefully in Robertson 1970.
30. Traprain Law: the most recent survey is by Jobey (1976 but written in 1972) reviewing all the earlier literature, especially Hogg 1951 and Feachem 1958.
31. Richmond 1961, 148–9.
32. The Roman material from Ireland was fully discussed in Ó'Ríordáin 1947 and more recently reassessed by Bateson 1973. Roman coins from Newgrange are considered by Carson and O'Kelly 1977.
33. Tacitus, *Agricola* 24.
34. Peacock and Thomas 1967.

9 Beyond the Rhine (pp.171–192)

1. The crossing of 55 and 53 BC: see *B.G.* 4.1–19, 6.29–44. Agrippa in Gaul and the campaign of 38 BC, Appain, *B.G.* 5.386; Dio 48.49.3.
2. A full account of Augustus's German campaigns and the events leading up to them is given by Wells (1976). The archaeological evidence is there presented in detail. See also Schönberger 1969, 144–51, with extensive references.
3. See Wells 1976, chapters 5 and 6 with full supporting archaeological detail.
4. Dio 60.29 and 30.
5. Koestermann 1957, 441–3; von Petrikovits 1966.
6. Tacitus, *Ann.* 1.50–2.26.
7. Schönberger 1969, 151–5.
8. The most accessible and perceptive discussion of the changes in German society from the first century BC to the first century AD will be found in E. A. Thompson's book, *The Early Germans*. Thompson argues that the accounts by Caesar and Tacitus can be regarded as reliable and that the differences in society presented by the two accounts reflect changes caused largely by proximity to the Roman world.
9. *B.G.* 6.22.
10. *B.G.* 6.23.
11. Tacitus, *Ger.* 15.
12. Tacitus, *Ger.* 11.
13. Tacitus, *Ger.* 14.
14. Tacitus, *Ger.* 15.
15. Tacitus, *Ann.* 2.62,3.
16. Arminius: Tacitus, *Ann.* 1.54–68; 2.7–20 for account of the major events of his career.
17. Tacitus, *Ann.* 2.88.
18. *B.G.* 4.2.
19. Tacitus, *Ger.* 5.
20. The literature on Roman imports in Germania is very considerable. The most thorough survey is the seminal account by Eggers (1951) which is summarized and enlivened in a masterly way by Wheeler (1954) who reproduces a series of useful maps. The numerous attempts to find pattern and meaning in the occurrence of Roman material beyond the frontiers have been summarized

conveniently by Hedeager (1978a, 192–8), who then proceeds (199–216) to offer a systematic quantitative analysis of her own.

21. Tacitus, *Ann.* 62.
22. For the distribution of Roman goods in Bohemia: Motykova-Sneidrova 1963 and 1967, and Sakař 1970, the latter giving a general overview.
23. Pliny, *Nat. Hist.* 37.45.
24. Tacitus, *Ger.* 41.
25. Tacitus, *Ger.* 42.
26. Tacitus, *Ann.* 2.45.
27. Tacitus, *Ann.* 11.14.
28. Tacitus, *Ann.* 11.19.
29. Hedeager (1978a) argues convincingly for the existence of two zones — a buffer zone and barbarian Germany beyond — basing her arguments on the differential distribution of artefacts. Her interpretation of the evidence differs a little from that offered here. She prefers to see the buffer zone as one in which a market economy exists with limited use of money. She argues that this is the direct result of the area having already undergone a 'Celtic' development during which *oppida* had emerged.
30. For Lübsow, see Eggers 1950. A convenient general discussion of this category of graves is given by Wheeler (1954, chapter 4) and Todd (1977).
31. Johansen 1923.
32. The fullest account of the cultural groups and burial practices of eastern Germania is given by Godłowski (1970). Todd (1975, chapter 2) provides a useful summary.
33. Schulz 1933 and 1953.
34. See e.g. Svoboda 1972, for the cemetery at Piestany.
35. A detailed discussion of the eastern Danish burials is given by Hedeager (1978b). Her views are summarized with further comments on interpretation by Jensen (1982, 244–9).
36. For Gotland, settlement and economy, see Hagberg 1967.
37. The literature concerning Dutch and German Roman Age settlements is considerable. For a useful overview of the German evidence, Schmid 1978 (with references); for Feddersen Wierde, Haarnagel 1973; for Flögeln, Zimmermann 1978; for Wijster, Van Es 1967. There is much more besides. Both Wheeler 1954 and Todd 1975 offer general summaries, up-to-date for their time of publication. The processes of interaction between Roman and native are at last beginning to receive careful attention: Van Es 1966 (for general view of settlement in Friesland), Brandt 1983 (for summary of research in Assendelver Polders) and Bloemers 1983 (for a broad view of acculturation along the Lower Rhine).
38. For an up-to-date summary of the Danish evidence, with useful references to specific sites, see Jensen 1982, 204–22.
39. Schönberger 1969, 171–7.
40. For recent discussion of *laeti*, see Günther 1975 and Böhme 1974.

Bibliography

ADCOCK, F. 1956: *Caesar as a Man of Letters* (Cambridge).

AKURGAL, E. 1956: 'Les fouilles de Phocée et les sondages de Kymé', *Anatolia* 1, 3–14.

ALCOCK, L. 1980: 'The Cadbury Castle Sequence in the First Millennium BC', *Bull. Board of Celtic Studies* 18, 656–718.

ALLEN, D.F. 1963: 'Celtic coins from South Ferriby', *Hull Museums Publication* 214, 33–6.

ALLEN, D.F. 1969: 'Monnaies à la Croix', *Num. Chron.* 90, 35–77.

ARCELIN, P., ARCELIN-PRADELLE, C. & GASCO, Y. 1982: 'Le village protohistorique du Mont-Garou (Sanary, Var)', *Doc. d'Archéol. Méridionale* 5, 53–128.

ARNEL, J., MAJUREL, R. & PRADÈS, H. 1974: *Le Port de Lattara (Lattes, Hérault)* (Montpellier).

ARRIBAS, A. 1962: *The Iberians* (London).

AUDIN, A. 1956: *Essai sur la topographie de Lugdunum* (Lyon).

BADIAN, E. 1966: 'Notes on Provincia Gallia in the Late Republic', in Chevallier, R. (ed.), *Mélanges d'archéologie et d'histoire offerts à André Piganiol* (Paris).

BADIAN, E. 1968: *Roman Imperialism in the Late Republic* (Oxford).

BARRUOL, G. 1969: *Les peuples préromains du Sud-Est de la Gaule* (Paris).

BATESON, J.D. 1973: 'Roman material from Ireland: a re-consideration', *Proc. Royal Irish Academy* 73, 21–97.

BENEDICT, C.H. 1941: *A History of Narbo* (Lancaster, Pa).

BENEDICT, C.H. 1942: 'The Romans in Southern Gaul', *American Journ. Philology* 63, 38–50.

BENOÎT, F. 1947: 'Les fouilles d'Entremont en 1946', *Gallia* 5, 81–97.

BENOÎT, F. 1954: 'Les fouilles d'Entremont en 1953–4', *Gallia* 12, 285–94.

BENOÎT, F. 1957: *Entremont. Capitale celto-ligure des Saylens de Provence* (Aix-en-Provence).

BENOÎT, F. 1959: 'L'économie du littoral de la Narbonnaise a l'epoque antique', *Rev. d'Études Ligures* 25, 87–110.

BENOÎT, F. 1961: *L'Épave du Grand Congloué à Marseille* (*Gallia* Supp. 14: Paris).

BENOÎT, F. 1965: 'Recherches sur l'Hellénisation du Midi de la Gaule', *Pub. Ann. Fac. Lettres Aix* NS, 43.

BENOÎT, F. 1966: 'Topographie antique de Marseille: Le théatre et le mur de Crinas', *Gallia* 24, 1–20.

BENOÎT, F. 1968a: 'Résultats historiques des fouilles d'Entremont (1946–1967)', *Gallia* 26, 1–31.

BENOÎT, F. 1968b: *Nice et Cimiez antiques* (Nice).

BENOÎT, F. 1972: 'L'évolution topographique de Marseille. Le port et l'enceinte a la lumiere des fouilles', *Latomus* 31, 54–70.

BENOÎT, F. 1981: *Entremont* (Paris).

BESSET, F. & PERICHON, R. 1964: 'Contribution a l'étude de quelques sites fortifiés du Department de la Loire', *Celticum* 9, 63–74.

BIRCHALL, A. 1965: 'The Aylesford-Swarling culture: the problem of the Belgae reconsidered', *Proc. Prehist. Soc.* 31, 241–367.

BLOEMERS, J.H.F. 1983: 'Acculturation in the Rhine/Meuse basin in the Roman period: a preliminary survey', in Brandt & Slofstra (eds.) 1983, 159–210.

BOARDMAN, J. 1980: *The Greeks Overseas* (third edition, London).

BÖHME, H.W. 1974: *Germanische Grabfunde des 4 bis 5 Jahrhunderts zwischen unterer Elbe und Loire. Münchner Beiträge zur Vor-und Frühgeschichte* 19 (Munich).

BONNAMOUR, L. 1975: 'Le port Gaulois et gallo-romain de Châlon', *Mém. de la Soc. d'Histoire et d'Archéologie de Châlon-sur-Saône* 45, 61–73.

BOUDET, R. 1986: *L'oppidum gaulois de Montmerlhe à Laissac (Aveyron). Campagne 1985* (typescript interim report).

BOULOUMIE, B. 1982: 'Saint-Blaise et Marseille au VIᵉ siècle avant J-C. L'hypothèses étrusque', *Latomus* 41, 74–91.

BRANDT, R. 1983: 'A brief encounter along the northern frontier', in Brandt & Slofstra (eds.) 1983, 129–46.

BRANDT, R. & SLOFSTRA, J. (eds.) 1983: *Roman and native in the Low Countries* (BAR Int. Ser. 184: Oxford).

BREEZE, D.J. 1982: *The northern frontiers of Roman Britain* (London).

BREEZE, D.J. & DOBSON, B. 1985: 'Roman military development in North England', *Britannia* 16, 1–20.

BRETZ-MAHLER, D. 1971: *La Civilisation de la Tène I en Champagne* (*Gallia* Supp. 23: Paris).

BRIARD, J. 1965: *Les Dépôts bretons et L'Age du Bronze atlantique* (Rennes).

BROUGHTON, T.R.S. 1952: *The Magistrates of the Roman Republic* (New York).

BROWN, F.E. 1951: 'Cosa I: History and Topography', *Mem. American Acad. Rome* 20, 5–113.

BROWN, F.E. 1980: *Cosa: the Making of a Roman Town* (Ann Arbor).

BROWN, R.A. 1986: 'The Iron Age and Romano-British Settlement at Woodcock Hall, Saham Toney, Norfolk', *Britannia* 17, 1–58.

BRUNT, P.A. 1962: 'The army and the land in the Roman Revolution', *Journ. Roman Studies* 52, 69–86.

BRUNT, P.A. 1971a: *Social conflicts in the Roman Republic* (London).

BRUNT, P.A. 1971b: *Italian Manpower*, 225 BC–AD 14 (Oxford).

BUCHNER, G. 1966: 'Pithekoussai: oldest Greek colony in the West', *Expedition* (Summer 1966), 4–12.

BUCHNER, G. 1970: 'Mostra degli scavi de Pithecusa', *Dialoghi di Archeologia* 3, 85–101.

BUCHSENSCHUTZ, O. 1984: *Structures d'Habitats et Fortifications de L'âge du Fer en France Septentrionale* (*Mem. Soc. Prehist. Francaise*, Tome 18: Paris).

BURNHAM, B.C. & JOHNSON, H.B. (eds.) 1979: *Invasion and Response. The Case of Roman Britain* (BAR 73: Oxford).

CABOTSE, J. & PÈRICHON, R. 1966: 'Céramique gauloises et gallo-romaines de Roanne (Loire)', *Gallia* 24, 29–75.

CAMPARDOU, J. 1957: 'L'oppidum préromain de Pech-Maho à Sigean (Aude)', *Études Roussillonnaises* 6, 35–65.

CARANDINI, A. 1980: 'Il vigneto e la villa del fondo di Settefinestre nel Cosano: un caso di produzione per il mercato transmarino', *Mem. American Acad. Rome* 36, 1–11.

CARANDINI, A. 1985: *Settefinestre: una villa schiavistica nell'Etruria Romana* (3 vols.) (Moderna).

CARANDINI, A. & SETTIS, S. 1979: *Schiavi e padroni nell'Etruria Romana. La villa di Settefinestre dallo scavo alla mostra* (Bari).

CARANDINI, A. & TATTON-BROWN, T. 1980: 'Excavations at the Roman Villa of "Sette Finestre" in Etruria, 1975–9. First interim report', in Painter, K. (ed.), *Roman Villas in Italy. Recent excavations and research* (London), 9–44.

CARSON, R.A.G. & O'KELLY, C. 1977: 'A catalogue of the Roman coins from Newgrange, Co. Meath and notes on the coins and related finds', *Proc. Royal Irish Academy* 77, 35–56.

CARY, M. 1924: 'The Greeks and ancient trade with the Atlantic', *Journ. Hell. Studies* 44, 166–79.

CLAVEL, M. 1970: *Béziers et son territoire dans l'Antiquite* (Paris).

CLAVEL-LÉVÊQUE, M. 1975: 'Pour une problématique des conditions économiques de l'implantation romains dans le Midi gaulois', *Cahiers Ligures de Préhistoire et d'Archéologie* 24, 35–75.

CLAVEL-LÉVÊQUE, M. 1977: *Marseille grecque, la dynamique d'un impérialisme marchand* (Marseille).

CLEMENTE, G. 1974: *I Romani nella Gallia meridionale (II-I sec. a.C)* (Bologna).

CLERC, M. 1927–9: *Massalia, Histoire de Marseille dans l'Antiquité, des origines à la fin de l'Empire romain d'Occident* (Marseille).

CLIFFORD, E.M. 1961: *Bagendon — a Belgic Oppidum* (Cambridge).

COLBERT DE BEAULIEU, B. 1971: 'La limite septentrionale des monnaies à la croix et la politique de Rome', *Revue Belge de Numismatique* 117, 115–31.

COLLIS, J. 1977: 'Pre-Roman burial rites in north-western Europe', in Reece (ed.) 1977, 1–12.

COOK, J.M. 1962: *The Greeks in Ionia and the East* (London).

CORDER, P. & DAVIES PRYCE, T. 1938: 'Belgic and other Early Pottery found at North Ferriby, Yorks', *Antiq. Journ.* 18, 262–77.

COTTON, M.A. 1957: 'Muri Gallici', in Wheeler & Richardson 1957, 159–225.

COUPRY, J. 1964: 'Les fouilles d'Olbia à Hyères', *Comptes Rendus de l'Academie des Inscriptions et Belles Lettres*, for 1964, 313–21.

CRAWFORD, M.H. 1977: 'Republican *denarii* in Romania: the suppression of piracy and the slave-trade', *Journ. Roman Studies* 67, 117–24.

CRUMMY, P. 1980a: 'Cropmarks at Gosbecks, Colchester', *Aerial Archaeol.* 4, 77–82.

CRUMMY, P. 1980b: 'Camulodunum', *Current Archaeol.* 7, 6–10.

CUNLIFFE, B.W. 1971: 'Some Hill-forts and their Cultural Environments', in Jessen, M. and Hill, D. (eds.), *The Iron Age and its Hillforts* (Southampton), 53–69.

CUNLIFFE, B.W. 1976: 'The origins of urbanization in Britain', in Cunliffe, B.W. and Rowley, R.T., *Oppida: the beginnings of urbanization in Barbarian Europe* (BAR Int. Ser. 11: Oxford), 135–61.

CUNLIFFE, B.W. (ed.) 1981: *Coinage and society in Britain and Gaul* (CBA 38: London).

CUNLIFFE, B.W. 1981: 'Money and society in pre-Roman Britain', in Cunliffe (ed.) 1981, 29–39.

CUNLIFFE, B.W. 1982: 'Britain, the Veneti and beyond', *Oxford Journ. Archaeol.* 1:1, 39–68.

CUNLIFFE, B.W. 1983: 'Ictis: was it here', *Oxford Journ. Archaeol.* 2:1, 123–6.

CUNLIFFE, B.W. 1984a: 'Iron Age Wessex: continuity and change', in Cunliffe & Miles (eds.) 1984, 12–45.

CUNLIFFE, B.W. 1984b: 'Relations between Britain and Gaul in the first century BC and early first century AD', in Macready & Thompson (eds.) 1984, 3–23.

CUNLIFFE, B.W. 1987: *Hengistbury Head, Dorset: Vol. 1, Neolithic to Roman* (OUCA monog. 13: Oxford).

CUNLIFFE, B.W. & MILES, D. (eds.) 1984: *Aspects of the Iron Age in Central Southern Britain* (OUCA Monog. 2: Oxford).

CUNLIFFE, B.W. & ROWLEY, R.T. (eds.) 1978: *Lowland Iron Age Communities in Europe* (BAR Int. Ser. 48: Oxford).

DANNELL, G.B. 1979: 'Eating and drinking in pre-conquest Britain: the evidence of Amphorae and Samian trading, and the effect of the invasion of Claudius', in Burnham & Johnson (eds.) 1979, 177–84.

D'ARMS, J.H. 1980: 'Senators' involvement in commerce in the late Republic: some Ciceronian evidence', *Mem. American Acad. Rome* 36, 77–88.

DAUBIGNEY, A. 1981: 'Relations marchandes méditerranéennes et procès des rapports de dépendance (*Magu*-et ambactes) en Gaule protohistorique', *Colloquio internazionale su forme di contatto e processi di trasformazione nelle società antiche, Cortone 24–30 mai 1981.*

DAYET, M. 1962: 'Qui était Togirix?', *Rev. archéol. de l'Est* 13, 82–98.

DEBORD, J. 1982: 'Premier bilan de huit années de fouilles à Villeneuve-Saint-Germain (Aisne) 1973–1980', in Durand, M. (ed.), *Vallée de l'Aisne: cinq années de fouilles protohistorique* (*Rev. Archéol. de Picardie* numero special: Amiens), 213–64.

DEBORD, J. & SCHEERS, S. 1984: 'Les monnaies gauloises tardives en argent attribuables aux Suessiones trouvées à Villeneuve- Saint-Germain (Aisne)', in Cahen-Delhaye, A., Duval, A., Leman- Delerive, G. and Lemon, P. (eds.), *Les Celtes en Belgique et dans le Nord de la France (Rev. du Nord* numero special: Lille), 69–74.

DÉCHELETTE, J. 1904: *Les fouilles du Mont Beuvray* (Paris/Autun).

DÉCHELETTE, J. 1904: *Les Vases céramiques ornés de la Gaul romaine* (Paris).

DEHN, W. & FREY, H-O. 1962: 'Die absolute Chronologie der Hallstatt- und Frühlatenezeit Mitteleuropas auf Grund des Südimports', *Congresso Internazionale della Scienze Preistoriche e Protostoriche* 6 *Atti*, 3, 197–208.

DEMOULE, J-P. & ILETT, M. 1985: 'First millennium settlement and society in northern France: a case study from the Aisne Valley', in Champion, T.C. and Megaw, J.V.S. (eds.), *Settlement and Society aspects of West European prehistory in the first millennium* BC (Leicester), 214–21.

DION, R. 1970: 'Transport de l'étain des îles Britanniques à Marseille à travers la Gaule préromaine', *Actes du 93ème Congrès national des Sociétés savantes. Tours 1968* (Paris), 423–38.

DOBSON, B. 1970: 'Roman Durham', *Trans. Arch. and Archaeol. Soc. of Durham and Northumberland* NS 2, 31–43.

DORE, J. & GREENE, K.T. 1977: *Roman pottery studies in Britain and Beyond* (BAR Supp. Ser. 30: Oxford).

DRIEHAUS, J. 1965: '"Fürstengräber" und Eisenerze zwischen Mittelrhein, Mosel und Saar', *Germania* 43, 32–49.

DRINKWATER, J.F. 1975: 'Lugdunum: natural capital of Gaul', *Britannia* 6, 133–40.

DRINKWATER, J.F. 1978: 'The rise and fall of the Gallic Iulii', *Latomus* 37, 817–50.

DRINKWATER, J.F. 1983: *Roman Gaul* (London).

DUBOIS, C. & GUILBAUT, J.E. 1980: 'Mines de cuivre antique dans le Séronais (Pyrénées ariégeoises)', *Mines et fonderies.*

DUNBABIN, T.J. 1948: *The Western Greeks* (Oxford).

DUNCAN-JONES, R. 1974: *The economy of the Roman Empire* (Cambridge).

DUNNING, G.C. 1976: 'Salmonsbury, Burton-on-the-Water, Gloucestershire', in Harding (ed.) 1976, 76–118.

DUPRAT, E.H. 1935: *Tauroentum: le Brusq-Six-Fours* (Marseille).

DUVAL, A. 1975a: 'Quelques aspects nouveaux de la sepulture d'Inglemare', *Rev. Soc. Sav. Hte-Normandie, lettres et sciences humaines* 77, 35–46.

DUVAL, A. 1975b: 'Sépultures de La Tène finale et civilisation des *oppida* en Haute-Normandie', in Duval, P-M. and Kruta, V. (eds.), *L'habitat et la nécropole à l'âge du Fer en Europe occidentale et centrale* (Paris), 35–44.

DUVAL, A. 1984: 'Regional Groups in Western France', in Macready & Thompson (eds.) 1984, 78–91.

DUVAL, A. & BLANCHET, J-C. 1974: 'La tombe à char d'Attichy (Oise)', *Bull. S.P.F. etudes et travaux* 1, 401–8.

DYSON, S.L. 1978: 'Settlement patterns in the *Ager Cosanus*: the Wesleyan University Survey, 1974–1976', *Journ. Field Archaeol.* 5, 251–68.

EARLE, T.K. & ERICSON, J. (eds.) 1977: *Exchange Systems in Prehistory* (London).

EBEL, C. 1976: *Transalpine Gaul. The emergence of a Roman Province* (Leiden).

ECHALLIER, J.C. 1982: 'La provenance des amphores massaliotes', *Doc. d'Archéol. Meridionale* 5, 139–44.

EGGERS, H.J. 1950: 'Lübsow, ein germanischer Fürstensitz der älteren Kaiserzeit', *Präh. Zeitschr.* 34–5, 58–111.

EGGERS, H.J. 1951: *Der römische Import im freien Germanien* (Hamburg).

ES, W.A. van 1966: 'Friesland in Roman Times', *BROB* 15–16, 37–68.

ES, W.A. van 1967: 'Wijster, a Native Village beyond the Imperial Frontier', *Palaeohistoria* 11.

EUZENNAT, M. 1976: *Les fouilles de la Bourse à Marseille* (CRAI 1976), 529–52.

EUZENNAT, M. & SALVIAT, F. 1968: *Les fouilles de Marseille* (Mars-Avril 1968) (CRAI 1968), 145–59.

FEACHEM, R.W. 1958: 'The fortifications on Traprain Law', *Proc. Soc. Antiq. Scot.* 89 (for 1955–1956), 284–9.

FEVRIER, P-A. 1973: 'The origin and growth of the cities of Southern Gaul to the third century A.D. An assessment of the most recent archaeological discoveries', *Journ. Roman Studies* 63, 1–28.

FINLEY, M.I. 1959: 'Was Greek civilization based on slave labour?', *Historia* 8, 154–64.

FINLEY, M.I. (ed.) 1960: *Slavery in Classical Antiquity* (Cambridge).

FINLEY, M.I. 1973: *The Ancient Economy* (London).

FITZPATRICK, A. 1985: 'The distribution of Dressel 1 amphorae in North-west Europe', *Oxford Journ. Archaeol.* 4:3, 305–40.

FORMIGÉ, J. 1949: *Le trophée des Alpes: la Turbie* (*Gallia* Supp. 2: Paris).

FRANKENSTEIN, S. & ROWLANDS, M.J. 1978: 'The internal structure and regional context of Early Iron Age society in south-western Germany', *Bull. Inst. Archaeol. Lond.* 15, 73–112.

FREIDIN, N. 1982: *The Early Iron Age in the Paris Basin* (BAR Int. Ser. 131: Oxford).

FRERE, S.S. 1974: *Britannia* (second edition: London).

FREY, H-O. 1955: 'Eine etruskische Bronzeschnabelkanne', *Annales Litt. de l'Univ. de Besançon* ser. 2, 2:1, 4–30.

FULFORD, M. 1985: *Guide to the Silchester Excavations. The Forum Basilica 1982–4* (Reading).

GALLET DE SANTERRE, H. 1962: 'A propos de la céramique grecque de Marseille', *Rev. des Etudes Anciennes* 64, 378–403.

GALLET DE SANTERRE, H. 1977: 'La diffusion de la céramique Attique aux Vᵉ et IVᵉ siècles avant J.-C. sur les rivages Français de la Méditerranée', *Rev. Archéologique de Narbonnaise* 10, 33–57.

GALLET DE SANTERRE, H. 1978: *Ensérune* (Paris).

GALLET DE SANTERRE, H. 1980: *Ensérune. Les silos de la terrasse est* (Supp. a *Gallia* 39: Paris).

GALLIOU, P. 1982: *Les amphores tardo-républicaines découvertes dans l'ouest de la France et les importations de vins italiens à la fin de L'age du Fer* (Brest).

GALLIOU, P. 1983: *L'armorique romaine* (Braspars).

GALLIOU, P. 1984: 'Days of Wine and Roses? Early Armorica and the Atlantic Wine Trade', in Macready & Thompson (eds.) 1984, 24–36.

GARCÍA Y BELLIDO, A. 1948: *Hispania Graeca* (Barcelona).

GARNSEY, P., HOPKINS, K. & WHITTAKER, C.R. (eds.) 1983: *Trade in the Ancient Economy* (London).

GEIZER, M. 1968: *Caesar: Politician and Statesman* (Oxford).

GÉRIN-RICHARD, H. de 1927: 'La sanctuaire de Roquepertuse', *Soc. de Stastique . . . de Marseille, vol. de centenaire*, 3–53.

GODŁOWSKI, K. 1970: 'The Chronology of the Late Roman and Early Migration periods in Central Europe', *Prace Archeologiczne* 11.

GOUDINEAU, C. 1980: 'La Gaule méridionale', in Duby, G. (ed.), *Histoire de la France urbaine, 1 La ville antique* (Sevil), 143–93.

GOUDINEAU, C. 1983: 'Marseilles, Rome and Gaul from the third to the first century BC', in Garnsey, Hopkins & Whittaker (eds.) 1983, 76–86.

GRAHAM, A.J. 1964: *Colony and Mother City in Ancient Greece* (Manchester).

GREEN, D. 1954: 'Early Irish Society', in Dillon, M. (ed.), *Early Irish Society* (Dublin), 22–35.

GREENE, K. 1972: *Guide to pre-Flavian fine wares c. AD 40–70* (Cardiff).

GRENIER, A. 1931–60: *Manuel d'archéologie gallo-romaine* (Paris).

GRIMES, W.F. 1951: *The Prehistory of Wales* (Cardiff).

GROSBELET, B. & PÈRICHON, R. 1965: 'L'implantation gauloise et gallo-romaine à la peripherie de l'oppidum de Joevre (Loire)', *Ogam* 17, 313–25.

GUENNON, G. 1981: *La Cité des Coriosolites* (Rennes).

GÜNTER, R. 1975: 'Germanische Laeten, Foederaten und Gentiles im nördlichen und nordöstlichen Gallien in der Spätantike', in Grünert, H. (ed.), *Römer und Germanen in Mitteleuropa* (Berlin), 225–34.

GUY, M. 1955: 'Les ports antique de Narbonne', *Rev. d'Etudes Ligures* 21, 213–40.

GUY, M. 1973: 'Le cadre géographique et géologique de Montlaurès', in *Narbonne Archéologie et histoire* (Montpellier), 27–43.

HAARNAGEL, W. 1973: 'Vor- und Frühgeschichte des Landes Wursten', in Lehe, E. (ed.), *Geschichte des Landes Wursten*, 17–128.

HACHMANN, R. 1976: 'The problem of the Belgae seen from the Continent', *Inst. of Archaeol. Bull.* 13, 117–37.

HACHMANN, R., KOSSACK, G. & KUHN, H. 1962: *Völker zwischen Germanen und Kelten Schriftquellen, Bodenfunde und Namengut zur Geschichte des nördlichen Westdeutschlands um Christi Geburt* (Neumünster).

HAFFNER, A. 1976: *Die westliche Hunsrück-Eifelkultur* (Berlin).

HAGBERG, U.E. 1967: *The Archaeology of Skedemosse I-II* (Stockholm).

HANSON, W.S. & CAMPBELL, D.B. 1986: 'The Brigantes: from Clientage to Conquest', *Britannia* 17, 73–90.

HARDEN, D.B. 1972: *The Phoenicians* (Harmondsworth: 3rd edition).

HARDING, D.W. (ed.) 1976: *Hillforts. Later Prehistoric Earthworks in Britain and Ireland* (London).

HÄRKE, H. 1979: *Settlement types and patterns in the West Hallstatt Province* (BAR Int. Ser. 57: Oxford).

HARRIS, W.V. 1980: 'Towards a Study of the Roman slave trade', *Mem. American Acad. Rome* 36, 117–40.

HARTLEY, B. 1977: 'Some wandering potters', in Dore & Greene (eds.) 1977, 251–61.

HASELGROVE, C. 1984: 'Romanization before the Conquest: Gaulish precedents and British consequences', in Blagg, T.F.C. and King, A.C. (eds.), *Military and Civilian in Roman Britain* (Oxford), 5–63.

HATT, J-J. 1945: 'Essai d'une comparaison entre la céramique celtique d'Aulnat-Sud et la céramique gallo-romaine précoc de Gergovie', *Bull. hist. et sci. de l'Auvergne* 64, 36–48.

HATT, J-J. 1949: 'Aperçus sur l'evolution de la céramique commune gallo-romaine, principalement dans le nord-est de la Gaule', *Rev. etud. anc.* 51, 100–28.

HATT, J-J. 1961. 'Le Pègue, habitat hallstattien et comptoir ionien en Haute Province', *Atti del settimo Congresso inter. di Arch. classica* 3, 177–86.

HAWKES, C.F.C. 1977: *Pytheas: Europe and the Greek Explorers* (Oxford).

HAWKES, C.F.C. 1984: 'Ictis disentangled, and the British Tin Trade', *Oxford Journ. Archaeol.* 3:2, 211–33.

HAWKES, C.F.C. & DUNNING, G.C. 1931: 'The Belgae of Gaul and Britain', *Archaeol. Journ.* 87, 150–335.

HAWKES, S.C. 1963: 'Some Belgic brooches from South Ferriby', *Hull Museums Publication* 214, 23–31.

HEDEAGER, L. 1978a: 'A Quantative Analysis of Roman Imports in Europe North of the Limes (0–400 AD), and the Question of Roman-Germanic exchange', *Studies in Scandinavian Prehistory and Early History* 1, 191–216.

HEDEAGER, L. 1978b: 'Processes towards State Formation in Early Iron Age Denmark', *Studies in Scandinavian Prehistory and Early History* 1, 217–223.

HENCKEN, H.O'N. 1932: *The Archaeology of Cornwall and Scilly* (London).

HIRTH, K.G. 1978: 'Interregional trade and the formation of prehistoric gateway communities', *American Antiquity* 43, 35–45.

HOGG, A.H.A. 1951: 'The Votadini', in Grimes, W.F. (ed.), *Aspects of Archaeology in Britain and Beyond* (London), 200–13.

HOLMES, T.R. 1899: *Caesar's Conquest of Gaul* (London).

HOPKINS, K. 1978a: *Conquerors and Slaves* (Cambridge).

HOPKINS, K. 1978b: 'Economic growth and towns in classical antiquity', in Abrahams, P. & Wrigley, E.A. (eds.), *Towns in Societies* (Cambridge), 35–79.

HOPKINS, K. 1980: 'Taxes and Trade in the Roman Empire', *Journ. Roman Studies* 70, 101–25.

HUNDT, H-J. 1969: 'Über vorgeschichtliche Seidenfunde', *Jahr. Röm-Germ. Zentralmus.* 16, 59–71.

HUNN, J.R. 1980: 'The earthworks of Prae Wood', *Britannia* 11, 21–30.

JACKSON, K.H. 1964: *The Oldest Irish Tradition: a Window on the Iron Age* (Cambridge).

JACOBSTAHL, P. 1944: *Early Celtic Art* (Oxford).

JANNORAY, J. 1955: *Ensérune: Contribution à l'étude des civilisations préromaines de la Gaule méridionale* (Paris).

JEHASSE, J. 1963: 'Les fouilles d'Aleria: le plateau et ses problemes', *Gallia* 21, 77–110.

JEHASSE, J. & J. 1973: *La nécropole préromaine d'Aleria* (*Gallia* Supp. 25: Paris).

JENSEN, J. 1982: *The Prehistory of Denmark* (London).

JOBEY, G. 1976: 'Traprain Law: a summary', in Harding (ed.) 1976, 191–204.

JOFFROY, R. 1954: *Le Trésor de Vix (Côte-d'Or)* (Paris).

JOFFROY, R. 1960: 'Le bassin et le trépied de Saint-Colombe (Côte-d'Or)', *Fondation Eugène Piot: Monuments et Mémoirs* 51, 1–23.

JOHANSEN, K.F. 1923: 'Hoby-fundet', *Nordiska Fortidsminder* II, Hefte 3.

JUCKER, H. 1973: 'Altes und Neues zur Grächwiler Hydria', in *Zur griechischen Kunst: Festschrift Hansjörg Bloesch* (Bern), 42–62.

JULLIAN, C. 1908–26: *Histoire de la Gaule*, in 6 volumes (Paris).

KENT, J. 1981: 'The origins of coinage in Britain', in Cunliffe (ed.) 1981a, 40–42.

KIMMIG, W. 1983a: 'Die griechische Kolonisation im westlichen Mittelmeergebiet und ihre Wirkung auf die Landschaften des westlichen Mitteleuropa', *Jahrbuch RGZM* 30, 3–78.

KIMMIG, W. 1983b: *Die Heuneburg an der oberen Donau* (Stuttgart).

KIMMIG, W. & HELL, H. 1958: *Vorzeit an Rhein und Dönau* (Lindau).

KOESTERMANN, E. 1957: 'Die Feldzüge des Germanicus 14–16n. Chr', *Historia* 6, 429–79.

KOSSACK, G. 1959: *Südbayern während der Hallstattzeit* (Berlin).

KOSSACK, G. 1972: 'Hallstattzeit', in Kunkel, O. (ed.), *Vor- und frühgeschichtliche Archäologie in Bayern* (Munich), 85–100.

LABROUSSE, M. 1968: *Toulouse antique, des origines à l'établissement des Wisigoths* (Paris).

LANGLOTZ, E. 1966: *Die kulturelle und künstlerische Hellenisierung der Küsten des Mittelmeers durch die Stadt Phokaia* (Köln).

LANGOUET, L. 1977: 'The fourth century Gallo-Roman site at Alet (Saint-Malo)', in Johnston, D.E. (ed.), *The Saxon Shore* (CBA Res. Rep. 18: London), 38–45.

LANGOUET, L. 1984: 'Alet and Cross-Channel Trade', in Macready & Thompson (eds.) 1984, 67–77.

LEACH, P. & THEW, N. 1985: *A Late Iron Age 'Oppidum' at Ilchester, Somerset* (Bristol).

LE BIHAN, J.P. 1984: *Villages Gaulois et parcellaires Antiques au Braden en Quimper* (Cahiers de Quimper Antique 1: Quimper).

LEVICK, B. 1971: 'Cicero, Brutus 43.159ff., and the foundation of Narbo Martius', *Classical Quarterly* 21, 171–9.

LOUIS, M. & TAFFANEL, O & J. 1955–60: *Le premier âge du fer languedocien* 3 vols.: I, *Les habitats* (1955); II, *Les nécropoles à incinération* (1958); III, *Les Tumulus: Conclusions* (1960) (Bordighera).

MACREADY, S. & THOMPSON, F.H. (eds.) 1984: *Cross-Channel trade between Gaul and Britain in the pre-Roman Iron Age* (London).

MANACORDA, D. 1978: 'The Ager Cosanus and the Production of the Amphorae of Sestius: new evidence and a reassessment', *Journ. Roman Studies* 68, 122–31.

MATTINGLY, H. 1922: 'Some Historical Coins of the Late Republic', *Journ. Roman Studies* 12, 230–3.

MATTINGLY, H. 1958: 'The Foundation of Narbo Martius', *Hommages à Albert Grenier: Collection Latomus* 57, 1159–71.

MAXWELL, G.S. 1980: 'The native background to the Roman occupation of Scotland', in Hanson, W.S. & Keppie, L.J.F. (eds.), *Roman Frontier Studies 1979* (BAR Int. Ser. 71: Oxford), 1–13.

MAXWELL, I.S. 1972: 'The Location of Ictis', *Journ. Royal Inst. of Cornwall* 6:4, 293–319.

MAY, J. 1984: 'The major settlements of the Later Iron Age in Lincolnshire', in Field, N. & White, A. (eds.), *A Prospect of Lincolnshire* (Lincoln), 18–22.

McCANN, A.M. 1979: 'The harbour and fishery remains at Cosa, Italy', *Journ. Field Archaeol.* 6, 391–411.

McCANN, A.M. 1985: 'The Roman port and fishery at Cosa: a centre of trade in the late Roman Republic', in Raban, A. (ed.), *Harbour Archaeology* (BAR Int. Ser. 257: Oxford), 115–56.

MENEZ, Y. 1985: *Les céramiques fumigée de l'ouest de la Gaule (Cahiers de Quimper Antique 2*: Quimper).

MESPLÉ, P. 1951: 'L'Atelier de potier gallo-romain de Galane à Lombez (Gers)', *Gallia* 15, 41–62.

MIDDLETON, P.S. 1979: 'Army supply in Roman Gaul: an hypothesis for Roman Britain', in Burnham, B.C. & Johnson, H.B. (eds.), *Invasion and Response: the case of Roman Britain* (BAR 73: Oxford), 81–98.

MIDDLETON, P.S. 1983: 'The Roman army and long distance trade', in Garnsey, P. & Whittaker, C.R. (eds.), *Trade and Famine in Classical Antiquity* (Cambridge), 75–83.

MOHEN, J-P. 1980: *L'Age du Fer en Aquitaine* (Paris).

MOREL, J-P. 1975: 'L'expansion phocéenne en occident: dix années de recherches (1966–1975)', *Bull. Corresp. Hellénique* 99, 853–96.

MOREL, J-P. 1985: 'Le céramique campanienne en gaul interne', in *Les Ages du fer dans la Vallée de la Saône (Rev. Arch. de Est et du Centre-est* 16ᵉ supp.: Paris), 182–7.

MOTYKOVA-SNEIDROVA, K. 1963: 'Die Anfänge der römischen Kaiserzeit in Böhmen', *Fontes Arch. Pragenses* VI.

MOTYKOVA-SNEIDROVA, K. 1967: 'Weiterentwicklung und Ausklang der älteren römischen Kaiserzeit in Böhmen', *Fontes Arch. Pragenses* XI.

MUCKLEROY, K. 1981: 'Middle Bronze Age trade between Britain and Europe: a maritime perspective', *Proc. Prehist. Soc.* 47, 275–97.

MURRAY, O. 1980: *Early Greece* (London).

NAPOLÉON III 1865: *Histoire de Jules César* (Paris).

NASH, D. 1976: 'Reconstructing Poseidonios's Celtic Ethnography; some considerations', *Britannia* 7, 111–26.

NASH, D. 1978a: 'Territory and state formation in Central Gaul', in Green, D., Haselgrove, C. & Spriggs, M. (eds.), *Social Organization and Settlement* (BAR Int. Ser. 47: Oxford), 455–75.

NASH, D. 1978b: *Settlement and Coinage in Central Gaul* c. 250–50 BC (BAR SS 39: Oxford).

NASH, D. 1985: 'Celtic territorial expansion and the Mediterranean World', in Champion & Megaw (eds.) 1985, 45–67.

NEUFFER, E.M. 1974: *Hallstatt: frühe Kelten in Baden-Württemberg* (Freiburg).

O'CONNOR, B. 1980: *Cross-Channel relations in the Bronze Age* (BAR Int. Ser. 91: Oxford).

OCTOBON, F.C.E. 1962: *Castellaras et Camps. Enceintes Celto-Ligures du Departement des Alpes-Maritimes* (Nice).

O'RÍORDÁIN, S.P. 1947: 'Roman Material in Ireland', *Proc. Royal Irish Academy* 51 (C3), 35–82.

PARKER, A.J. 1984: 'Shipwrecks and ancient trade in the Mediterranean', *Archaeol. Review Cambridge* 3:2, 99–107.

PATERSON, J. 1978: 'Transalpine gentes: Cicero, De Re Publica 3.16', *Classical Quarterly* 28, 452–8.

PAULI, L. 1985: 'Early Celtic society: two centuries of wealth and turmoil in central Europe', in Champion & Megaw (eds.) 1985, 23–43.

PEACOCK, D.P.S. 1984: 'Amphorae in Iron Age Britain; a Reassessment', in Macready & Thompson (eds.) 1984, 37–42.

PEACOCK, D.P.S. & THOMAS, A.C. 1967: 'Class E Imported Post Roman Pottery: a suggested origin', *Cornish Archaeol.* 6, 35–46.

PEARCE, S.M. 1983: *The Bronze Age Metalwork of South Western Britain* (BAR 120: Oxford).

PELLETIER, A. 1966: 'De la Vienne gauloise à la Vienne romaine: essai d'étude stratigraphique', *Cahiers Rhodaniens* 13, 144–54.

PENHALLURICK, R.D. 1986: *Tin in Antiquity* (London).

PÈRICHON, R. 1960: 'Note préliminaire sur les récherches a l'oppidum de Joevre (Loire)', *Celticum* 1, 205–12.

PERRAUD, A. 1955: *Le Pègue, préface de Marseille?*

PESCHEL, K. 1971: 'Zur Frage der Sklaverei bei den Kelten während der vorrömischen Eisenzeit', *Ethnographisch-Archäologische Zeitschrift* 12, 527–39.

PICON, M. & GARMIER, J. 1974: 'Un atelier d'Ateius à Lyon', *Rev. archeol. de l'Est et du Centre-Est* 24, 71–6.

POLANYI, K. 1957: 'The economy as instituted process', in Polanyi, K., Arensburg, C. & Pearson, H.W. (eds.), *Trade and Markets in the Early Empires* (Glencoe).

POLANYI, K. 1963: 'Ports of Trade in Early Societies', *Journ. Economic Hist.* 23, 30–45.

POLANYI, K. 1975: 'Traders and Trade', in Sabloff & Lamberg-Karlovsky (eds.) 1975, 133–54.

PREYNAT, J-P. 1962: 'L'oppidum d'Essalois', *Ogam* 14, 287–314.

PREYNAT, J-P. 1982: 'Evolution de l'oppidum d'Essalois de la Tène 2 au debut de notre ere', in Collis, J., Duval, A. & Pèrichon, R., *Le Deuxième Age du fer en Auvergne et en Forez* (St. Etiènne), 106–14.

PURCELL, N. 1985: 'Wine and wealth in Ancient Italy', *Journ. Roman Studies* 75, 1–19.

PY, M. 1968: 'Les fouilles de Vaunage et les influences grecques en Gaul meridionale, commerces et urbanisation', *Rev. d'Études Ligures* 34, 57–106.

PY, M. 1978: *L'oppidum des Castels à Nages, Gard, fouilles 1958–1974* (Supp. à *Gallia* XXXV).

PY, M. 1982: 'Civilisation indigène et urbanisation durant la Protohistoire en Languedoc-Roussillon', *Ktema* 7, 101–19.

RALSTON, I.B.M. 1984: 'Les caractères de l'habitat à La Tène III: les structure urbaines et leur correspondances avec les entitiés politiques', in *Recherche sur la naissance de l'urbanisation au Ier siècle avant J.-C. dans le Centre d'après les nouvelles données archéologiques* (Levroux), 169–98.

RAMIN, J. 1974: 'L'espace économique en Gaul. Les documents historiques concernant les mines', in Chavallier, R. (ed.), *Littérature gréco-romaine et géographie historique* (*Caesarodunum* IX bis: *Mélanges offerts à Roger Dion*), 417–37.

RANCOULE, G. 1979: 'Sondages Stratigraphique à la Cité de Carcassonne (Aude)', *Doc. d'Archeol. Meridionale* 2, 107–18.

RANCOULE, G. & GUIRAUD, L. 1979: 'Fond de cabane gaulois dan le secteur minier de Lastours (Aude)', *Bull. Soc. d'Et. Sci. de l'Aude* 79, 33–8.

RANCOULE, G. & RIGAUD, L. 1978: 'La fosse à amphores No 38 de Lascombe, commune de Lastours (Aude)', *Bull. Soc. d'Et. Sci. de l'Aude* 78, 27–33.

RANCOULE, G. & SOLIER, Y. 1977: 'Les mines antiques des Corbières audoises', *Fédération hist. du Languedoc*, 24–39.

RATHBONE, D.W. 1981: 'The development of agriculture in the 'Ager Cosanus' during the Roman Republic: problems of evidence and interpretation', *Journ. Roman Studies* 71, 10–23.

REILLE, J-L. 1985: 'L'analyse pétrographique des céramiques et le problème de la provenance des amphores massaliètes (VIème-IIème s. av. J.-C.)', *Doc. d'Archéol. Meridionale* 8, 101–12.

RENAUD, J. 1962: 'Notes sur l'oppidum d'Essalois, Loire. Le trace et la structure du rampart', *Ogam* 14, 57–67.

RICHARD, J.C.M. 1972: 'Monnaies gauloises du Cabinet numismatique de Catalogne', *Melanges de la Casa de Velazquez* 7, 51–87.

RICHMOND, I.A. 1961: 'Ancient Geographical Sources for Britain north of Cheviot', in Richmond, I.A. (ed.), *Roman and Native in North Britain* (London), 131–55.

RICQ-DE BOVARD, M. 1985: 'Le problème de l'origine des amphores massaliètes', *Doc. d'Archéol. Meridionale* 8, 113–8.

RIDGEWAY, D. 1973: 'The First Western Greeks: Campanian Coasts and Southern Etruria', in Hawkes, C.F.C. & S.C. (eds.), *Greeks, Celts and Romans. Studies in Venture and Resistance*, 5–38.

RIEK, G. 1962: *Der Hohmichele* (Berlin).

RIGBY, V. 1987: 'Early gaulish imported table wares (at Hengistbury)', in Cunliffe 1987, 276–80.

RIVET, A.L.F. (ed.) 1966: *The Iron Age in Northern Britain* (Edinburgh).

ROBERTSON, A.S. 1970: 'Roman finds from non Roman sites in Scotland', *Britannia* 1, 198–226.

ROLLAND, M.H. 1951: *Fouilles de Saint-Blaise (Bouches-du-Rhone)* (Supp. à *Gallia* 3).

ROLLAND, M.H. 1956: *Fouilles de Saint-Blaise (1951–1956)* (Supp. à *Gallia* 7).

ROLLAND, M.H. 1964: 'Saint Blaise', *Gallia* 22, 569–72.

ROLLAND, M.H. 1958: *Fouilles de Ganum 1947–1956* (Supp. à *Gallia* 16).

ROLLAND, M.H. 1960: *Glanum: Saint Remy de Provence* (Paris).

ROMAN, Y. 1983: *De Narbonne à Bordeaux. Un axe economique au l^{er} siècle avant J.-C.* (Lyon).

ROMAN, Y. 1985: 'Les amphores romaines et l'histoire economique de la Gaule, II^{er} siècle avant — Ier siècle après J.C.: bilan et pérspectives', in *Les Ages du Fer dans la Vallée de la Saône* (*Rev. Archaeol. de Est et du Centre-est* 16e supp.: Paris), 190–9.

ROWLANDS, M.J. 1980: 'Kinship, alliance and exchange in the European Bronze Age', in Barrett, J. & Bradley, R. (eds.), *The British Later Bronze Age* (BAR 83: Oxford), 15–55.

ROYMANS, N. 1983: 'North Belgic Tribes in the 1st century BC: a historical-anthropological perspective', in Brandt & Slofstra (eds.) 1983, 43–70.

SABLOFF, J.A. & LAMBERG-KARLOVSKY, C.C. (eds.) 1975: *Ancient Civilization and Trade* (Albuquerque).

SAKAŘ, V. 1970: 'Roman Imports in Bohemia', *Fontes Arch. Pragenses* 14.

SALMON, E.T. 1969: *Roman Colonization under the Republic* (London).

SALVIAT, F. & EUZENNAT, M. 1973: *L'Histoire de Marseille* (Toulouse).

SALWAY, P. 1981: *Roman Britain* (Oxford).

SANDARS, N.K. 1957: *Bronze Age Cultures in France* (Cambridge).

SANTROT, M-H. & J. 1979: *Céramiques Communes Gallo-Romaines d'Aquitaine* (Paris).

SANTROT, M-H. & J. 1984: 'Céramiques savonneuses grises', in Tasseaux, D. & F. *et al.*, *Aulnay de Saintonge: un camp militaire Augusto Tiberian en Aquitaine* (*Rev. Aquitaine* 2), 105–56.

SCHEERS, S. 1977a: *Traité de numismatique celtique. 2: La Gaule Belgique* (Paris).

SCHEERS, S. 1977b: 'La circulation des monnaies gauloises sur le territoire trevire', *Bull. Antiq. Luxembourgeoises* 8, 26–32.

SCHEERS, S. 1981: 'The origins and evolution of coinage in Belgic Gaul', in Cunliffe (ed.) 1981, 18–23.

SCHMID, P. 1978: 'New archaeological results of settlement structures (Roman Iron Age) in the north-west German Coastal area', in Cunliffe & Rowley (eds.) 1978, 123–46.

SCHODER, R. 1974: 'Graeco-Roman Antipolis on the French Riviera', *Antipolis* 1, 1–7.

SCHÖNBERGER, H. 1969: 'The Roman Frontier in Germany: an archaeological Survey', *Journ. Roman Studies* 59, 144–97.

SCHULTEN, A. 1926: *Sertorius* (Leipzig).

SCHULTEN, A. 1945: *Tartessos* (Madrid: 2nd edition).

SCHULZ, W. 1933: *Das Fürstengrab und das Grabfeld von Hassleben* (*Römischen-Germanische Forschungen* 7: Berlin and Leipzig).

SCHULZ, W. 1953: *Leuna. Ein germanischer Bestattungsplatz der spätrömischen Kaiserzeit* (Berlin).

SELLWOOD, L. 1984: 'Tribal boundaries viewed from the perspective of Numismatic Evidence', in Cunliffe & Miles (eds.) 1984, 191–204.

SHEFTON, B.B. 1979: *Die "rhodischen" Bronzekannen* (Mainz).

SNODGRASS, A.M. 1977: *Archaeology and the rise of the Greek State* (Cambridge).

SNODGRASS, A. 1986: 'A salon science?', *Antiquity* 60, 193–8.

SOLIER, Y. 1961: 'L'Oppidum de Pech-Maho (fouilles 1961)', *Bull. de la Com. archéologique de Narbonne* 25, 126–47.

SOLIER, Y. 1976: 'Pech Maho oppidum préromain (VIᵉ-IVᵉ s. av. J.C.)', *IXᵉ Congrès UISPP, Livret guide de l'excursion C3, Provence et Languedoc méditerranéen, sites protohistoriques et gallo-romains*, 253–62.

SOLIER, Y. 1979: 'Découverte d'inscriptions sur plombs en écriture ibérique dans un entrepôt de Pech Maho (Sigean)', *Rev. Archéol. de Narbonnaise* 12, 55–124.

SOLIER, Y. & FABRE, H. 1969: 'L'oppidum du Moulin à Peyriac-de-Mer, fouilles 1966–1967–1968', *Bull. Soc. d'Études Sci. de l'Aude* 69, 69–106.

SOUTOU, A. 1969: 'Répartition géographique de plus anciennes monnaies gauloises à la croix', *Ogam* 21, 155–69.

SPINDLER, K. 1983: *Die frühen Kelten* (Stuttgart).

STAEHELIN, F. 1948: *Die Schweiz in römischer Zeit* (Basel).

STEAD, I.M. 1976: 'A La Tène III burial at Welwyn Garden City', *Archaeologia* 101, 1–62.

STEAD, I.M. 1976: 'The earliest burials of the Aylesford culture', in Sieveking, G. de G., Longworth, I.H. & Wilson, K.E. (eds.), *Problems of Economic and Social Archaeology* (London), 401–16.

STEVENS, C.E. 1951: 'Britain between the invasions (BC 54–AD 43): A study in Ancient Diplomacy', in Grimes, W.F. (ed.), *Aspects of Archaeology in Britaiñ and Beyond* (London), 332–44.

STEVENS, C.E. 1980: 'North-West Europe and Roman politics (125–118)', in Deraix, C. (ed.), *Studies in Latin Literature and Roman History II* (*Collection Latomus* 168), 71–97.

SWOBODA, B. 1972: *Neuerworbene römische Metallgefässe aus Stràže bei Pieštàny* (Arch. Slovaca Fontes 11).

SYDENHAM, E.A. 1952: *The Coinage of the Roman Republic* (London).

TAFFENAL, O. & J. 1956: 'Les civilisations préromaines dans la région de Mailhac (Aude)', *Rev. d'Etudes Roussillonnaises* 5, 7–29; 103–30.

TAFFENAL, O. & J. 1960: 'Deux tombes de chefs à Mailhac (Aude)', *Gallia* 18, 1–37.

TCHERNIA, A. 1968–70: 'Premiers résultats des fouilles de Juin 1968 sur l'épave 3 de Planier', *Études Classiques* 3, 51–82.

TCHERNIA, A. 1978: 'The Roman wreck of La Madrague de Giens', *Prog. in Underwater Science* 3, 19–24.

TCHERNIA, A. 1983: 'Italian wine in Gaul at the end of the Republic', in Garnsey, Hopkins & Whittaker (eds.) 1983, 87–104.

TCHERNIA, A. 1986: *Le vin de l'Italie Romaine* (Rome).

TCHERNIA, A., POMEY, P. & HESNARD, A. 1978: *L'épave romaine de la Madrague de Giens (Var) (Campagnes 1972–1975) (Gallia* Supp. 34: Paris).

THILL, G. 1966: 'Goeblingen-Nospelt', *Hemecht* 18, 482–91.

THILL, G. 1967: 'Goeblingen-Nospelt', *Hemecht* 19, 87–98, 149–213.

THOMPSON, E.A. 1965: *The Early Germans* (Oxford).

TIERNEY, J.J. 1960: 'The Celtic Ethnography of Posidonius', *Proc. Royal Irish Acad.* 60, 189–275.

TODD, M. 1975: *The Northern Barbarians 100 BC–AD 300* (London).

TODD, M. 1977: 'Germanic burials in the Roman Iron Age', in Reece, R. (ed.), *Burial in the Roman World* (CBA Res. Rep. 22: London), 39–43.

TURNBULL, P. 1984: 'Stanwick in the Northern Iron Age', *Durham Archaeol. Journ.* 1, 41–9.

TYRES, P. 1980: 'Correspondance entre la céramique commune de La Tène III du sud-est de l'Angleterre et du Nord de la France', *Septentrion* 44, 61–70.

VAN ARSDELL, R.D. 1983: 'A Note on the Earliest Types of British Potin Coins', *Spinks Numismatic Circular* 91, no. 1, 18.

VAN ARSDELL, R.D. 1986: 'An industrial engineer (but no papyrus) in Celtic Britain', *Oxford Journ. Archaeol.* 5:2, 205–21.

VERTET, H. 1961: 'Céramique de Saint-Rémy-en-Rollat (Allier)', *Gallia* 19, 218–26.

VICKERS, M. 1984: 'Hallstatt and Early La Tène chronology in central, south and east Europe', *Antiquity* 58, 208–11.

VIDAL, M. & MAGNOL, J-P. 1983: 'Les inscriptions peintes en caractères ibérique de Vieille-Toulouse', *Rev. Archéol. de Narbonnaise* 16, 1–28.

VILLARD, F. 1960: *La céramique grecque de Marseille* (Paris).

VON PETRIKOVITS, H. 1966: 'Arminius', *Bonner Jahr.* 166, 175–93.

WACHER, J. 1975: *The Towns of Roman Britain* (London).

WARD-PERKINS, J.B. 1940: 'The pottery of Gergovia in relation to that of other sites in Central and South-Western France', *Archaeol. Journ.* 97, 37–87.

WEBSTER, G. 1978: *Boudica* (London).

WEDLAKE, W.J. 1958: *Excavations at Camerton, Somerset* (Camerton).

WELLS, C.M. 1976: *The German Policy of Augustus* (Oxford).

WELLS, P.S. 1980: *Culture contact and culture change* (Cambridge).

WESTERMANN, W.L. 1955: *The Slave Systems of Greek and Roman Antiquity* (Philadelphia).

WHEELER, R.E.M. 1943: *Maiden Castle* (Oxford).

WHEELER, R.E.M. 1954: *Rome Beyond the Imperial Frontiers* (London).

WHEELER, R.E.M. 1954: *The Stanwick Fortifications* (Oxford).

WHEELER, R.E.M. & RICHARDSON, K.M. 1957: *Hill-Forts of Northern France* (London).

WHITE, K.D. 1970: *Roman Farming* (London).

WHITTAKER, C.R. 1978: 'Land and Labour in North Africa', *Klio* 60, 331–62.

WHITTAKER, C.R. 1980: 'Inflation and the economy in the fourth century AD', in King, C.E. (ed.), *Imperial revenue, expenditure and monetary policy in the fourth century* (BAR Supp. Ser. 76: Oxford), 1–22.

WIGHTMAN, E.M. 1977: 'Military arrangements, native settlements and related developments in early Roman Gaul', *Helinium* 17, 105–26.

WIGHTMAN, E.M. 1985: *Gallia Belgica* (London).

WILL, E.L. 1979: 'The Sestius amphoras: a reappraisal', *Journ. Field Archaeol.* 6, 339–50.

WILL, E.L. 1982: 'Greco-Italic amphoras', *Hesperia* 51, 338–56.

WILLIAMS, D.F. 1981: 'The Roman Amphora trade with Late Iron Age Britain', in Howard, H. & Morris, E.L. (eds.), *Production and Distribution: a Ceramic Viewpoint* (BAR Int. Ser. 120: Oxford), 123–32.

WILLIAMS, D.F. 1987: 'Amphorae (from Hengistbury)', in Cunliffe 1987, 271–5.

WOODHEAD, A.G. 1962: *The Greeks in the West* (London).

ZIMMERMANN, W.H. 1978: 'Economy of the Roman Iron Age settlement Flögeln, Lower Saxony — husbandry, cattle farming and manufacture', in Cunliffe & Rowley (eds.) 1978, 147–66.

ZÜRN, H. 1970: *Hallstattforschungen in Nordwürttemberg* (Stuttgart).

Index